Freedom Books

YOU DON'T SAY

YOU DON'T SAY

Sometimes Liberals Show Their True Colors

FRED GIELOW

The photograph on the cover and title page
is copyrighted by Kenneth W. Fink and is used with permission.
Cover design by Brian Vigna.

Library of Congress Cataloging-in-Publication Data:

An application to the Library of Congress for this data was submitted 12 weeks prior to publication, but was not received during that time. An inquiry attempting to determine application status was greeted with a recorded message stating that no inquiries are accepted unless at least 24 weeks have elapsed since the date the application was submitted. [Bureaucracy in action!] When received, Cataloging-in-Publication Data will be available from the publisher, and will be shown here in subsequent printings.

Direct all inquiries to Freedom Books,
17234 Boca Club Boulevard #102, Boca Raton, Florida, 33487-1268.

Printed in the United States by Malloy Lithographing, Ann Arbor, Michigan.

First printing, part 1: 1998

ISBN: 0-9603938-2-X

I think, therefore I am.

- René Descartes[1] (1596-1650)
Le Discours dc la Méthode, IV

I feel, therefore I am.

- The quintessential liberal

To:

The Patriots,
proud and honorable Americans . . .

. . . who love their country, cherish freedom, and treasure the principles defined by the Declaration of Independence, U.S. Constitution, and Bill of Rights.

. . . who hate not their government, but rather the destruction of their freedoms, blatant disregard for the Constitution, and the fraud and deception practiced by selfish politicians.

. . . who so prize freedom they will fight the fights, battle the battles, and make the ultimate sacrifice to assure survival of this democratic republic, as conceived by the wisdom and inspiration of our Founding Fathers.

ACKNOWLEDGMENTS

Thanks are due my brother, Jim, who devoted many hours to review my work, provided needed editing, and offered sage advice.

I owe particular thanks to Reed Irvine, whose moral support and aid have been immeasurable. Without Reed's belief in my work, it's likely this book's ultimate destiny would have been abandonment.

Thanks, too, to Tom DeWeese for use of his article as this book's Conclusion, to Pat Matrisciana for his kindness and support, to Morton Blackwell, David Horowitz, Oliver North, and Pat Buchanan for their encouragement, to John Wheeler for his valued critique and recommendations, to Nancy Sperry for her able proof reading, to Alice Holinbeck for her steadfast moral support, and to Chris Ruddy for his help in my search for a publisher.

Last but not least, thanks to you, intrepid reader, for allowing me to "whisper in your ear" some ideas, facts, and perspectives. I trust this book will be not only entertaining, but thoroughly thought provoking as well.

CONTENTS

Quotation numbers are in parentheses.

INTRODUCTION

If you want to find the jealous embrace of attained power, go to the Liberal ideologue, who must have total power in order to achieve his total reform, his rapid creation of Utopia.

- Gary Wills[2]
What Is Conservatism? 1964

The guilt of the liberal causes him to feel obligated to try to do ***something*** *about any and every social problem, to cure every social evil . . . even if he has no knowledge of the suitable medicine or, for that matter, of the nature of the disease; he must do* ***something*** *about the social problem even when there is no objective reason to believe that what he does can solve the problem - when, in fact, it may well aggravate the problem instead of solving it.*

- James Burnham[3]
Suicide of the West, 1964

[T]he liberal crusader is focused on the negative. He is trying to stamp out all evil with a coercive hand of big government, and winds up destroying much of what is good in the process.

- Edwin Feulner[4]
President, The Heritage Foundation

hen it comes to eating, you've got to hand it to Venus de Milo, but when it comes to compassion, you've got to hand it to liberals. They're the ones who are caring, giving, loving. They're the ones concerned about the environment, people on welfare, the homeless. They want to take away guns so no one will ever again be shot. They race to dispense with a life to guarantee a mother's "choice." They, in the interest of compassion and concern, wish to deny people expression of their religious beliefs. And the rest of us are just plain evil. Or so we're told.

So we're told, that is, by the Propaganda Machine (my label for the mainstream media, the entertainment industry, and much of the education establishment). The mighty and influential Propaganda Machine is largely populated by, surprise: liberals!

But is it really true all liberals are virtuous and all conservatives evil? Reasonable people will chuckle at the idea. Everyone knows there are good and bad apples in every barrel.

So, let's examine a few apples from the liberal barrel. Let's look at some actual statements from these noble and compassionate folks. Let's just see how compassionate and loving these liberals really are.

But to make things interesting, after each quotation I've provided five potential authors. Your challenge then, should you choose to accept it, is to guess which of the five actually made the quoted remark. Answers are conveniently revealed on the page following each quote.

Now you may wish to quarrel with me over some of those on whom I've pinned the label "liberal." (By the way, I'm not saying all those named herein are liberals.) So let me give you my definition of the term. I'd say a liberal is anyone who favors larger government, more government control, or world government. A liberal considers animals, birds, and plants more important than people, and protection of the environment more important than the well being of human beings. A liberal does not believe in the sanctity of the traditional family, nor the sanctity of life, either in the womb or in later years whenever living becomes "inconvenient". A liberal has no qualms about robbing Peter to pay Paul, and in fact encourages the government to take *your* money so it may be given to others whom liberals consider more worthy.

Our liberal brethren believe good motivations always triumph over bad outcomes: If the U.S. will just unilaterally disarm, all our enemies will do likewise and join us in everlasting peace. If we will just let the government take our rifles and hand guns, there will never again be violence in our streets. If we will just give people on welfare more money, recipients will use it wisely to quickly rebuild their lives and become hardworking, productive citizens. If we will just give government more power, it will regulate us and control us to everyone's benefit, and we'll all live happily ever after.

Yeah, right. But so goes the liberal Pollyanna.

In an article titled "Inside the Liberal Mind," Grant Russell wrote: "The liberal believes (as did Marx, Engels, Stalin, Castro) that if he can erase the thoughts of society and replace them with the idea that man is by nature good, then men will learn to work hard, share, have compassion, be tolerant, and be law-abiding without the need for force. Liberals believe that if they could control the minds of one generation and erase greedy thoughts [and] intolerance, and teach the common good and brotherly love in a classless society, then men would become naturally good. *In order to accomplish this new way they must be totally intolerant of any ideas other than their own."*[5] [Emphasis in the original.]

Russell continued: "The liberal cries for tolerance of every evil, but is absolute in his intolerance of those who disagree with him . . . . The liberal hates free speech. He does not tolerate any speech that disagrees with him. Realism is not allowed in the education system. Books are screened to see that God is removed (*God is a realist*). Filth is taught as literature, perversion as normal, sin as good, and iniquity is displayed on all fronts to make society more tolerant of evil."[6]

Our liberal friends have it backwards. They believe (though they may not admit it) that government should be all powerful and should dispense freedom in accord with the needs of the State. Conservatives believe *we the people* are endowed by *our Creator* with certain unalienable rights and that *we the people* should yield to government only enough power as is necessary to protect those rights, provide for the common defense, and maintain good relations among the states.

Whereas liberals believe in the state, conservatives believe in the people. Syndicated columnist and talk show host Armstrong Williams observed, "Conservatives trust people and their neighbors to solve most of their problems, while liberals believe most people are unable to act responsibly without government direction."[7]

Putting it another way Williams said, "Unlike liberals, who believe government to be the panacea for all societal problems, conservatives still have faith in the power of the individual. Conservatives have watched as liberals have wasted billions of dollars on government programs that have done nothing more than exacerbate the problems they were initiated to confront."[8] He went on to say, "Conservatives maintain that the problems facing our families, the problems facing our schools, and the problems facing our neighborhoods can and should be solved by our families, schools, and neighborhoods - not faceless bureaucrats in government agencies."[9]

Syndicated columnist Linda Bowles offered this analysis: "Clearly, new-age liberals are not liberal at all in the classic sense, but control freaks. While passionately rejecting the idea that anyone has the right to impose values upon anyone else, they rush to impose their own ideological folly and cultural prejudices upon others."[10]

She added: "We have strayed far from the two basic principles which guided the Founders: the principle of limited government which empowers the people, and the principle of moral responsibility which makes that empowerment possible."[11]

Henry Grady Weaver, in *The Mainspring of Human Progress,* wrote: "Most of the major ills of the world have been caused by well-meaning people who ignored the principle of individual freedom. The harm done by criminals, murderers, gangsters, and thieves is negligible in comparison with the agony inflicted upon human beings by the professional do-gooders, who attempt to set themselves up as gods on earth and who would ruthlessly force their views on all others - with the abiding assurance that the end justifies the means."[12]

Pope John Paul II observed that "freedom does not consist in doing what we want, but choosing to do what we ought."[13]

Take a look at the 76 quotations from liberals presented in the following pages. Look closely for the compassion, caring, and loving. Sometimes you will search in vain.

A number of these statements will chill your bones . . . or at least they ought to! These are sentiments of many of our leaders, some our *top* leaders. Do you agree with them? Is this the leadership you want for our country? Will these people and their vision take us where *you* want America to go?

Look, I didn't make up what's quoted here. These statements are no figment of my imagination. Each contains liberal thinking as reported by one or more sources. Yes, some are amusing, some ridiculous, but some are frightening enough to scare your socks off!

See if you can guess who said what. If you score over 50%, you win a prize: the realization you've got our friends the liberals pegged!

LOVE THY NEIGHBOR

Omnia vincit amor: et nos cedamus amori. (Love conquers all things; let us too surrender to Love.)

- Virgil[14] (70-19 B.C.)
Eclogues II

A new Commandment I give unto you, That ye love one another.

- John 13:34[15]

1. CHRISTIANS

Who said this?

> *The evaporation of four million [Christians] who believe in this crap [the Second Coming of Christ] would leave the world an instantly better place.*

Was it:

A. **Andrei Codrescu.** Editor, *Exquisite Corpse.*
B. **Terry Madison.** Editor, *World Vision.*
C. **Matthew Rothschild.** Editor, *The Progressive.*
D. **Robin M. Thompson.** Editor-in-chief, *Rosicrucian Digest.*
E. **Ronald D. Williams.** Editor, *Foursquare World Advance.*

The answer is

A. **Andrei Codrescu.**

When/where:

Spoken during the "All Things Considered" program on taxpayer-subsidized National Public Radio, December 19, 1995.

Source:

"Stupid Quotes," *The Limbaugh Letter,* February 1996, page 7, quoting the Associated Press.[16]

1. Andrei Codrescu with his new book, *The Dog with the Chip in His Neck,* in West Orange, New Jersey, November 18, 1996.

Comments:

What intrigues me about Codrescu's quotation is the intolerance he and many other liberals display in rare, unguarded moments. Codrescu would no doubt describe himself as caring and concerned, one who sympathizes with the plight of downtrodden people, yet his compassion apparently doesn't extend to millions of Christians, who he would gladly vaporize in the interest of making the "world a better place." It's an amazing and baffling thought process.

Codrescu later apologized "for the language, but not for what I said." Well now, what kind of an apology is that?

But Codrescu isn't a lone anti-Christian soldier. Dwight L. Kinman describes the results of a national poll.[17] The question: "Of the three groups in America - Neo-Nazis; white supremacists; and fundamental, Bible-believing Christians - which is the most dangerous?" The *majority* answered "Fundamental, Bible-believing Christians."

2. COMPASSION

Who said this?

> *[I]t's compassionate to spend money - even if there is not money there to spend and even if you're heaping debt on the next generation.*

Was it:

A. **Margaret Carlson.** Journalist, *Time* Magazine.

B. **Eleanor Clift.** Former White House correspondent. Contributing editor for *Newsweek* Magazine. Commentator on the McLaughlin Group television program.

C. **Mara Liasson.** Reporter, National Public Radio.

D. **Lisa Myers.** Reporter, NBC News.

E. **Barbara Walters.** Former writer-producer for WNBC-TV. Former Today Show co-host. Former newscaster for the ABC Evening News. Co-host of the 20/20 television show. Named Woman of the Year in Communications (1974). Winner of the Lifetime Achievement Award (International Women's Media Foundation, 1992). Winner of numerous other awards.[18]

The answer is

D. **Lisa Myers.**

2. Lisa Myers.

When/where:

On a CNBC-TV special "Meet the Media" program, October 23, 1995.

Source:

"Quote of the Week," *Human Events,* December 8, 1995, page 1.

Comments:

Liberals are anxious to help the poor, the disadvantaged, the homeless, the oppressed, and I say a hearty *Bravo* to such compassion! 'Tis noble and honorable, indeed.

But where is justice when the pursuit of compassion leads liberals to plunder the haves to give to the have nots? By what right do they steal from *future generations* to give to those "needy" individuals *they* consider more worthy? As has been sagely observed: "The government can't give you anything it hasn't first taken away."[19]

When liberals pirate the legitimate reward of those who achieve through hard work, creativity, and risk, they make a mockery of freedom and the fundamental principals of this country. How many sports records will be broken if the winning athlete is rewarded with a quick trip to the guillotine?

Sometimes compassion seems to blind liberals to all the consequences of their actions; compassion alone seems sufficient to create their motivation and then subsequently to rationalize the outcome. Both the end and the means are therefore justified in the name of "caring," even if the results are utterly disastrous.

3. COMPASSION

Who said this?

> *I hope his wife feeds him [Clarence Thomas, Justice the U.S. Supreme Court] lots of eggs and butter and he dies early like many black men do, of heart disease . . . . He is an absolutely reprehensible person.*

Was it:

A. **Samuel Andrew (Sam) Donaldson.** Veteran ABC News reporter. Former ABC News White House correspondent. Panelist on This Week with David Brinkley. Co-anchor on the Primetime Live television show. Cancer sufferer.[20]

B. **Julianne Malveaux.** *USA Today* columnist. Pacifica Radio talk show host.

C. **Dee Dee Myers.** Former press secretary for the Dukakis-for-President campaign, Diane Feinstein-for-Governor campaign, and Clinton-for-President campaign. Former presidential press secretary. Former co-host of the Equal Time television show. Cycling enthusiast. Major league baseball fan.[21]

D. **Cokie Roberts.** News commentator.

E. **Maxine Waters.** U.S. Representative (D, California).

The answer is

B. **Julianne Malveaux.**

When/where:

Remarks made on the PBS program "To the Contrary," November 4, 1994.

Source:

"The Most Embarrassing Quotes of the Liberal Media," *Human Events,* November 7, 1997.[22]

3. Perhaps warning labels should be posted on selected remarks from the more caustic liberals.

Comments:

How about ABC reporter Nina Totenberg's remark about conservative Senator Jesse Helms, during her appearance on Inside Washington in 1995: "If there is . . . justice, he'll get AIDS," she said, "or one of his grandchildren will get it."[23]

Remember now, it's liberals who call conservatives "mean spirited", not the other way around.

A newsletter distributed at a 1995 New Hampshire AFL-CIO convention included this notice: "Drive home safely, and remember: if you must drink and drive, try to do it when Phil Gramm is crossing the street."[24]

Some might interpret such a poor-taste "joke" as merely good-natured humor, but change the name from Phil Gramm to David Bonior, Tom Daschle, or Richard Gephardt - let that remark be spoken by a conservative - and just listen to the uproar! Apologies would be demanded, resignations implored, and the din would be deafening.

But when "compassionate" liberals like Ms. Malveaux and Ms. Totenberg make hate utterances, there is but mild snickering, if any reaction at all, from the all-powerful Propaganda Machine.

4. COMPASSION

Who said this?

> *[Aborted fetuses] are wasted if we don't eat them . . . . I wash them with clear water until they look transparent white and then steam them. Making soup is best. Fetuses are smelly and not everybody can take the stink.*

Was it:

A. A doctor practicing medicine in the People's Republic of China.
B. A nurse stationed in Bangladesh.
C. A religious leader living in Burma.
D. A restaurant owner living on the outskirts of Pyongyang, North Korea.
E. A Thailand army captain stationed in Ayutthaya, Thailand.

The answer is

A. A doctor in the People's Republic of China.

When/where:

Reported in the *Eastern Express,* a Hong Kong-based newspaper.

Source:

"Is China Selling Aborted Fetuses?" *Human Events,* May 12, 1995, page 7.

4. The good doctor gives new meaning to the phrase "Chinese food".

Comments:

The Source says: "According to the article, state-run hospitals and private clinics are now selling aborted fetuses, at about 10 Hong Kong dollars [$1.25 U.S.] each, as a food that can cure a range of maladies and promote healthy skin and organs. The *Eastern Express* reporters wrote that one doctor explained to them that the fetuses 'can make your skin smoother, your body stronger, and are good for your kidneys.'"

At the Luo Huo Clinic in Hubei Province, one doctor said she ate more than a hundred fetuses in six months, about one every other day!

In his book, *Global Taxes for World Government,* Cliff Kincaid reports: "In June of 1995 a law went into effect in China mandating automatic abortions for fetuses judged to be 'defective' (i.e., retarded or having spina bifida). Can the murder of the elderly be far behind? As many as eighty million people were killed in China as part of the Communist revolution. A few million more wouldn't make any difference to the Communist dictators."[25]

"[O]nce euthanasia is accepted for some people, under what seem like ethical circumstances, it can be expected that the practice will be applied by government to others against their will . . . . Nazi Germany serves as a concrete example of how a government-run euthanasia program works in practice."[26]

Raise your hand if you agree with Margaret Mead: "The unadorned truth is that we do not need now, and will not need later, much of the marginal labor - the very young, the very old, the very uneducated, and the very stupid."[27]

5. COMPASSION

Who said this?

> *[The defendant] is a good man, except that he sometimes kills people.*

Was it:

A. **Rosemary Barkett.** Judge, U.S. Court of Appeals. Justice, Florida State Supreme Court. Ex-nun. Co-author with Justice McDonald of a death sentence dissent which states in part: "[T]he death penalty [in this case] is not warranted and is disproportionate to the majority of hate slayings, at least where the victim is black and the perpetrator is white . . . ."[28]

B. **Anthony Bisceglie.** Attorney for Theodore (Ted) Kaczynski, the admitted "Unabomber," who sent mail bombs that killed three and injured 23 others during an 18-year period.

C. **Al Cowlings.** Close friend of Orenthal James (O.J.) Simpson.

D. **Geoffrey Fieger.** Attorney representing Dr. Jack Kevorkian.

E. **Stephen Jones.** Attorney representing Timothy McVeigh.

The answer is

A. **Rosemary Barkett,** winner of the See-No-Evil Award "for a decision in which a judge turns a blind eye to crime - insisting that criminals are victims of society." This June 1997 Jester Award, issued by the Family Research Council to highlight "outrageous" examples of judicial tyranny, recognized her extensive "coddling" of convicted criminals in opinions on the Florida Supreme Court and the 11th U.S. Circuit Court of Appeals.[29]

5. U.S. Senators Connie Mack (R, Florida, left) and Bob Graham (D, Florida) flank Florida Supreme Court Justice Rosemary Barkett at a Senate Judiciary Committee hearing on Barkett's nomination to the 11th U.S. Circuit Court of Appeals in Atlanta, Georgia, February 3, 1994.

When/where:

In court during comments made while she vacated a death sentence.

Source:

"The Misanthrope's Corner," by Florence King, *National Review,* September 25, 1995, page 104.

Comments:

I think the point of Ms. King's column and her reference to Ms. Barkett was to draw attention to the tendency to let blind compassion, the blood and guts of liberalism, get in the way of common sense. Some would call it turning the other cheek, but how often does one turn the other cheek, if inevitably it's then pummeled? Do you release all the prisoners in the jails in a spirit of compassion and forgiving? Do you throw down your weapons at the feet of your enemy in such a spirit? Just where do you draw the line and proclaim right is right and wrong is wrong?

And such is the liberal's dilemma. Everyone admires compassion, but at what point does compassion make the transition from caring and concern to utter foolishness?

6. CONSERVATIVES

Who said this?

> *[Jack Kemp] is a rare combination - a nice conservative. These days, conservatives are supposed to be mean. They're supposed to be haters.*

Was it:

A. **Betty Friedan.** Author, *The Feminine Mystique,* 1963.
B. **Al Gore.** Spoken during the televised vice-presidential candidate debate, 1996.
C. **Dan Rather.** Former White House correspondent. CBS-TV news reporter, commentator, and editorialist. Author of several books including *Memoirs, I Remember* (1991). Recipient of numerous awards including dedication of the Dan Rather Communications Building at Sam Houston State University, Huntsville, Texas.[30]
D. **Charlie Rose.** Television talk show host on PBS.
E. **Bill Schneider.** Political analyst.

The answer is

E. **Bill Schneider.**

When/where:

Remarks made during a CNN broadcast of "Inside Politics," August 9, 1996.

Source:

"Stupid Quotations," *The Limbaugh Letter,* October 1996, page 10.[31]

6. Bill Schneider, CNN, 1993.

Comments:

Here we have a typical example of liberal propaganda: a smear wrapped in a sugar-coated compliment. Al Gore pulled the same trick on Jack Kemp during the vice-presidential candidates' debate in 1996. He basically parroted Schneider's remark.

Kemp, however, seemed completely buffaloed by the Trojan Horse Gore had presented to him. Apparently focusing on the "praise", he appeared oblivious to the fact that with his ever-so-sweet remark Gore had neatly and cleverly slandered all Republicans!

Such is the way of our friends the liberals. They make every effort to trick, trounce, or trample their opponent, rather than debate an issue with facts and truth. Perhaps that's because they're wise enough to understand that for many positions they take on the issues, facts, and truth can't win their debates.

Senator Christopher Dodd (D, Connecticut), Democratic National Committee co-chair, remarked on the Don Imus radio show just before the 1996 election: "Eight more days and I can start telling you the truth again. It's killing me, I'll tell you."[32]

Senator Dodd, it's killing the American people, too.

7. CONSERVATIVES

Who said this?

> *In South Africa we'd call it apartheid. In Nazi Germany we'd call it fascism. Here [in the U.S.] we call it conservatism. These people are attacking the poor.*

Was it:

A. **Reverend Ralph Abernathy.** Clergyman and civil rights leader.
B. **Reverend Louis Farrakhan.** Minister and leader of the Nation of Islam.
C. **Reverend Jesse Jackson.** Ordained minister of the Baptist Church in 1968. Unsuccessful U.S. presidential candidate. Clergyman. Civil rights leader.
D. **Reverend Martin Luther King.** Clergyman and civil rights leader.
E. **Reverend Alfred Charles (Al) Sharpton.** Founder and president of the National Youth Movement, Inc. Junior pastor at the Washington Temple Church of God in Christ. Minister. Recipient of several awards.[33]

The answer is

C. **Reverend Jesse Jackson.**

7. Jesse Jackson in Washington, D.C. on Solidarity Day, September 19, 1981.

When/where:

In an article in *The Fort Lauderdale Sun-Sentinel.*

Source:

"Stupid Quotes," *The Limbaugh Letter,* November 1996, page 4.

Comments:

"If the plight of Negroes as a group continues to be a hardship," says Anne Wortham in her book *The Other Side of Racism,*[34] "it is, to a large degree, because so many individuals in that group either do not know or refuse to accept the fact that self-determination and self-identity can be neither achieved nor destroyed by political means."

Responding to those "who would enslave us with welfare statism," Ms. Wortham declares: "No! The equality you urge on us is not a requirement of our existence . . . . We reject your attempts to make us exceptions to the rules of human existence simply because of our skin color. We do not want the results of our action to be *equal* to everyone else's . . . . We do not want a guaranteed livelihood paid for by the expropriated resources of others. We do not want to be spared the responsibility and risks of surviving by our own means . . . . We do not want positions of employment we are unqualified to hold. We do not want 'preferential treatment' in order to be spared the risks of competition by achievement . . . . We want no rewards we have not earned. We only want to be free!"[35]

When a group is singled out for special treatment, some members of that group race to stand in line for the handouts. Others, however, react with "a kind of demoralization," according to Professor Shelby Steele, because "the quality that earns us preferential treatment is an implied inferiority."[36]

8. EXTREMISTS

Who said this?

> *Extremists [those individuals who insist on clinging to this country's Founding Fathers' vision of America] fail to provide a viable pathway from the cold war to the global village.*

Was it:

A. **David Bonior.** U.S. Representative (D, Michigan).

B. **Thomas John (Tom) Brokaw.** Former White House correspondent for NBC. Host of numerous specials, including: A Conversation with Mikhail Gorbachev. Winner of the Alfred I. DuPont Award. NBC news anchorman.[37]

C. **Hillary Rodham Clinton.** Attorney. Former counsel on the Nixon impeachment inquiry staff of the Judiciary Committee in the U.S. House of Representatives. Former chair, ABA Commission on Women in America. Former chair, Legal Services Corp. First Lady.[38]

D. **Ira Magaziner.** Former senior advisor to President Clinton and principal instigator of the 1342-page Clinton Health Care Plan.

E. **Colin Powell.** Former chairman of the Joint Chiefs of Staff. Reluctant politician.

The answer is

C. **Hillary Rodham Clinton.**

When/where:

In her book, *It Takes a Village - And Other Lessons Children Teach Us,* published by Simon and Schuster, 1996.

Source:

"Hillary's Global Village," by William Norman Grigg, *The New American,* March 4, 1996, page 38.

8. Hillary Rodham Clinton speaking at a White House luncheon she hosted for *Parents Magazine* honorees, May 22, 1997.

Comments:

If, as suggested, we discard the vision of our Founding Fathers, just whose vision will we then adopt in its place? Do you suppose it might be that of Hillary Rodham Clinton? And do you suppose we'd be allowed a choice if Mrs. Clinton and company could have their way?

The Source observes: "Since coming to power in 1993, the Clinton vanguard has tirelessly urged the enrichment of AFDC [Aid for Dependent Children], Head Start, and other federal welfare programs as a means of 'investing in children'. Such 'investments' not only create an incentive for single parenthood, but also make the federal government the surrogate father. By subsidizing the mother, the state effectively controls the home."

So perhaps we've already been introduced to the Clinton "vision of America". It's implementation may already be well underway.

9. INTELLIGENCE

Who said this?

> *The United States has some of the dumbest people in the world. I want you to know that. We know that.*

Was it:

A. **Ted Bundy.** Serial killer.

B. **Ted Danson.** Actor in off-Broadway plays, motion pictures, and television. Star of the NBC-TV series Cheers. Recipient of Best Comedy Actor Golden Globe Award, American Comedy Award, People's Choice Award for Favorite Male Television Performer, Best Actor Emmy, among other awards.[39]

C. **Ted Kennedy.** Politician. U.S. Senator (D, Massachusetts).

D. **Ted Koppel.** Host of the television show Nightline.

E. **Ted Turner.** CEO of Turner Broadcasting Network and CNN networks. Vice president, Time-Warner. Owner, Atlanta Braves. Chief advisor to Mikhail Gorbachev's Green Cross International. Donor of $1,000,000,000 (9 months pay) to the UN.[40] Source of a recommendation to junk *The Star Spangled Banner* as our national anthem because it's too "warlike".[41]

The answer is

E. **Ted Turner.**

When/where:

In an article in the *U.S. News & World Report.*

Source:

"Stupid Quotes," *The Limbaugh Letter,* September 1996, page 10.

9. Ted Turner, September 18, 1997, announcing he'll donate one billion dollars to the United Nations over the next 10 years. American Sovereignty Action Project director Cliff Kincaid says the gift is illegal. "Article 17 of the UN Charter says the expenses of the organization shall be borne by the member states," says Kincaid. "It does not authorize the UN to raise revenue from any other source."

Comments:

If indeed the American public has been dumbed down, then you, Mr. Turner, ought to look to your own kind - liberals - to take responsibility for this outrage.

For example, as Tom DeWeese reveals in his *DeWeese Report*:[42] "In Oregon, high school seniors . . . no longer receive diplomas that indicate academic achievement. Instead, they are issued the Certificate of Initial Mastery . . . [but] such a document does not imply academic achievement. It simply means that a student has met the proper standards for attitudes, values, and beliefs as set down by the education establishment.

"One such student received his Certificate of Initial Mastery showing that he had met the standards for: Involved Citizen, Quality Producer, Self-Directed Learner, Constructive Thinker, Effective Communicator, and Collaborative Contributor.

"The Certificate explains that the student can now 'Quantify, Apply Math/Science, Understand Diversity, Deliberate on Public Issues, Interpret Human Experience, and Understand Positive Health Habits.' What the student cannot do is diagram a sentence, conjugate a verb, or spell. English is not taught at his school - nor was he taught Algebra, Geometry, Trigonometry, Civics, or Biology."[43]

Maureen DiMarco, top education adviser to California Governor Pete Wilson, explained: "Our state's educational leaders decided it was terribly insulting for kids to have to learn number tables or how to spell words. So we ended up with math books without arithmetic, and literature books without reading."[44]

The Washington Times reports: "Only Cyprus and South Africa performed worse than U.S. 12th-graders on a test of general knowledge in mathematics and science . . . ." "Even the best and brightest didn't measure up: American high school seniors studying pre-calculus, calculus, or physics placed next to last in advanced mathematics and last in physics."[45]

A Pennsylvania student brought home a math paper she was given in the public school. One of the problems stated there were four birds in a nest and one flew away. The question: "How do you think the bird felt that flew away from the nest?"[46]

A report titled "Outcome-Based Education"[47] surveys the damage: "Kids . . . are to make their own decisions based on feelings and whims . . . . [Teachers] teach there is no right way to spell a word; no right way to pronounce it; no meaning in it; no absolutes. Life becomes meaningless . . . What follows this despair is a total desolation with nothing left but mysticism. Those raised on mysticism and superstition are easy to lead - easy to program - easy to enslave."

We see that caring and compassionate liberals wish to change the learning experience from the acquisition of information and the refinement of the thinking process to the sharpening of sensitivities and the development of feelings.

"Professor" Rush Limbaugh observes: "After years of hearing conservatives decry the decline in SAT scores, the Educational Testing Service decided to try to shut us up: They simply padded the average reading and math scores by 100 points - which more than made up for the 80-point drop in average SAT scores since 1964."[48]

The "professor" continues: "Are liberals embarrassed in the face of overwhelming evidence of the failure of their educational ideas and prescriptions? No, of course not! They never are, because they never admit their ideas and prescriptions have failed."[49]

The objective of the liberal's education is principally attitudinal, not academic. It is designed to mold sociable, compliant workers. Required competencies for students are: to participate as a member of a team (thereby discouraging individual creativity and accomplishment), to negotiate to reach a decision (values and judgement don't count), to work with cultural diversity (any culture or belief is OK), to achieve mental visualization (forget reading, writing, arithmetic), to maintain high self-esteem (whether warranted or not . . . and by the way, according to whose measuring stick?), to be able to make decisions (on what basis, pray tell?), to demonstrate integrity and honesty (how can you argue with that . . . if the words mean what you and I think they mean), and to achieve sociability.[50]

The U.S. Labor Department publishes manuals for schools called SCANS (Secretary's Commission on Achieving Necessary Skills) which direct the above-described Outcome Based Education (OBE) programs. SCANS Commissioner Thomas G. Sticht, said in 1987: "What may be crucial . . . is the dependability of a labor force and how well it can be managed and trained - not its general education level . . . . Ending discrimination and changing values are probably more important than reading in moving low-income families into the middle class."[51]

This is not wild conjecture or science fiction pap, this is going on in public schools around the country right now, and has been for years.

Here's more evidence: "In Pennsylvania, a child's belief system, not his academic knowledge, was tested. His score was permanently recorded on a computerized dossier which could indicate his political leanings, personal problems, family finances, medical records, and personal background data . . . . Eventually, this information would be used in high-stake decision-making to control who would graduate, who would work, and what type of health care services the school would provide. The school would be used as a model for administering a national agenda . . . . Any child not meeting subjective and vague outcomes outlined by Outcome-Based Education (OBE) would be [a candidate] for remediation."[52]

It looks as though the predictions of the "father of Outcome-Based Education," Professor Benjamin Bloom, are becoming reality. In his book, *All Our Children Learning*[53] he said, "The purpose of education and the schools is to change the thoughts, feelings and actions of students."[54]

Whatever happened to the "three Rs"?

10. RACISM

Who said this?

> *Blacks and Hispanics were too busy eating watermelons and tacos to read the fine print on the phony insurance policies.*

Was it:

A. **Billy Carter.** Brother of President Jimmy Carter. Alleged namesake of Billy Beer.

B. **Roger Clinton.** Brother of President Bill Clinton. Singer. Former cocaine addict. Former drug dealer.[55]

C. **Phil Donahue.** Former television talk show host. Recipient of Emmy Awards for the Best Daytime Talk Show (1977, 1979, 1982), the Peabody Award (1980), Best Talkshow Host (1988), Margaret Sanger Award (Planned Parenthood Federation of America, 1987), and others.[56]

D. **Geraldo Rivera.** Host of the Rivera Live television show.

E. **Mike Wallace.** Author, *Close Encounters* (1984). Commentator and co-editor of the 60 Minutes television program on CBS. Recipient of many awards including the Robert Sherwood Award, 18 Emmy Awards, George Foster Peabody Awards, DuPont Columbia Journalism Awards, among others.[57]

The answer is

E. **Mike Wallace.**

10. Mike Wallace at the 1991 People's Choice Awards.

When/where:

Spoken during preparation of a 60 Minutes television program on insurance fraud in 1981.

Source:

The 60 Minutes Deception, video produced by Citizens for Honest Government, 1997.

Comments:

According to the Source, Wallace later apologized but received no reprimand from CBS.

In the video, syndicated columnist Deroy Murdock commented: "I think it's amazing a guy like Mike Wallace, [who] is considered an open-minded, decent, warmhearted liberal, would refer to Blacks and Hispanics as eating watermelons and tacos and therefore are too busy doing that to read insurance policies. That's [an] incredibly bigoted remark and it's amazing that when someone who is a member of the Liberal Media Establishment talks that way he's very quickly forgiven and people sort of put it behind them and move on. And if a conservative journalist had said that, he'd still be excoriated and probably would have been fired and never heard from again."

Remember Fuzzy Zoeller's not-so-funny comment about fried chicken and collard greens. One little remark he thought at the time was humorous, and the press came down on him like an avalanche! He had to apologize a zillion times![58]

You may consider Mike Wallace a bigot based on his 1981 comments, but he's also an admitted liar. The Source quotes him as saying, "You don't like to lie baldly, but I have." Why would anyone wish to pay attention to this man?

11. RACISM

Who said this?

> *[S]ome nigger, some junior high [school] nigger kicks Steve's ass while he was trying to help his brothers out . . . . Steve had the nigger down . . . . He had the nigger down; he let him up . . . .*

Was it:

A. **Billy Carter.** Brother of President Jimmy Carter. Alleged namesake of Billy Beer.
B. **Roger Clinton.** Brother of President Bill Clinton. Singer. Former cocaine addict. Former drug dealer.[59]
C. **Phil Donahue.** Former television talk show host. Recipient of Emmy Awards for the Best Daytime Talk Show (1977, 1979, 1982), the Peabody Award (1980), Best Talkshow Host (1988), Margaret Sanger Award (Planned Parenthood Federation of America, 1987), and others.[60]
D. **Geraldo Rivera.** Host of the Rivera Live television show.
E. **Mike Wallace.** Author, *Close Encounters* (1984). Commentator and co-editor, 60 Minutes television Program on CBS. Recipient of many awards including the Robert Sherwood Award, 18 Emmy Awards, George Foster Peabody Awards, DuPont Columbia Journalism Awards, among others.[61]

The answer is

B. **Roger Clinton.**

11. Roger Clinton, during an interview in Los Angeles, October 21, 1992.

When/where:

Arkansas State Police surveillance video taken June 27, 1984, 11:33 p.m..

Source:

The Mena Cover-Up: Drugs, Deception, and the Making of a President, video produced by Americans Against Government Corruption, 1996.

Comments:

Remember when you were a kid and someone would insult you or call you a name? "Sticks and stones can break my bones, but *names* can never hurt me!" How many times did you use that little bromide, or hear others use it?

Today it's strangely out of fashion. Now the politically correct reaction to name calling is wild outrage. Apparently what's important now is not dispelling hard feelings and anger but cultivating them! And liberals are leading this charge.

Article I of the Bill of Rights states: "Congress shall make no law . . . abridging the freedom of speech . . . ." Yet, liberals, with their endorsement and enforcement of "politically correct" speech seem anxious to turn Article I on its ear. I say: revive and resurrect Article I. Let people say what they please. Let the crude, callus, and careless among us reveal themselves by their free and open expression of what's on their mind. Let them demonstrate their rudeness and antisocial behavior with their words instead of their deeds.

Seven minutes after Roger Clinton's repeated use of the "N" word, the video shows him snorting a line of cocaine laid out on the coffee table before him. Roger is quoted as saying, "I've got to get some [cocaine] for my brother; he's got a nose like a vacuum cleaner."[62]

12. RACISM

Who said this?

> *I'll have them niggers voting Democratic for the next two hundred years.*

Was it:

A. **James Carville.** Advisor to President Clinton.

B. **President Lyndon Baines Johnson.**

C. **Dick Morris.** Former advisor to President Clinton. Author of the book, *Behind the Oval Office: Winning the Presidency in the Nineties.* Alleged toe fancier.

D. **Mark Rosenbaum.** American Civil Liberties Union (ACLU) legal director.

E. **Charles Schumer,** U.S. Representative (D, New York).

The answer is

B. **Lyndon Baines Johnson.**

When/where:

Speaking to two governors about his true motivations regarding his support of civil rights legislation, while aboard Air Force One, as described in Ronald Kessler's book, *Inside the White House.*

Source:

"Behind the Lines," *The American Sentinel,* Issue #606, September 1997, page 9.

12. Lyndon Baines Johnson.

Comments:

Ronald Kessler reports further that a steward who witnessed the incident said, "That was the reason he was pushing the bill; it was strictly a political ploy for the Democratic party. He was phoney from the word 'go'."

I suppose you'd have to add that Johnson was a racist, too.

What strange circumstances we live in today. When it was revealed that Mark Fehrman used the "N" word years ago while discussing dialog for a movie, the media hounded him out of his job, home, and reputation. (Granted, it wasn't too smart to swear under oath he had never used the word.) But when it's revealed a president, a liberal president of the United States used the forbidden "N" word, the media react with deafening silence.

Balint Vazsonyi, director, Center for the American Founding, makes an interesting point: "Social justice is not to be confused with genuine concern for those who suffer . . . . The search for social justice provides a cover for the destruction of our legal system by setting unattainable goals, by fueling discontent, by insinuating a permanent state of hopelessness . . . . Social Justice . . . is what anyone says it is on any given day."[63]

13. RACISM

Who said this?

> *This is the time of the black man's rise and the white man's demise.*

Was it:

A. **Angela Davis.** Former U.S. Communist Party vice- presidential candidate. Executive director for Jesse Jackson's Rainbow Coalition.

B. **Louis Farrakhan.** Controversial U.S. religious leader. Organizer of the Million Man March.

C. **Jesse Louis Jackson.** Founder/executive director, Operation PUSH (People United to Serve Humanity). Democratic candidate for nomination for U.S. president. Founder and national president of the Rainbow Coalition. Interviewer, Both Sides with Jesse Jackson television show. Recipient of several awards including Humanitarian Father of the Year Award (1971) and Third Most Admired Man in America (Gallop Poll, 1985).[64]

D. **Carrie Meek.** U.S. Representative (D, Florida).

E. **Khallid Muhammad.** Close associate of Nation of Islam Leader Louis Farrakhan.

The answer is

E. **Khallid Muhammad.**

When/where:

During the Million Man March, October 1995.

Source:

"Quote of the Week," *Human Events,* October 27, 1995, page 1.

13. Former Nation of Islam official Khallid Abdul Muhammad speaks to a crowd of about 1,000 people May 28, 1994 in Los Angeles, telling them the enslavement of blacks has resulted in a holocaust "100 times worse than any other."

Comments:

Once again we encounter a simply outrageous statement, made in a public forum, yet the Propaganda Machine refuses to offer even a peep of criticism of one of its own . . . a liberal. Other Muhammad statements are even worse.[65] When will the media return to the tradition of evaluating and commenting upon the worth and substance of a person's *ideas* without regard to his or her color, race, gender, sexual preference, or other class distinction? But note it's the *liberals* who continue to focus on class distinction.

When Louis Farrakhan comments, as he did at a news conference in Tehran, Iran: "God will not give Japan and Europe the honor of bringing down the United States. This is an honor God will bestow on Muslims,"[66] why is outrage withheld? If we refuse to challenge *ideas* because of the race, creed, or color of those who utter them, then we have raised political correctness to the point of absurdity. We've also raised it to the point where it will rule.

In his book *The Disuniting of America - Reflections on a Multicultural Society,* author Arthur M. Schlesinger, Jr. notes: "The cult of ethnicity exaggerates differences, intensifies resentments and antagonisms, drives ever deeper the awful wedges between races and nationalities. The endgame is self-pity and self-ghettoization."[67]

Schlesinger quotes Theodore Roosevelt: "The one absolutely certain way of bringing this nation to ruin, of preventing all possibility of its continuing to be a nation at all, would be to permit it to become a tangle of squabbling nationalities, an intricate knot of German-Americans, Irish-Americans, English-Americans, French-Americans, Scandinavian-Americans, or Italian-Americans, each preserving its separate nationality."[68]

Certainly were Teddy Roosevelt with us today, he would add to his list African-Americans, Native-Americans, and Mexican-Americans, among others.

Schlesinger summarizes: "But even in the United States, ethnic ideologues have not been without effect. They have set themselves against the old American ideal of assimilation. They call on the republic to think in terms not of individual but of group identity and to move the polity from individual rights to group rights. They have made a certain progress in transforming the United States into a more segregated society. They have done their best to turn a college generation against Europe and the Western tradition. They have imposed ethnocentric, Afrocentric, and bilingual curricula on public schools, well designed to hold minority children out of American society. They have told young people from minority groups that the Western democratic tradition is not for them. They have encouraged minorities to see themselves as victims and to live by alibis rather than to claim the opportunities opened for them by the potent combination of black protest and white guilt. They have filled the air with recrimination and rancor and have remarkably advanced the fragmentation of American life."[69]

Speaking of group rights versus individual rights, Balint Vazsonyi makes an insightful observation in the Hillsdale College publication *Imprimis:* "Group rights are the negation of individual rights. Group rights say, in effect, 'You cannot and do not have rights as an individual - only as a member of a certain group.' The Constitution knows nothing about groups. Groups have no standing in the eyes of the law . . . . Individual rights and group rights are mutually exclusive."[70]

With group rights, who will look after *your* rights, if you're not in the *right* group?

Group rights are the liberal's battle cry: special (group) rights for blacks, special (group) rights for homosexuals, special (group) rights for women. For liberals, equality of opportunity is insufficient; equal *results* has become the focus and objective. And liberals want *their* hands on the controls to dole out rights in accord with *their* compassion and caring. But, as Philip K. Howard observes in his book, *The Death of Common Sense,* "Rights give open-ended power to one group, and it comes out of everybody else's hide."[71]

A letter to the *Human Events* editor provides interesting insight in this regard: "There are enormous differences . . . between equality of opportunity and equality of result. The former is capitalism, the latter is socialism."[72]

In his book, *Right from the Beginning,* Pat Buchanan observes: "So long as a people, any people, blames the real injustices in its past for all its present misfortunes, it forfeits its future. So long as a people, any people, seeks its salvation through politics, it will seek in vain. Only when the Irish buried their resentment and hatred of the British in the soil of their new country, America, did they get on with building their dreams."[73]

Buchanan adds: "If we Americans no longer share the same religious creed, the same code of morality, and manifestly we do not, the day is not far off when we will no longer share the same idea of virtue or freedom or patriotism, because, ultimately, these, too, are rooted in one's deepest beliefs, one's 'religious' beliefs."

14. REPUBLICANS

Who said this?

> *The republicans are the real threat. They are the real threat to our women, they are the real threat to our children, they are the real threat to the clean water, the clean air, the rich landscape in America. They are the real threat to fairness, to equality, to an enlightened Supreme Court.*

Was it:

A. **Mario Cuomo.** Politician. Former governor of New York. Briefly, a talk show host.

B. **Peter Charles Jennings.** Former Canadian television network anchorman. Producer of numerous network documentaries. Anchorman, Peter Jennings Reporting. Recipient of a number of awards including seven Emmy Awards for news reporting.[74]

C. **Larry Zeiger King.** Writer. Broadcaster. Radio and television personality. Movie actor. Talk show host of Larry King Live. Recipient of many broadcasting awards.[75]

D. **Tony Lake.** President Clinton's one-time choice for CIA director.

E. **Charles Rangel.** U.S. Representative (D, New York).

The answer is

A. **Mario Cuomo.**

14. Mario Cuomo.

When/where:

At the 1966 Democrat convention, as quoted in *The New York Post.*

Source:

"Stupid Quotes," *The Limbaugh Letter,* October 1996, page 11. ALSO: The November 1996 issue, page 5.

Comments:

Hey, Mario, don't be bashful,
if you don't like Republicans, just say so!

Representative John Lewis (D, Georgia) wasn't quite so verbose, but was equally caustic when he shouted out that the Republicans are "coming for our children, they're coming for the poor, they're coming for the sick, the elderly, the disabled."[76]

Al Gore took his turn at bat to slander the opposition with this charge: "The Republican leadership in this Congress is conducting a jihad on the environment . . . . If [the Republican budget] bill ever became law, our drinking water would be dirtier, would make more people sick, and would kill more people. Our air would be dirtier, make more people sick, and kill more people . . . . What [Republicans] want to do is make war on the kids of this country."[77]

Left-wing journalist Robert Scheer described Republicans as cold-hearted creatures who "would rather kill people than raise taxes."[78]

But perhaps the prize should go to *Washington Post* columnist Mary McGrory, who expressed her compassion on the subject of Republicans: "Human sacrifice is much in vogue right now. The Republican Right thinks that people who get on its nerves, especially women, should be sent to the stake . . . ."[79]

Gosh, if their hate-filled comments are ever reported widely by the mainstream media, liberals just might lose their highly touted reputation for compassion!

FREEDOM

Posterity, you will never know how much it has cost my generation to preserve your freedom. I hope you will make good use of it.

- John Quincy Adams[80]

[B]ecause you have never lost your freedom, because you have never been conquered, because you have never had all your possessions taken from you, you are now willing to surrender your freedom, independence, and autonomy by inches. You simply don't notice it, but, one inch at a time, it slips away.

- A German girl[81] who spent her childhood in East Berlin

15. COMMUNISM

Who said this?

> *I would think that if you understood what Communism was, you would hope, you would pray on your knees, that we would someday become communists.*

Was it:

A. **Earl Browder.** Head of the Communist Party in the U.S.
B. **Rachel Carson.** In her book *Silent Spring.*
C. **Jane Fonda.** Actress. Activist in the anti-nuclear, feminist, and peace movements. Producer. Star of Jane Fonda's New Workout & Weight-Loss Program (1986), Jane Fonda's New Pregnancy Workout & Total Birth Program (1989), and other videos. Recipient of many awards. Daughter of Henry Fonda. Wife of Ted Turner.[82]
D. **John Kenneth Galbraith.** Author of numerous books including *American Capitalism* (1952), *The Great Crash* (1955), *The Liberal Hour* (1960), *Annals of an Abiding Liberal* (1979). Economist, Harvard University.[83]
E. **Alger Hiss.** Former senior State Department official who was convicted of perjury for denying he had given secret U.S. documents to Whittaker Chambers for transfer to the Soviet Union. Secret agent for the Soviet Union.[84] Secretary-general of the San Francisco conference at which the United Nations was founded.

The answer is

C. **Jane Fonda.**

When/where:

At a gathering of students at Michigan State University, 1970.

Source:

The News Manipulators, by Reed Irvine, Joseph Goulden, and Cliff Kincaid, Book Distributors, Incorporated, 1993, page 292.

15. Jane Fonda at the Savoy Hotel in London for the filming of a television show, January 1965.

Comments:

If you or I made the plea preached by Jane Fonda, it would be inconsequential, for you and I have no power or influence. But Jane is connected to highly influential people around the country, around the world. She rubs noses with the elite, she parties with the power brokers, heck, she's married to one. Unfortunately, she's not alone with her liberal wishes and agendas.

The back lots of the movie industry, the hallowed halls of academia, the brightly lit television studios, the magazine and newspaper newsrooms all hum with the liberal beat. Silently, now not so subtly, steadily, these great voices of the Propaganda Machine sing out their message across the land.

Do you get the message? Do you buy it? What will it mean for your children and their children? What will it mean for the future of this once-great country? And for the world?

16. FAMILY

Who said this?

> *Childbearing [should be] a punishable crime against society, unless the parents hold a government license . . . . All potential parents [should be] required to use contraceptive chemicals, the government issuing antidotes [only] to citizens chosen for childbearing.*

Was it:

A. **David Brower.** Founder (1969), Friends of the Earth. Chairman, Earth Island Institute. Twice nominated for the Nobel Peace Prize.

B. A representative of the Chinese Communist government.

C. **Hillary Rodham Clinton.** Former chair the Children's Defense Fund ("Their name shouldn't be the Children's Defense Fund; it should be the Defense Fund for the Welfare State," asserts Robert Pambianco of the Capital Research Center). Former chair of the Legal Services Corporation. Author. Named Outstanding Layman of the Year (Phi Delta Kappa). Named one of the 100 Most Influential Lawyers (*American National Law Journal*). Recipient of numerous other awards.[85]

D. A representative of the U.S. Department of Education.

E. A representative of the U.S. Department of Health & Human Services.

The answer is

A. **David Brower.**

When/where:

Quoted from *Now Is the Dawning of the New Age New World Order,* by Dennis Lawrence Cuddy, Hearthstone Publications, 1991.

Source:

Trashing the Planet, by Dixy Lee Ray with Lou Guzzo, copyright © 1990 by Regnery Publishing, page 169. All rights reserved. Reprinted by special permission of Regnery Publishing, Incorporated.[86]

16. "I inherited the American dream," says David Brower in his San Francisco office in 1979, "and I wanted to see my children inherit that same dream. Berkeley Hills was my wilderness. Now my children can no longer see them."

Comments:

The Source quotes Kenneth Boulding, originator of the "Spaceship Earth" concept as saying: "The right to have children should be a marketable commodity, bought and traded by individuals but absolutely limited by the state."

Dixy Lee Ray says David "Brower believes 'other people's children' constitute pollution and are therefore an environmental concern."

"But enough," Dixy Lee Ray continues. "The common threads of belief that seem to run through these opinions are Malthusian ideas of finite resources, limits to growth, forced population control, a distrust of human beings, a belief in the omnipotence of the State and its ability to control individual choice, and a rejection of science, technology, and industrialization. Does this represent the convictions of most Americans? No way!"

17. FAMILY

Who said this?

> *We really don't know how to raise children. If we want to talk about equality of opportunity for children, then the fact that children are raised in families means there's no equality . . . . In order to raise children with equality, we must take them away from families and communally raise them.*

Was it:

A. **David Brower.** Founder (1969), Friends of the Earth. Chairman, Earth Island Institute. Twice nominated for the Nobel Peace Prize.

B. A representative of the Chinese Communist government.

C. **Hillary Rodham Clinton.** Former chair the Children's Defense Fund ("Their name shouldn't be the Children's Defense Fund; it should be the Defense Fund for the Welfare State," asserts Robert Pambianco of the Capital Research Center). Former chair of the Legal Services Corporation. Author. Named Outstanding Layman of the Year (Phi Delta Kappa). Named one of the 100 Most Influential Lawyers (*American National Law Journal*). Recipient of numerous other awards.[87]

D. A representative of the U.S. Department of Education.

E. A former representative of the U.S. Department of Health & Human Services.

The answer is

E. **Dr. Mary Jo Bane,** former Clinton Administration assistant secretary of administration for children and families in the U.S. Department of Health and Human Services. Now, professor of public policy at Harvard's Kennedy School of Government.

17. Mary Jo Bane, educational researcher, in her office at Harvard University, September 22, 1972.

When/where:

Not specified by Source.

Source:

"Target: Total Government," by William Norman Grigg, *The New American,* September 16, 1996, page 29.[88]

Comments:

Proposals have already been made to license parents.[89] Norman Grigg (Source) notes that any parent-licensing system would "enshrine in law a presumption of parental incompetence."

Professor David Lykken of the University of Minnesota says, "if children were born to unlicensed parents, the state would intervene immediately. Licenses would be checked in hospital maternity wards. Unlicensed parents would lose their children permanently . . . ."[90]

Grigg also quotes Professor Gene Stephens, University of South Carolina, who in 1981 said: "In most cases, certified couples would be allowed to have their own natural children. In some instances, however . . . couples will be licensed to breed, but will give up their children to other people licensed to rear them."

Welcome to the New World Order!

18. FAMILY

Who said this?

> *Each child belongs to the state.*

Was it:

A. **Larry Flint.** Publisher/editor, *Hustler* magazine.
B. **Anita Hill.** Government worker who gained national attention when she accused Supreme Court nominee Clarence Thomas of sexual harassment.
C. **Bob Chase.** President of the National Education Association (NEA).
D. **William Seawell.** Professor of education, University of Virginia.
E. **Donna Shalala.** U.S. Secretary for Health and Human Services. Dubbed "high priestess of political correctness" for supporting harsh "speech codes" at the University of Wisconsin where she was chancellor.[91] "Outed" in April 1993 as a closeted lesbian by her own press secretary, Victor Zonana (homosexual and co-founder of the National Lesbian & Gay Journalists Association).[92]

The answer is

D. **William Seawell.**

18. Dr. Seawell served as professor of education at the University of Virginia and chair of the Department of Administration and Supervision. He was also associate executive secretary of the Virginia School Boards Association and consultant to the State Board of Education and 10 school divisions.

When/where:

As quoted in Dr. Sheldon Richman's 1994 book *Separating School and State,* page 51, published by the Future of Freedom Foundation, Fairfax, Virginia.

Source:

"Whose Children?" by William Norman Grigg, *The New American,* July 21, 1997, page 4.

Comments:

The Source states: "As the resources of the Rockefeller, Carnegie, Ford, and other foundations became available to underwrite their designs, subversives and collectivists within the school system became brazen about their intentions. In 1932, George S. Counts, a Fabian Socialist who taught at Columbia University Teachers College, instructed his followers that 'teachers should deliberately reach for power and then make the most of their conquest' by seeking to 'influence the social attitudes, ideals, and behavior of the coming generation.'"

And just what kind of influence, training, and behavior did Counts have in mind? Grigg continues: "The 'knowledge' the educrats had in mind, of course, was not the moral and intellectual wisdom needed to live responsibly in a free society, but the propaganda required to win blind obedience to the arbitrary dictates of an all-powerful state. Students, in fact, would be conditioned to view the state (not the family) as the most important of all loyalties and institutions and (eventually) to love Big Brother."

Grigg adds, "The state would equip its students with enough 'knowledge' to perform certain tasks in the interests of the state, but not enough to think independently or to yearn for freedom."

Now, more than 65 years later, the public education bureaucracy is bold and confident in its usurpation of parental rights. Consider as illustration the recent incident in a Pennsylvania public school, as described by the Source: "On March 19, 1996 at the J.T. Lambert Intermediate School in East Stroudsburg, Pennsylvania, 59 eleven-year-old girls were herded into the school nurse's office, told to remove their clothes, and forced to undergo a genital examination. Many of the children began crying, only to be berated for acting like 'babies'. Some of them tried to escape. School authorities explained after the fact the children were [being] inspected for abnormalities or symptoms of venereal disease and that parents had been given the opportunity to exempt their children from the exam. However, several of the traumatized girls had been examined over the explicit objections of their parents."

The Source quotes Katie Tucker, whose 11-year-old daughter was one of those forcibly examined. Katie Tucker told the press: "The girls were scared. They were crying and trying to run out of the door, but one of the nurses was blocking the door so they couldn't leave. My daughter told the other nurse that 'My mother wouldn't like this. I want to call her.' And they said, 'No.' And my daughter said, 'I don't want this test done.' And the nurse said, 'Too bad.'"

Dr. Ramlah Vahanvaty responded to parental criticism by dismissing it as a product of "ignorance". "Even a parent doesn't have the right to say what's appropriate for a physician to do," Dr. Vahanvaty declared, insisting that the forcible violation of eleven-year-old girls was "in the best interest of the children."

Portrait of today's American family: father, mother, child, and (not pictured) big government. Who's in charge?

Parents were outraged, properly so, and complained to the school board. The board, however, was not only unsympathetic, it rebuffed the criticism, took no action to condemn examinations, and as a matter of fact, said the examinations would continue![93] Rutherford Institute attorneys are working on the case, but as of this writing, there is no resolution.

Norman Grigg continues: "To the extent that government at any level had any role in family policy, it was to be a local responsibility. In contemporary America, however, 'family policy' is defined by the central government, and the public school system is the primary means through which federal intervention in the home is facilitated. After all, as Hillary Rodham Clinton maintains, 'it takes a village to raise a child' - 'village' in this instance referring to the state."

Dr. Allan C. Carlson, editor and publisher of *The Family in America* newsletter, asserts that the idea of "freeing the individual from family and religious authority led *ironically* and *inevitably* to the grander oppressions of the twentieth century . . . . Man and women have been 'liberated' from meaningful ties to children, parents, and kin, in order to become servants and dependents of the parental state."[94]

The Source quotes Sheldon Richman, author of *Separating School and State,* as saying: "The future of education, and of America as a free society, depends on the liberation of the American family from the grip of the public school."

I might add that it depends on the liberation of the child from the grip of the state, as well. Hillary Rodham Clinton represented well the liberal view when she remarked, "There's no such thing as other people's children."[95]

19. FAMILY

Who said this?

> *Every child is our child.*

Was it:

A. Preamble to the "United Nations Convention on Rights of the Child" treaty.
B. Slogan used by AFDC (Aid for Dependent Children).
C. Slogan used by the Children's Defense Fund.
D. Slogan used by UNICEF (UN International Children's Emergency Fund).
E. Slogan used by the YMCA (Young Men's Christian Association).

The answer is

D. UNICEF slogan.

When/where:

UNICEF slogan.

Source:

"Your Child, the Global Citizen," by William Norman Grigg, *The New American,* July 21, 1997, page 40.[96]

19. UNICEF symbol.

Comments:

So there you have it. And you thought your child was *your* child. How old fashioned.

In another article, "Supplanting Parents," Grigg states: "Early intervention programs such as Head Start and Early Start extend the influence of the federal government literally into the nursery, and - as President Clinton declared as he signed the Goals 2000 Act in 1994 - the intention is to enroll every American child into Head Start 'or another program like it.'"[97]

Grigg says "the objective is to instill in students a disposition to look upon the state, and not the family, as worthy of the individual's highest loyalty."

Consider this quotation: "We must remove the children from the crude influence of their families . . . . We must take them over and, to speak frankly, nationalize them . . . ." In essence that's the policy in the U.S. public school system today, but the quotation was actually a statement to Soviet educators by Communist Party officials in 1918. "From the first days of their lives they will be under the healthy influence of Communist children's nurseries and schools. There they will grow up to be real Communists."[98]

The Soviet game plan seems to be playing out right here.

20. FREEDOM

Who said this?

> *[W]hen we got organized as a country . . . we wrote a fairly radical [U.S.] Constitution with a radical Bill of Rights, giving a radical amount of individual freedom to Americans . . . so a lot of people say there's too much personal freedom . . . . When personal freedom's being abused, you have to move to limit it.*

Was it:

A. **Roseanne Barr.** Comedienne. Star of the Roseanne television show. Star of the film *She-Devil,* 1989.

B. **Bill Clinton.** Former Arkansas governor. President of the United States.

C. **Katherin Graham.** Retired publisher of *The Washington Post.* President of the Washington Post Company, publisher of the *Washington Post.* Owner of *Newsweek.* Member, Council on Foreign Relations. Fellow, American Academy of Arts and Sciences. Member, National Press Club.[99]

D. **Robert Bernard Reicht.** Author of *The Next American Frontier* (1983), *The Work of Nations* (1991), and other books. Close friend of Bill Clinton. Fellow Rhodes Scholar. Former U.S. Labor Secretary.[100]

E. **George Stephanopoulos.** Contributor to *Newsweek* and ABC News at the same time he was counselor to the President, advising Clinton on the Paula Jones matter.

20. Bill Clinton, January 7, 1996.

The answer is

B. **Bill Clinton.**

When/where:

During a television appearance April 19, 1994.

Source:

"Target: Total Government," by William Norman Grigg, *The New American,* September 16, 1996, page 27.[101]

Comments:

Hey, we're talking really dangerous "radicals" here, like George Washington, Alexander Hamilton, Ben Franklin, James Madison, and the other Signers of the U.S. Constitution. Golly, who can trust *those* guys?

The Source points out that from Clinton's perspective, the "federal government retains plenary powers to take away 'excessive' freedom." However, students of the Declaration of Independence know this flies in the face of a fundamental principle: "We hold these truths to be self-evident, that all men are created equal, that they are *endowed by their Creator with certain unalienable rights,* that among these are life, liberty, and the pursuit of happiness . . . ."

These words apparently don't impress Senator Bob Kerry (D, Nebraska): "I don't think the problem is that we don't have enough freedom," said he. "For gosh sakes, I've got so much freedom, I don't know what to do with it all."[102]

In a *Chicago Tribune* poll 27% of the respondents said the guarantee of free speech in the First Amendment to the U.S. Constitution goes "too far in the rights it guarantees."[103]

Berkeley Law Professor Robert Post says: "The whole point of the Constitution is to limit at some point and in some way popular will."[104] The Signers must be flipping in their graves.

21. FREEDOM

Who said this?

> *[The federal government should] make national service mandatory and assign the Selective Service System the task of locating 18-year-olds and matching them with national service slots.*

Was it:

A. **Roberta Achtenberg.** Former Assistant Secretary for Fair Housing, HUD. Board member of the United Way.
B. **Edward Fouhy.** Former ABC and CBS executive. Head of the Pew Center for Civic Journalism.
C. **Lani Guinier.** Nominee to head the Civil Rights Division of the Justice Department.
D. **John F. Kennedy, Jr.** Editor, *George Magazine.* Son of President and Mrs. J. F. Kennedy.
E. **Scott Shuger.** Consultant to the federal government on National Service.

The answer is

E. **Scott Shuger.**

When/where:

In an article in the January 1996 issue of *The Washington Monthly.*

Source:

"Service of Slavery?" by William Norman Grigg, *The New American,* July 21, 1997, page 46.

21. *"Hmm. Suppose I choose not to volunteer. I wonder what the consequences would be. A fine, maybe? Prison? Some kind of freeze out of the job market? Just how will the government go about enforcing a behavior it wishes to impose on the American people?"*

Comments:

President Clinton apparently agrees with Mr. Shuger's suggestion. As he said at the volunteering summit in Philadelphia in 1997, "[I]f you're asked in school, 'What does it mean to be a good citizen,' I want the answer to be . . . you have to obey the law, you've got to go to work or be in school, you've got to pay your taxes and, oh, yes, you *have to serve* . . . ." [Emphasis added.] So, there it is: compulsory volunteerism, an amazing oxymoron from your friendly federal government.

William Norman Grigg (Source) says "In other words, national service is seen by Mr. Clinton as a means of teaching students that the state must intervene to solve the nation's social ills and that, consequently, their duty to the state transcends any other loyalty."

Grigg also quotes Thomas Moralis, father of two straight-A students denied high school diplomas for refusing to meet school "community service" requirements: "What they're trying to do is enslave our society by taking our children's rights away. Young people who go through these programs learn to submit, and later on they won't mind giving up a few more of their rights when the government says it's necessary."

22. LIFE

Who said this?

> *[The scarcity of world resources imposes] a duty to die . . . [a] responsibility to end one's life in the absence of any terminal illness . . . a duty to die even when one would prefer to live . . . .*
>
> *A duty to die is more likely when you have already lived a rich and full life. You have already had a full share of the good things life offers.*

Was it:

A. **Al Franken.** Author of *Rush Limbaugh is a Big Fat Idiot - and Other Observations,* which was followed by a book by J. P. Mauro titled: *Al Franken is a Buck-Toothed Moron - and Other Observations.*

B. **Ruth Bader Ginsburg.** General counsel for the ACLU (1973-1980). Supporter of the Equal Rights Amendment and the homosexual agenda. U.S. Supreme Court Justice.[105]

C. **John Hardwig.** Professor of medical ethics and social political philosophy at East Tennessee State University.

D. **Ralph Nader.** Consumer affairs activist. Socialist.[106]

E. **Dr. Ruth Westheimer.** (Karola Ruth Siegel Westheimer.) Psychologist. Sexologist. Television personality. Author of several books including *The Art of Arousal* (1993) and *Dr. Ruth's Encyclopedia of Sex* (1994).[107]

The answer is

C. **John Hardwig.**

When/where:

In his article in the March/April 1997 issue of *The Hastings Center Report.*

Source:

"'Duty' to Die" ("Insider Report"), *The New American,* July 7, 1997, page 6.

22. How many candles is too many candles?

Comments:

The Source asks: "What about those who have reached their eighth and ninth decades and haven't exhausted their enthusiasm for life? 'To have reached the age of, say 75 or 80 years, without being ready to die is itself a moral failing, the sign of a life out of touch with life's basic realities,' lectures Professor Hardwig."

Reacting to Professor Hardwig's assertions, columnist Nat Hentoff quipped: "John Hardwig says 'we fear death too much.' My sense is that we do not fear bioethicists enough."

Richard Lamm, advisor to the Clintons on health care, was quite blunt about the matter: "Old people have a duty to die and get out of the way."[108]

You, too, may think Hardwig's and Lamm's ideas are absurd, but a change in moral values is gradually creeping across the countryside. Jack Kevorkian's "gentle" pushes over the precipice, which many people strongly support, are but a small step from a systematic plan of euthanasia. Look at what's going on in Holland. There, more than a thousand patients are *involuntarily* euthanized each year, about three every day. Pediatricians are killing mentally retarded babies and those with other birth defects.[109]

From appearances, the medical establishment in this country seems anxious or at least ready for a change of ethical robes in anticipation of following Holland's lead.

23. RELIGION

Who said this?

> *The wrong kind of faith leads to division and conflict. Prejudice and contempt cloaked in the presence of religion or political conviction are no different. These forces have nearly destroyed our nation in the past. We shall overcome them. We shall replace them with a generous spirit of a people that feel at home with one another.*

Was it:

A. **Fidel Castro.** President, Cuba.
B. **Bill Clinton.** Governor, Arkansas, 1979-1981, 1983-1992. President, U.S., 1992-present.
C. **Louis Farrakhan.** Clergyman. Father of nine children. Recipient of the designation of sheikh and imam by attendees at the International Islamic People's Conference (sponsored by Farrakhan and Moammar Gadhafi).[110]
D. **Al From.** President, Democratic Leadership Council.
E. **Oprah Winfrey.** Popular television talk show host. Actress. Producer. Recipient of numerous awards including Woman of Achievement Award (NOW, 1986), Emmy for Best Daytime Talkshow Host (1987, 1991, 1992), and America's Hope Award (1990).[111]

The answer is

B. **Bill Clinton.**

When/where:

In his inaugural address, January 20, 1997.

Source:

Facts, Truth, Evidence that Will Affect All Americans, support material for David Wegener's video *Barbed Wire on America,* page 17.

23. Bill Clinton, May 8, 1993.

Comments:

It sounds as though Mr. Clinton is suggesting that he, with infinite liberal wisdom, has decided what constitutes the "wrong kind of faith." One would then naturally presume he has also decided what constitutes the *right* kind of faith.

"We shall overcome," the president asserts, "these forces [that] have nearly destroyed our nation . . . ." Well, well, well! Just how does he intend to do so? With politically correct laws? With politically correct police? With politically correct prison terms for all those whose views and faith don't correspond with Mr. Clinton's?

The liberal, compassionate Clinton administration first intimidated, then destroyed the "faithful" at Waco, Texas. Seventy-eight men, women, and children were harassed, gassed, and torched by government forces.[112] Is *your* faith "approved" by Mr. Clinton? Do *you* belong to "acceptable" organizations, as determined by the liberal bureaucrats? Are *you* thinking "proper" thoughts?

My understanding is that the First Amendment to the U.S. Constitution addresses that topic: providing a guarantee of the right to free speech and religious freedom. Mr. Clinton doesn't seem to think so.

24. RELIGION

Who said this?

> 1. *Christianity promotes a deep cultural pathology of human greed and addictions.*
>
> 2. *We must rethink our ideas about God; we should place less emphasis on Christ as a person and a redeemer. We should put the Bible away for 20 years while we radically rethink our religious ideas.*

Was it:

A. **Larry Abraham** and **Franklin Sanders.** Authors of *The Greening,* Soundview Publications, Atlanta, Georgia, 1993.

B. **Father Thomas Berry.** Gaia worshiper. Dissident Catholic priest. Leader of the Temple of Understanding in New York City.

C. **Mikhail Gorbachev.** Former Russian dictator. Leader of the World Green Cross.

D. **Hugh Hefner.** Publisher, *Playboy* magazine.

E. **Virginia Wetherell.** Secretary, Department of Environmental Protection.

The answer is

B. **Father Thomas Berry.**

When/where:

1. Not specified by Source.
2. In Berry's book *Dream of the Earth,* published by Sierra Club Books.[113]

Sources:

1. *Special Report - Who is Leading the Attack on American Liberty?,* by David A. Russell, 1996, page 85.[114]
2. "Invasion of Green Religion," *ēco•logic,* November/ December 1995, page 27.[115]

24. Father Thomas Berry. We can test his hypothesis about Christianity promoting greed and addictions by simply asking the question: are non-Christians less greedy and have they fewer addictions?

Comments:

The *ēco•logic* source reports that the Cathedral of St. John the Divine, home of the Temple of Understanding, is also home of both the Gaia Institute and the Lindesfarne Association, which were nurtured by, of all people, then-Senator Al Gore. In 1994 then-Vice-President Al Gore delivered a sermon in that august cathedral, proclaiming: "God is not separate from the earth," the Gaia religion's central tenet.[116]

The New York City cathedral on occasion could readily pass as a kind of indoor zoo. Crab, bass, mussels, and other water creatures live in an "Earth Shrine" habitat there. One wall is decorated with orchids, ferns, mosses, and aquatic plants. At a service celebrating the Feast of St. Francis, with a robed Al Gore sermonizing, nature was "honored" by parading a camel and elephant up and down the aisles, while worshipers carried a bowl of compost and worms in a procession to the altar.[117]

I saw a video of one of those services on television. Dogs, snakes, and animals of all descriptions were delivered to the altar to receive a blessing from a woman cleric. "God bless you," she said, greeting each creature by name, "in the name of the Father, and of the Son, and of the Holy Spirit."[118]

25. RELIGION

Who said this?

> *The two big mistakes [are] the belief . . . that there's a man in the sky with ten things he doesn't want you to do and you'll burn for a long time if you do them . . . and private property, which I think is at the core of our failure as a species.*

Was it:

A. **Alan Alda.** Actor. Director. Writer. Star of the award-winning television series M*A*S*H.

B. **Dan Becker.** Energy program director, the Sierra Club.

C. **George Carlin.** Comedian.

D. **Whoopi Goldberg.** Comedienne. Television and motion pictures star. Winner of an Oscar for Best Supporting Actress in *Ghost,* (1990).

E. **Howard Stern.** Radio talk show host. Recording artist of "50 Ways to Rank Your Mother" and others. Host of pay-per-view television specials including "Howard Stern's Negligee and Underpants Party," "The Miss Howard Stern New Year's Eve Pageant," and others. Libertarian candidate for N.Y. State governor (1994). Honored by having a rest stop on I-295 in New Jersey named after him.[119]

The answer is

C. **George Carlin.**

When/where:

In an interview that appeared in the March/April 1997 issue of *Mother Jones.*

Source:

"When Left-Wing Stars Speak as 'Experts'," by L. Brent Bozell, III, *Human Events,* April 25, 1997, page 20.

25. George Carlin, many years prior to his *Mother Jones* interview.

Comments:

Now you may wish to pooh-pooh the rantings and ravings of the likes of George Carlin. And indeed, I'd like to, too, for his outbursts are basically inconsequential when one looks at the big picture.

But Carlin's perspective on religion or a view close to it, seems to appear all too frequently in the public school classroom, and *there* it isn't inconsequential at all. Berit Kjos tells us about Professor Sidney Simon's book, *Values Clarification - A Handbook of Practical Strategies for Teachers and Students:* "Among the classroom exercises which soon filtered into textbooks and schools everywhere was a tactic called 'values voting'. The teacher simply asks questions dealing with personal values. The students say 'yes' by raising their hands, 'no' by pointing their thumbs down. They discuss the answers. Consider some of the questions: for example, 'How many of you would choose to die and go to heaven, if it meant playing a harp all day?' [And] 'How many of you think you will continue to practice religions, just like your parents?'"[120]

What in heaven's name are questions like these doing in your son's or daughter's classroom?

26. RELIGION

Who said this?

> *Every child who believes in God is mentally ill.*

Was it:

A. **Dr. Paul Brandwein.** Leading U.S. child psychologist.

B. **James Carville.** Former Clinton campaign manager and Democratic strategist, who, in one of his campaigns to defame people, said of Paula Jones April 7, 1994: "Drag a $100 bill through a trailer camp, and there's no telling what you'll find." He also said, "Ken Starr is one mistake away from not having any kneecaps."[121]

C. **Jeffrey Dahmer.** Serial killer.

D. **Carl Jung.** Swiss psychiatrist.

E. **Dr. Benjamin McLane Spock.** Child care "expert". People's Party candidate for U.S. president (1972) and vice president (1976). Author of *Baby and Child Care,* 50 million copies of which have been printed, making it the best-selling nonfiction book after the Bible.[122] Spock once said, "To save children from radiation I became a public supporter of a test ban treaty and co-chairman of SANE [National Committee for a Sane Nuclear Policy] in 1962, which led eventually to full-time opposition to the Vietnam War, conviction for conspiracy, [and] conversion to socialism."[123]

The answer is

A. **Dr. Paul Brandwein.**

When/where:

Not specified by Source.

Source:

Bill Clinton: Friend or Foe? by Ann Wilson, 1994, page 175.[124]

26. Are they to be rounded up and dispatched to nearby insane asylums?

Comments:

The Source quotes Dr. Sidney Simon, lecturer and educator, who instructs teachers: "We do not need any more preaching about right and wrong. The old 'thou shalt nots' simply are not relevant. Values Clarification is a method for teachers to change the values of children without getting caught."

A mathematics teaching guide used in California advises: "Your job is . . . not to judge the rightness and wrongness of each student's answer. Let those determinations come from the class."[125]

Perhaps most distressing is a passage from the book *Weep for Your Children* praising the Values Clarification/Situation Ethics program being taught today in America's public schools: "It's OK to lie. It's OK to steal. It's OK to have premarital sex. It's OK to cheat or to kill if these things are part of your value system, and you clarified these values for yourself. The important thing is not what values you choose, but that you have chosen them yourself freely and without coercion of parents, spouse, priest, friends, ministers, or social pressure of any kind."[126]

This is the rich harvest Humanism has yielded, and many subscribers now eagerly partake of its bounty. The concepts of right and wrong have simply vanished along with outhouses, garters, and 45-RPM records.

27. RELIGION

Who said this?

> 1. *Fundamental, Bible-believing people do not have the right to indoctrinate their children in their religious beliefs because we, the state, are preparing them for the year 2000, when America will be part of a one-world global society and their children will not fit in.*
>
> 2. *The reason we have to regulate . . . church schools is that . . . children that are not trained in state-controlled schools will not fit in.*

Was it:

A. **Michael Eisner.** CEO and chairman of the board of the Walt Disney Company.
B. **Richard Gephardt.** U.S. Representative (D, Montana).
C. **Peter Hoagland.** U.S. Representative (D, Nebraska).
D. **Michael John McCloskey.** Member of the steering committee, Blueprint for the Environment. Vice chairman, American Committee on International Conservation. Chairman, Sierra Club. One who spoke the wisdom: "Trees and rocks have rights to their own freedom, to go their own way untrammeled and unfettered by man."[127]
E. **Sir Peter Scott.** Chairman of the Fauna Society.

The answer is

C. **Peter Hoagland.**

27. Peter Hoagland, 1989.

When/where:

A. While speaking with Pastor Everett Sileven on the radio, 1983.
B. While commenting during a televised debate.

Sources:

1. *Bill Clinton, Friend or Foe?* by Ann Wilson, 1994, page 170.[128]
2. *Facts, Truth, Evidence that Will Affect All Americans,* support material for David Wegener's video *Barbed Wire on America,* page 32.

Comments:

In her booklet strangely titled *Body Snatching and the New World Odor,* author Shirley Correll includes a quotation from UNESCO (United Nations Educational, Scientific, and Cultural Organization) Publication 356: "As long as the child breathes the poisoned air of nationalism (patriotism), education in world-mindedness can produce only rather precarious results. As we have pointed out, it is frequently the family that infects the child with extreme nationalism. The school should therefore . . . combat family attitudes that favor jingoism (war mongering) . . . . We shall presently recognize in nationalism the major obstacle to the development of worldmindedness . . . . [E]ach member nation . . . has a duty to see to it that nothing in its curriculum, course of study and textbooks is contrary to UNESCO's aims."[129]

In other words, the UN is writing the rules! The UN is now your board of education and UN ideology is right on track to transcend national rights, state rights, and personal rights.

Have a nice day.

28. SOVEREIGNTY

Who said this?

You're wasting your time, man. We're going to take your country whether you like it or not. You know there are so many of us. Now you know, you might as well give it up, man. We're going to control your government and everything because of sheer numbers. Don't you realize we have the freedom to vote now and that we're out-reproducing you people six to one? Who do you think's going to be running this state, man? Give it up. Take a vacation. You've had it, man. Now we're going to take your country from you - something the Japs couldn't do. We're going to do it easy and you're going to help us - your government - cause you're stupid.

Was it:

A. A caller to The American Immigration Control Foundation.
B. A caller to the California Coalition for Immigration Reform.
C. A caller to C-SPAN during a morning call-in program.
D. A caller to **Rush Limbaugh** on his radio program.
E. A caller to **Pete Wilson,** governor, California.

The answer is

B. Unidentified Hispanic male who left a recorded message for the California Coalition for Immigration Reform (CCIR).

28. The Nation of Aztlan: the seven southwestern (shaded) states.

When/where:

Believed to be during 1996.

Source:

*9*1*1,* a publication of CCIR, Volume IV, Issue 12, December 1996, page 2.

Comments:

There are many supporters of the idea that much of the southwest U.S. should be deeded to Mexico so it can be transformed into the Nation of Aztlan. Some of our politicians are more outspoken on the subject than others.

"Mexico, some of us say, is the country this land used to belong to," said Mike Hernandez, Los Angeles city council, June 1997.[130]

"As goes the Latino population, so goes California and so goes America. That is what southwest voters must do, you must stand for our Latino future . . . ."[131] So spoke Henry Cisneros, then HUD Secretary, July 1995.

"We're proud to stand with you against Proposition 187. We'll fight it in other states as well. We're counting on you. You really hold the key. Hispanics are on the move." Words of encouragement from vice-president Al Gore in 1995.[132]

So much for the melting pot.

Cliff Kincaid says: "America's immediate threat is a movement of Mexicans - here and abroad - who are actively plotting to get the territory taken during the Mexican-American War, which they call Aztlan, returned to Mexico."[133]

Thomas Chittum, author of *Civil War Two,* tells us: "Like it or not, ignore it or not, the Mexicans are taking the southwest back, and short of sealing our border with Mexico there is precious little we can do about it."[134]

29. SOVEREIGNTY

Who said this?

> *The time of absolute and exclusive sovereignty . . . has passed.*

Was it:

A. **Bruce Babbitt.** Former head of the League of Conservation Voters (a radical environmental group). U.S. Secretary of the Department of Interior. One who is sometimes referred to as "Bruce the Green Goose."[135]

B. **Boutros Boutros-Ghali.** Egyptian politician. Former member of the Central Committee of the Arab Socialist Union. Author of various publications. Former United Nations Secretary General.[136]

C. **Erskine Bowles, Jr.** President Clinton's chief of staff.

D. **Keith Olbermann.** Television commentator of the nightly news broadcast The Big Show on MSNBC.

E. **Ernesto Zedillo.** Mexico President.

The answer is

B. **Boutros Boutros-Ghali.**

When/where:

As stated in his June 1992 report, *An Agenda for Peace.*

Source:

"Coming Shift in UN Leadership," by John F. McManus, *The New American,* November 11, 1996, page 44.[137]

29. Boutros Boutros-Ghali at UN Headquarters in New York City, during a rare news conference in which he discussed UN peacekeeping operations, January 5, 1995.

Comments:

The Source says Boutros Boutros-Ghali declared the UN should intervene within national borders over issues of ecological damage, disruption of family life, unchecked population growth, disparity between rich and poor, drought, ozone depletion, etc. By definition such intrusion by a foreign power would signal the extermination of U.S. sovereignty.

In a 1996 speech at England's Oxford University, Boutros-Ghali called for UN power to tax international financial transactions, fossil fuel use, and international air travel - another slap at U.S. sovereignty. UN General Secretary Kofi Annan said, "The U.S. can go to hell. We are in charge now."[138]

I have a question for all those anxious for one-world government: who, pray tell, will speak for *your* interests in the powerful UN world bureaucracy? The single U.S. vote in such a body (we'll have no veto power) could be negated by any other country in the world! And *will be* if UN General Assembly history is any measure.

U.S. Representative Roscoe Bartlett (R-Maryland) says: "There are people who genuinely believe that our interests are best served if we become weaker and weaker and the UN becomes stronger and stronger . . . . These people are called globalists, new-world-order, one-world-government people. Our President [Clinton] is a globalist."[139]

30. SOVEREIGNTY

Who said this?

> *Nationhood as we know it will be obsolete, all states will recognize a single, global authority . . . . [N]ational sovereignty wasn't such a great idea after all.*

Was it:

A. **Madeleine Albright.** Former U.S. delegate to the UN. U.S. Secretary of State.
B. **Kofi Annan.** UN General Secretary.
C. **Susan Rachel Estrich.** Law educator. Columnist for *U.S.A. Today.* President, *Harvard Law Review.* Member of the national governing board of Common Cause. Political analyst and campaign manager for the Dukakis-for-President 1988 presidential campaign.[140]
D. **David Rockefeller.** Billionaire. Humanist. CFR (Council on Foreign Relations) kingpin. Founder of the Trilateral Commission.
E. **Strobe Talbott.** Rhodes Scholar. Former *Time* columnist. One-time college roommate of Bill Clinton. U.S. Deputy Secretary of State.

The answer is

E. **Strobe Talbott.**

When/where:

In his article titled "The Birth of the Global Nation," that appeared in the July 20, 1992 issue of *Time* Magazine.

Source:

The Phyllis Schlafly Report, June 1994, page 3, and October 1997, page 1.[141]

30. Strobe Talbott (left), December 28, 1993, at the announcement by Secretary of State Warren Christopher (right) of Talbott's nomination as Deputy Secretary of State.

Comments:

Phyllis Schlafly says of Mr. Talbott: "He is eager to get rid of nationalism and patriotism and to replace American independence and sovereignty with world government . . . . Talbott bragged about how national sovereignty has been diminished by the International Monetary Fund and the General Agreement on Tariffs and Trade (GATT) . . . . If the IMF and GATT are indeed diminutions of national sovereignty on the road to world government, the American people were never so advised."

In his book, *The Arrogance of Power,* Senator William Fulbright, former chairman of the Senate Foreign Relations Committee writes: "In the world family of nations, sovereignty is one of the key conditions of existence, and sovereignty is inviolate . . . . The day [sovereignty] breaks down will be the beginning of the end of world order and of a return to the rule of brute force."[142]

31. VOTING RIGHTS

Who said this?

> *[W]e must look into [proposals for giving non-citizens the right to vote].*

Was it:

A. **Mary Frances Berry.** Chair of the eight-member U.S. Commission on Civil Rights.
B. **Leonel Castillo.** Former commissioner of the INS (Immigration and Naturalization Service) under President Jimmy Carter.
C. **Jeoffrey Cowan.** Director, Voice of America.
D. **Doris Meissner.** Commissioner of the INS.
E. **Ross Perot.** Businessman. Founder of Electronic Data Systems Corp. Politician. U.S. presidential candidate (1992 and 1996).

The answer is

B. **Leonel Castillo.**

When/where:

At the Latino Leadership Summit Conference, Riverside, California, January 1995.

Source:

Border Watch, newsletter of The American Immigration Control Foundation, March 1995, page 4.

31. Leonel Castillo, head of the INS, March 1979.

Comments:

According to a May 5, 1996 *Washington Times* item titled "Immigrant Rights," in 1990 a total of 123,898 of San Francisco's 607,210 adults were noncitizens. That's real clout if it can be turned into voting power. The spokeswoman for California Secretary of State Bill Jones said he "will challenge the constitutionality of that [petition to let noncitizens vote] every step of the way . . . . Only citizens are granted the right to vote."[143]

Well, at least so far. Well, at least according to the law.

Mr. Castillo sounds a little timid in his comments about allowing noncitizens to vote, but Mr. Laughlin McDonald, head of the ACLU Voting Rights Project in Atlanta is not. In an interview June 11, 1997 he said, "These people have some claim to fair representation, whether they're citizens or not."[144]

I wonder what changes Mr. McDonald has in mind for the U.S. Constitution. "You've got to represent people whether they're voters or not," he said.[145]

Author Thomas Chittum describes the consequences: "If illegal aliens are allowed to vote, even in local elections, it will be another unmistakable signal that American citizenship, and therefore America itself, is finished."[146]

The headline of an article in *Human Events* sums up: "California Will Not Indict Illegal Foreign Voters."[147]

POWER AND CONTROL

Power gradually extirpates from the mind every humane and gentle virtue.

- Edmund Burke[148]
A Vindication of Natural Society, 1756

[T]here have existed, in every age and every country, two distinct orders of men - the lovers of freedom and the devoted advocates of power.

- Robert Y. Hayne[149]

There is scarce[ly] a [ruler] in a hundred who would not, if he could, get first all the people's money, then all their lands, and then make them and their children servants forever.

- Benjamin Franklin[150]
1787

32. ANIMALS

Who said this?

> 1. *Pet ownership is slavery.*
>
> 2. *I don't believe human beings have the "right to life." That's a supremacist perversion. A rat is a pig is a dog is a boy.*

Was it:

A. A member of the American Society for the Prevention of Cruelty to Animals (ASPCA).
B. A member of Animal Rights, Incorporated.
C. A member of the Humane Society.
D. A member of the International Primate Protection League.
E. A member of People for the Ethical Treatment of Animals (PETA).

The answer is

E. **Ingrid Newkirk,** cofounder and national director, People for the Ethical Treatment of Animals (PETA).

32. Ingrid Newkirk, PETA director, with her 11-year-old dog, "Conchita," in her Rockville, Maryland office, December 28, 1988.

When/where:

Not specified by Sources.

Sources:

1. "The Pagan Roots of Environmentalism," by Tom DeWeese, American Policy Center, as reproduced in *Special Report - Who Is Leading the Attack on American Liberty?,* by David A. Russell, president, Citizens for Constitutional Property Rights, Incorporated, 1996, page 87.
2. "The True Meaning of 'Animal Rights,'" by Kathleen Marquardt, *Insider's Report,* Newsletter of the American Policy Center, June 1997, page 3.

Comments:

Some folks might say Ms. Newkirk's compassion for animals is a little over done. She once said, "Mankind is the biggest blight on the face of the Earth. Six million people died in concentration camps, but six billion broiler chickens will die this year in slaughterhouses."[151] Do you suppose she is indeed suggesting that a human life is worth less than a thousand barnyard pullets?

In a revealing article titled "PETA Steps Up Pursuit of Radical Goals," author Daniel Oliver reports that the "animal rights movement, virtually unknown to Americans just 15 years ago, has grown from a handful of small, all-volunteer groups to several hundred nonprofit organizations, many well-funded and professionally staffed. With an estimated 10 million supporters and combined budgets of over $200 million, animal rights groups have targeted biomedical researchers, livestock and poultry farmers, hunters and trappers, and others whom they accuse of animal abuse. One of the most successful of the animal rights groups is People for the Ethical Treatment of Animals . . . . Its $11 million in annual revenue is derived mostly from 500,000 dues-paying members. Through a series of well-publicized corporate boycotts, letter-writing campaigns, celebrity galas, and other events, PETA has become the best-known animal rights organization . . . ."[152]

The article continues: "Animal rights organizations rely on the support of a generous but sometimes gullible urban public that is sympathetic to animals but knows little about how farm animals are raised, why hunting and trapping are necessary, and why animal research is needed for progress in medicine . . . . Animal rights organizations understand that most people have a natural sympathy for animals and can easily write a check that will leave them feeling that they have done something worthwhile."

But the compassionate PETA folk seem to have a dark side. A sidebar to Oliver's article states: "PETA's support for the Animal Liberation Front (ALF), an underground group of activists who firebomb fur stores, break into research laboratories to 'liberate' animals and destroy research and commit other illegal acts, shows the least savory side of its agenda. ALF is active in Australia, Canada, France, Great Britain, Holland, Germany, New Zealand, Sweden, South Africa, and the United States and is classified by the FBI as a terrorist organization . . . . The Justice Department estimates that expenditures for increased security at research laboratories have raised the cost of biomedical research by 10-20%, diverting scarce resources from lifesaving research."

Writing in *Human Events,* Susan E. Paris says, "Like many extremist groups, the animal rights movement cloaks its radical intentions under the guise of compassion, hoodwinking the public into believing animal extremists wish to strike a balance between human and animal interests. Yet, unlike the concept of animal welfare, which we all support, the animal rights agenda calls for a fundamental change in the relationship between humans and animals - from one of responsible stewardship to one of *absolute* equality."[153]

Kathleen Marquardt (Source 2) describes a dialog between Tom Regan, professor of philosophy, University of North Carolina, and an audience member who asked if Regan were in a lifeboat with a baby and a dog, and the boat capsized, would he rescue the baby or the dog? Regan replied, "If it were a retarded baby and a bright dog, I'd save the dog." One is left to speculate what Mr Regan's answer would have been if it were a "normal" baby and a "normal" dog.

Marquardt continues, saying PETA's stand on animal rights means "no hunting, fishing, trapping, livestock farming or ranching. No use of animals in science or education; no animal bone marrow to treat blood disorders. No meat, eggs, honey, leather, fur, wool, down, or even silk . . . . No zoos, aquariums, circuses, rodeos, or animal actors in films. No butter or ice cream . . . . Candies, gelatin, drywall, home insulation, candles, soap, glue, brake fluid, and heart valves - even the runway foam used for disabled aircraft - all would be forbidden under an animal rights regime . . . . [Also,] no milk for our children, no insulin for diabetics, and no guide dogs for the blind. No rat traps could mean the return of the bubonic plague. No pest control means widespread malaria . . . ."

Liberal Peter Singer, reputed "father of animal rights" has said: "Christianity is our foe. If animal rights is to succeed, we must destroy the Judeo-Christian religious tradition."[154] Another Singer quote: "When the death of a disabled infant will lead to the birth of another infant with better prospects of happy life, the total amount of happiness will be greater if the disabled infant is killed."[155] Compassionate folks, these animal rights advocates.

Should man's best friend be covered under the 13th Amendment (abolishment of slavery) and set free?

Yet PETA and the animal rights movement continue to receive favorable press reports and widespread popular approval. Although many animal lovers are growing suspicious of the PETA agenda ("They're not as naive as ten years ago," says Rod Strand of the Portland, Oregon-based National Animal Interest Alliance),[156] the younger generation nevertheless appears enthusiastic in its support. A 1991 Gallup Poll found that 67% of American teenagers support animal rights "somewhat" or "very much." [157]

33. CAPITALISM

Who said this?

> *We have ended the dreaded Communism, we must now end the dreaded capitalism . . . . We have to use less. Cutting our consumption by 75% is a very reasonable and relatively easily obtainable goal.*

Was it:

A. **Ian Fry.** Greenpeace International.

B. **Guss Arvo Kusta Halberg Hall.** National chairman, Communist Party, U.S.A. Communist Party candidate for U.S. president. Author of numerous writings including *For a Radical Change: The Communist View* (1966), and *Karl Marx: Beacon for Our Times* (1983).[158] (In 1948 Guss Hall was convicted of conspiring to overthrow the U.S. Government.[159])

C. **Andy Kerr.** Executive director, Oregon Natural Resources Council.

D. **Robert Strange Mc Namara.** Former banking executive. Former Ford Motor Company executive. Former president of the World Bank. Author of several books including *Blundering into Disaster* (1986) and *In Retrospect* (1995). Recipient of the Presidential Medal of Freedom with distinction and other awards. Secretary of Defense during the Kennedy and Johnson Administrations.[160]

E. **Bill Moyers.** Former chief correspondent for CBS Reports. News analyst, NBC News. Popular PBS personality. Author. Recipient of several awards. Fellow, American Academy for the Arts and Science.[161]

The answer is

C. **Andy Kerr.**

When/where:

During a speech at the Oregon Natural Resources Council 22nd Annual Conference in the fall of 1994.[162] The comment was also published in an "In My Opinion" article by Andy Kerr in *The Oregonian.*

33. Has Communism truly been eradicated from the face of the earth, or is it simply hibernating in anticipation of an approaching spring?

Source:

Special Report - Who Is Leading the Attack on American Liberty?, by David A. Russell, president, Citizens for Constitutional Property Rights, Incorporated, 1996, page 5.

Comments:

Not so fast, Mr. Kerr. There are those who aren't quite so willing to concede that the communist threat has been beaten into oblivion. Some believe "the dreaded Communism" is not only alive, but spunky. William F. Jasper, in his article "Conspiracy: Where's the Proof?" states: "Yes . . . there was a communist conspiracy. And there *is* a communist conspiracy. Communism has been, and remains, the single most dramatically significant phenomenon of our century. It has enslaved billions of souls across our globe and has murdered between 100 million and 300 million . . . ."[163] (This was penned *after* the fall of the Berlin Wall.)

Listen to what Mikhail Gorbachev himself said to the Politburo in November 1987: "Gentlemen, comrades, do not be concerned about all you hear about glasnost and perestroika and democracy in the coming years. These are primarily for outward consumption. There will be no significant internal change within the Soviet Union, other than for cosmetic purposes. Our purpose is to disarm the Americans and let them fall asleep."[164]

In 1989 Gorbachev reiterated his commitment to communism. Quoted in the *New York Times* he said, "I am a Communist, a convinced Communist! For some that may be a fantasy. But to me it is my main goal."[165]

In his book, *Toward a New World Order,* Don McAlvany cautions: "America is in grave danger! Communism is *not* dead, the Cold War is *not* over, peace has *not* arrived, and throughout the recent political upheaval in the U.S.S.R. the gargantuan Russian military has *not* been touched or diminished in any way."[166]

And what about the Chinese? They haven't exactly rolled over and shouted "Give me liberty or give me death." In 1994 the vice-chairman of the Chinese Communist Party, Mo Xiu-song, was asked, "Is the long-term aim of the Chinese Communist Party still world communism?" Mr. Mo's answer was unequivocal: "Yes, of course. That is why we exist."[167]

So while the Berlin Wall may have crumbled and the Russians may have convincingly cried "uncle", there nevertheless remains a potent and aggressive world movement intent upon achieving full communist domination.

But now let's talk about Mr. Kerr's draconian idea of cutting consumption by 75%. Sadly, Mr. Kerr is not a lone voice in the wilderness with such poppycock. Our esteemed vice president (the next president?) Mr. Al Gore pipes in: "Humankind has suddenly entered into a brand-new relationship with our planet. Unless we quickly and profoundly change the course of our civilization, we face an immediate and grave danger of destroying the worldwide ecological system that sustains life as we know it."[168]

So the big picture begins to emerge: Mr. Gore's push for electric cars and Mr. Kerr's plea for reduced consumption are all part of the same grand plan: We have to fix a terrible problem on earth, and *we* are the problem! All would be well with the planet if only we the people got our act together.

Fred Smith, president and founder of the Competitive Enterprise Institute states: "The doomsayers' viewpoint, shared by many conventional environmentalists, argues the human dilemma in Terrible Toos terms: There are *too* many of us! We consume *too* much! We rely *too* heavily on technology, which we understand *too* poorly! The human impact on the environment is directly related to our numbers, our affluence, and our reliance on technology . . . ."[169]

Smith continues: "Doomsayers dominate the published literature, with noted figures such as Paul Ehrlich, Barry Commoner, Herman Daly, Carl Sagan, and Jeremy Rifkin[170] all commanding major audiences throughout the world . . . . Public opinion polls, at least in the United States, suggest that to date the doomsayers have been more persuasive. Polling data indicate that most Americans seem to believe that the earth's condition is worsening, for example, overwhelming percentages believe that pollution is increasing."

If you poke around on the Internet you may come across the Green Cross International website.[171] Read through the history and you'll learn: "Mikhail Gorbachev, president of Green Cross International, and Maurice Strong, chairman of the Earth Council, met in the Hague in April 1994 and agreed to launch The Earth Charter initiative." Correct me if I'm wrong, but I don't remember voting for any such initiative.

Poke around some more on the Internet and you'll find the website for the Earth Charter Project.[172] Principle Seven states in part: "A basic sustainable level of per capita material consumption will have to be reached in accordance with the Earth's natural resource constraints. This requires both increasing the material consumption of the people now living in poverty and reducing material over-consumption by the rich minority . . . ."

Guess what, friends, *we* are the "rich minority". We Americans are responsible for all this nasty, despised material over-consumption. Billions and billions in the Third World live in "poverty", so get ready to do with less. Mr. Gorbachev and Mr. Strong have decided.

But, read on and you'll see in Principle 14, Global Sovereignty: "The protection of the Biosphere, as the Common Interest of Humanity, must not be subservient to the rules of state sovereignty, demands of the free market or individual rights. The idea of Global Sovereignty must be supported by a shift in values which recognize this Common Interest."

With their support and implementation of the Earth Charter, the Internationalists, liberals every one, wish to shred the U.S. Constitution, crush capitalism, and obliterate individual rights. Nice bunch, these folks!

Thus, the message translates to this: Give up your comforts, give up your pleasurable lifestyles, give up your dreams, give up your hope. Yield totally to that elite, all-wise, all-wonderful bunch of liberals who will rule the world forever more.

Sound frightening? I should say so! Particularly when so many honest, law-abiding, intelligent people in nations around the globe are willingly buying into this line of hogwash and are tripping over one another in a race to join this Great Lemmings' Crusade.

34. CONTROL

Who said this?

> *Food is power. We use it to change behavior. Some may call that bribery. We do not apologize.*

Was it:

A. **Maya Angelou.** Poet.
B. **Peter Arnett.** Journalist from New Zealand. Veteran war correspondent. Author of *Live from the Battlefield: 35 Years Inside the World's War Zones* (1994). Art collector. Gourmet cook.[173]
C. **Catherine Bertini.** Executive director, UN World Food Program.
D. **Vladimir Lenin.** Founder and leader of the Russian Communist Party.
E. **Joseph Stalin.** Political leader and dictator of the Soviet Union.

The answer is

C. **Catherine Bertini.**

When/where:

At the UN 4th World Conference on Women, Beijing, China, September 1995.

Source:

Special Report - Who Is Leading the Attack on American Liberty?, by David A. Russell, president, Citizens for Constitutional Property Rights, Incorporated, 1996, pages 35, 77, and 110.[174]

34. Catherine Bertini, during a press conference in Geneva, Switzerland, July 9, 1997.

Comments:

David Russell (Source) explains: "Hungry people can be easily manipulated and controlled." He says: "Those who seek world dominance know the power inherent in controlling land use, housing, food, and food-producing capabilities. They also know how to use the power of government laws and regulations to achieve their goals."

Once again we observe that the liberals' compassion is eclipsed by their overriding political agenda: control, domination, and limitless power.

35. DESTROYING CIVILIZATION

Who said this?

> *Isn't it the only hope for the planet that the industrialized civilizations collapse? Isn't it our responsibility to bring that about?*

Was it:

A. **Bella Abzug.** Radical feminist. Former Democratic New York congresswoman. Former head of the tax-funded Women's Environment and Development Organization.[175]
B. **Fidel Castro.** Revolutionary prime minister, Cuba.
C. **Ted Kaczynski.** The Unabomber. He kept close ties with radical environmentalist groups. He attended a University of Montana Earth First! meeting at which a "hit list" of "enemies" of the environment was distributed.[176]
D. **Barbra Streisand.** Actress. Composer. Director. Singer. Political activist.
E. **Maurice Strong.** Canadian environmentalist. Under- secretary-general of the UN. Secretary General of the 1992 Earth Summit. Special assistant to Kofi Annan, UN Secretary General. Close associate of former Soviet President Mikhail Gorbachev. Holder of several honorable degrees. Author of various journal articles.[177]

The answer is

E. **Maurice Strong.**

When/where:

In an interview with Jim Johnston for the *British Columbia Report,* May 18, 1992, Vol. 3, No. 37, page 22.

Source:

"Our Life & Times," *Media Bypass* magazine, June 1996, page 57.[178]

35. Maurice Strong, talking to reporters, June 1, 1992.

Comments:

Maurice Strong has been a longtime, outspoken advocate of "Sustainable Development", which is defined as policy that meets "the needs of the present without compromising the ability of future generations to meet their own needs."[179] The phrase came into prominence about the time President George Bush signed Agenda 21 at the June 1992 Earth Summit in Rio de Janeiro.[180]

In reality, however, Sustainable Development is a set of judgements by the likes of Maurice Strong and others about what activities on Earth are considered appropriate (by those in power) to "sustain" the planet. Strong wishes to limit or ban use of appliances, air conditioning, high meat intake, frozen foods, fossil fuels, etcetera, etcetera, etcetera. He proclaims: "Consumption in the United States must be reduced 60 percent."[181] He warns: "If we don't change, our species will not survive . . . ."[182]

Phyllis Schlafly says Sustainable Development is "the code word for global control of energy consumption."[183]

According to *The New American,* "under the concept of 'sustainability', government no longer serves the people; its purpose is to protect nature from people."[184]

David Russell has the last word: "Those who take part in this charade (Sustainable Development), willingly or unwittingly, will be doing their part towards destroying our freedom and ushering in global government."[185]

36. EDUCATION

Who said this?

> *Every child in America entering school at the age of five is insane because he comes to school with certain allegiances toward our Founding Fathers, toward his parents, toward our elected officials, toward a belief in a supernatural being, and toward the sovereignty of this nation as a separate entity. It's up to you, teachers, to make all these sick children well by creating the international child of the future.*

Was it:

A. **Marian Wright Edelman.** President, Children's Defense Fund.

B. **Dr. Joycelyn Elders.** Former U.S. Surgeon General who was labeled "Condom Queen" by critics of her enthusiasm for distributing condoms in Arkansas high schools. She said to *60 Minutes,* "I tell every girl . . . when she goes out on a date, put a condom in her purse."[186]

C. **Kathleen Lyons.** Spokeswoman for the National Education Association (NEA).

D. **Chester M. Pierce.** Professor, Department of Educational Psychiatry, Harvard University. Humanist. New World Order guru.

E. **Richard Wilson Riley.** Former member of the South Carolina House of Representatives and Senate. Recipient of the Harold W. McGraw, Jr. Prize in Education. U.S. Secretary of Education.[187]

36. What ideology, values, and morals are being pumped into the innocent minds of the kids in the public schools today?

The answer is

D. **Chester M. Pierce.**

When/where:

During his keynote address to 2000 teachers attending the Childhood International Education Seminar, Denver, 1973.

Source:

Brave New Schools, by Berit Kjos, Harvest House Publishers, 1995, page 160.[188]

Comments:

Mr. Pierce's words are alarming, but they are not new. William Benton, Assistant U.S. Secretary of State said almost the same thing at a UNESCO meeting in 1946.[189]

One of the most successful at the game of capturing the minds of a country's youth was a fellow by the name of Adolph Hitler. Writing in *The New American,* William Norman Grigg reports that in a May 1, 1937 speech the Fuhrer said: "This new Reich will give its youth to no one, but will itself take youth and give to youth its own education and its only upbringing."[190] That sounds to me a lot like the essence of Chester Pierce's message.

In a speech November 6, 1933 Hitler revealed his plan: "When an opponent says, 'I will not come over to your side,' I calmly say, 'Your child belongs to us already . . . . What are you? You will pass on. Your descendants, however, now stand in the new camp. In a short time they will know nothing else but this new community.'"[191]

So I must ask: In what camp will *your* children stand? Will they, too, know nothing but the "new community"?

37. EDUCA

Who said this?

> *I am convinced*
> *humankind's future must be wa*
> *in the public school classroom by teachers that correctly perceive their role as proselytizers of a new faith which will replace the rotting corpse of Christianity.*

Was it:

A. **John J. Dunphy.** Humanist.
B. **Sigmund Freud.** Austrian psychiatrist.
C. **Keith Geiger.** Outgoing president of the NEA (National Education Association, *a.k.a.,* the teachers' union), who received more than $300,000 in salary and benefits as president in 1996.[192]
D. **Alfred Kinsey.** Zoologist. Director, Institute for Sex Research. Author of the famous books *Human Sexuality and the Human Male,* 1948, and *Human Sexuality and the Human Female,* 1953, for which he used data derived from prisoners, rapists, homosexuals, pimps, male prostitutes, thieves, and others, according to co-author Judith Reisman's book, *Kinsey, Sex and Fraud: the Indoctrination of a People.*[193] Kinsey has been described as one who "indulged in sado-masochistic homosexual acts and filmed his wife having sex with fellow researchers at Indiana University."[194]
E. **John Phillipson.** Professor, Oxford University.

n J. Dunphy.

e:

umanist Magazine, January-February 1983.

ource:

Operation Vampire Killer 2000, revised 1996, published by Police Against the New World Order, page 31.

37. Rotting corpse?

Comments:

When Hitler began his movement to indoctrinate the country's youth, membership was relatively small. Hitler Youth membership totaled 108,000 in 1932, contrasting sharply with ten million or so German youth associated with nonpolitical organizations such as the Boy Scouts. Only 5 years later, however, ranks of the Hitler Youth swelled to nearly 8 million.

The following year Hitler made membership compulsory by enactment of a law conscripting all German youth. An article in *The New American* quotes leftist historian William Shirer as saying: "Recalcitrant parents were warned that their children would be taken from them and put into orphanages or other homes unless they enrolled" their children in Hitler's program.[195] Now *that's* an effective membership drive!

But it was Bill Clinton, not Adolph Hitler, who said: "Imagine an army of 100,000 young people restoring urban and rural communities and giving their labor in exchange for education and training . . . . [National Service] will harness the energy of our youth and attack the problems of our time. It literally has the potential to revolutionize the way young people all across America look at their country and feel about themselves."[196]

Retired General Colin Powell apparently agrees with the president. "People say, 'General, you can't make that mandatory. You're forcing children to do something against their will, that violates the First, 13th, 14th, and 15th Amendments,'" says the respected war hero. "My response is, they made me do algebra, and service is just as important as algebra."[197] *The New American* adds,

"For Colin Powell and other compassion fascists, the three "R's" are "readin', 'ritin', and regimentation."

Let us now learn of the sorry plight of Walter Freiwillig, senior at the Eleanor Roosevelt High School, in Glenview Township, New York State.[198] He was told that if he was unable to complete his school's community service requirement in a 3-month period, he would not be permitted to graduate. Such is distressing news, no doubt, to a student who had already been accepted at four Ivy League colleges . . . contingent, of course, upon his graduation.

Poor Walter insists he had indeed met the community service requirement, inasmuch as he had invested more than 400 hours of service after school and during summer vacations tutoring fourth-grade students in chemistry. This was noble service, to be sure, but it didn't quite meet the letter of the law.

You see, Walter's high school graduation prerequisites are patterned after the Federal Mandatory Community Volunteer Program Guidelines, which must be followed if the school district is to receive federal school funds, and these guidelines state that tutoring doesn't qualify for credit unless at least 50 percent of those tutored were children of underprivileged families. To be exact, the guidelines state that at least 50 percent of the beneficiaries of any volunteer project must be "economically, culturally, or environmentally disadvantaged, of black or Latino descent, or victims of AIDS or breast cancer."[199]

These insightful requirements were produced by (can you guess?) the President's Commission on Volunteerism. Yes, the federal government has not only determined that volunteering is compulsory, it has specified what is proper and what is improper volunteering. Gosh, I guess there's nothing left for the student to do but just put in his or her time. Doesn't the word "serfdom" begin to describe what's going on here?

Walter even offered to teach at a school in the Bronx, where he might have met the requirements, but that wasn't acceptable because school administrators thought his advanced chemistry instruction might encourage those tutored to experiment with dangerous substances, possibly even drugs.

It was suggested that Walter might wish to fulfill his obligation by demonstrating condom use rather than chemistry, but after reflection he decided not to take advantage of this generous invitation.

Goals 2000, the Educate America Act, makes the point quite unequivocally: "[A]ll students will be involved in activities that demonstrate community service."[200] If you don't like it, if you don't think it's right for your son or daughter, if you object to the intrusion on your freedoms, well, tough.

According to a 1994 article titled "Out of the Classroom, into the Community," volunteerism on a non-voluntary basis is well established throughout the country. "Community service is a mandatory part of the curriculum in more than 200 public and private schools nationwide."[201] (Note that private schools have also jumped on the forced volunteerism bandwagon.)

Once a seat of knowledge; now the site of intensive government indoctrination.

"[C]entral controls lead to tyranny and poverty, not peace and equality," states Thomas Sowell in his review of Friedrich Hayek's book *Road to Serfdom*. "Yet our lawmakers continue to pave the path to lifelong management of our children while raising the promise of 'local control' as a smokescreen to pacify concerned parents .... The goal of education is no longer to teach the kind of literacy, wisdom, and knowledge we once considered essentials of responsible citizenship; it is to train world citizens - a compliant international workforce, willing to flow with the storms of change and uncertainty. These citizens must be ready to believe and do whatever will serve a predetermined 'common good' or 'greater whole.' Educators may promise to 'teach students to think for themselves,' but if they finish what they have started, tomorrow's students will have neither the facts nor the freedom needed for independent thinking. Like Nazi youth, they will be taught to react, not to think, when told to do the unthinkable."[202]

So just what will your son or daughter learn today in this country's public schools? "It looks like he [or she] will learn to feel good even though he can't read, write, or calculate," concludes Phyllis Schlafly.[203] "That's called 'Self-Esteem.' He will learn that he should not try to achieve excellence because he must stick with the mediocrity of the class. That is called 'Outcome-Based Education,' (OBE) or 'Cooperative Learning.' The child will learn that every behavior or lifestyle is acceptable and must not be criticized. That is called 'Diversity' or 'Tolerance' .... And of course we all know that 'diversity' is the code word for the gay-lesbian agenda in the schools. Your child will learn that America is a bad and oppressive nation. That's called 'Multiculturalism' or 'National History Standards,' because that is what they teach. Your child will learn to make his own decisions without adult direction about which kind of sex and drugs to do. That is called 'Values Clarification' or 'Decision Making' . . . . Your child will learn in school that his parents' morals and religion are out of date. That's called 'Critical Thinking,' or as some people say, it's called 'Now let's criticize your parents.' Your child will learn that it's OK to spell words any way he wants. That's called 'Inventive Spelling' . . . . Your child will learn to look to the school to provide all of his medical needs. That's called 'School-Based Clinics,' or the 'medicalization of the schools' . . . . Your child will learn to confide in school counselors instead of in parents. That's called 'Guidance' . . . . And of course your child will learn to guess at words instead of sounding them out and to skip over words that he doesn't know. That is called 'Whole Language.'"

Is that the kind of education you want for your children? What happened to the "basics"? What happened to teaching the kids how to think? Who took "education" out of education?

[Just as an aside, did you know that almost 2 million students across the country are being given the drug Ritalin, a drug not unlike cocaine, to make them behave better in school?[204] Sure, it's mind altering and potentially addictive, but we don't want energetic, excited kids running around the classroom, do we? It would seem kids in school today are being *numbed* down in addition to being *dumbed* down!]

An OBE high school in Iowa gave students a test without parental knowledge or consent. Listed were 15 nationalities and religions, such as German-Americans, Hispanic-Americans, Jews, Catholics, Protestants, etc. The question: "Which of the above do you think would be most likely to eliminate an entire race?" Another question: "If you could eliminate an entire race, would you? If yes, which one?"[205]

Explaining why students today can't read, one teacher exclaimed, "we're attempting to make sure they have the right vitamins, the right minerals, the right condoms, the right family planning; I don't have time to teach them to read."[206]

So, the answer is home schooling, right? Well, not exactly. Take the case of Seth O'Hara, a Georgia home-schooled student who scored an impressive 1480 on his SAT test. Very impressive, indeed, but when Seth went knocking on the doors of the state's public universities, none would admit him. Why? Well, my goodness, because he was home schooled![207] The education industry looks after its own.

"The truth is," says Rush Limbaugh, "in the last thirty years, liberals have done to the schools what they did to the nation's major cities: brought them to near ruin . . . . Liberals wanted more money spent, and so it was spent. They wanted self-esteem taught, and so it was taught. They wanted multiculturalism, and they got it. They wanted sex education, and we have it. They wanted new math, inventive spelling, gender equity, recycling, and here it is. They wanted anti-drug and anti-violence programs, and we have them up the wazoo. They wanted no one to fail, and so we removed all means of measuring success. And what has all this gotten us? Ignorance, failure, illiteracy."[208]

"The fact is," says Tom DeWeese in *The DeWeese Report*, "in today's 'restructured' curriculum almost every single word uttered in the classroom, every lesson in a text book, every class project is there for a political or psychological reason."[209]

Says Bertrand Russell, writing in the UNESCO Journal *The Impact of Science on Society,* "Every government that has been in control of education for a generation will be able to control its subjects securely without the need of armies or policemen . . . ."[210]

Schlafly notes: "Outcome-Based Education is completely consistent with the Dewey philosophy of making socialization the goal rather than individual achievement."[211]

Referencing E.D. Hirsch Jr.'s book, *The Schools We Need,* Ms. Schlafly states, "He makes a broadside attack on the prevailing [public educational system's] pedagogical fads that 'process' should take priority over the acquisition of knowledge, that teachers do not need to know the subjects they teach, and that it is unnatural and unfair to challenge children academically through content-based curricula."[212]

Greek philosopher and teacher Diogenes (412-323 B.C.) observed: "The foundation of every state is the education of its youth." Today it would appear that in the U.S. we're not as interested in education as we are in indoctrination.

38. GUN CONTROL

Who said this?

> *This year will go down in history! For the first time a civilized nation has full gun registration. Our streets will be safer, our police will be more efficient, and the world will follow our lead into the future.*

Was it:

A. **James Brady.** Press secretary for President Ronald Reagan.
B. **Ong Teng Cheong.** President, Singapore (elected 1993).
C. **Bill Clinton.** President, United States (elected 1992, 1996).
D. **Adolph Hitler.** Dictator, Germany.
E. **Janet Reno.** U.S. Attorney General and object of criticism from attorney Jack Thompson regarding her lesbianism and drinking problem.[213]

The answer is

D. **Adolf Hitler.**

38. Adolph Hitler.

When/where:

1935.

Source:

Barbed Wire on America, video of a talk by David Wegener at the Prophecy Club®.[214]

Comments:

By seizing all the weapons, Hitler rendered the people defenseless, thereby making it easy to eliminate anyone who opposed him.[215]

Observed Thomas Jefferson: "When the government fears the people there is liberty; when the people fear the government, there is tyranny."[216] Adolf was clearly opting for the latter state of affairs.

James Madison said, "Americans need never fear their government because of the advantage of being armed, which the Americans possess over the people of almost every other nation."[217]

I suppose in making his gun registration statement, the German dictator was simply following advice outlined in *The Communist Rules of Revolution:* "Register all firearms, under any pretext, as a prelude to confiscating them."[218]

Do you sense a little *deja vu* going on right here in the good old U.S.A.?

In the U.S. House of Representatives, January 7, 1997, Mr. Alcee Hastings (D, Florida) introduced HR 186 IH, the "Handgun Registration Act of 1997": "To provide for the mandatory registration of handguns." The bill was referred to the Committee on the Judiciary.

When do you suppose it will be the law of the land?

39. GUN CONTROL

Who said this?

> *The most effective means of fighting crime in the United States is to outlaw the possession of any type of firearm by the civilian populace.*

Was it:

A. **James Brady.** Press secretary for President Ronald Reagan.
B. **Ong Teng Cheong.** President, Singapore (elected 1993).
C. **Bill Clinton.** President, United States (elected 1992, 1996).
D. **Adolph Hitler.** Dictator, Germany.
E. **Janet Reno.** U.S. Attorney General and object of criticism from attorney Jack Thompson regarding her lesbianism and drinking problem.[219]

The answer is

E. **Janet Reno.**

When/where:

During a speech at a B'nai B'rith meeting in Fort Lauderdale, Florida, 1991.

Source:

"Weekend Warriors," by Alan W. Bock, *National Review,* May 29, 1995, page 40.[220]

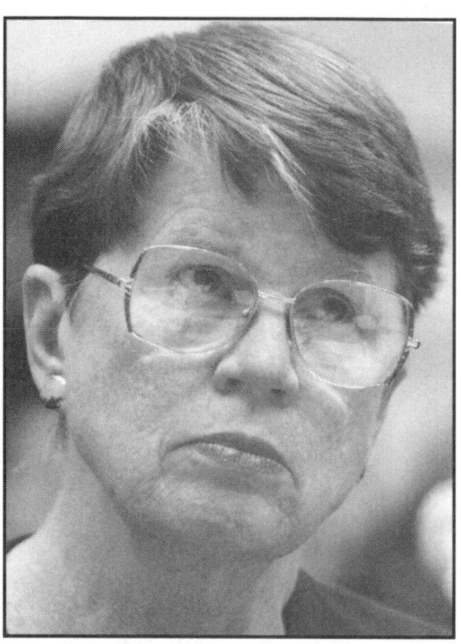

39. Janet Reno announcing she will not appoint an independent counsel to investigate alleged fund-raising violations by President Clinton and Vice President Gore, December 2, 1997.

Comments:

The commander's face is grim: two dozen years of military experience have deepened his furrowed brow and toughened his demeanor. He addresses his troops: "Listen up, men. At 0600 tomorrow morning we'll penetrate the jungle and begin our operation. Be advised that the enemy is well equipped with the latest-technology armaments. Our adversary is a rough and tough bunch of highly trained, professional fighters. They're fast, they're smart, they're efficient. So be alert! Be on guard for attacks from any direction. And . . . good luck, men! Oh, one more thing: For this assignment you won't be allowed to use any weapons or ammunition. Good Luck!"

How absurd, you say? No more absurd than preventing the general public from arming and protecting itself from gangsters, rapists, and thieves! Hey, it's a jungle out there!

40. GUN CONTROL

Who said this?

> *We cannot survive into the 21st century unless we remember the need to expand our wave to new thinking to the total disarmament of America.*

Was it:

A. A "confidential" memo from Handgun Control, Incorporated.

B. **Edward Fouhy.** Former ABC and CBS executive. Now heading the Pew Center for Civic Journalism.

C. **Albert R. (Al) Hunt.** Columnist. Former president of the Dow Jones Newspaper Fund. Regular participant, NBC's Meet the Press and CNN's Capital Gang. Former Washington Bureau Chief for the *Wall Street Journal.* Husband of Judy Woodruff.[221]

D. **Dean Morris.** Professor. Director, Law Enforcement Assistance Administration.

E. The Preamble to the Handgun Registration Act of 1997.

The answer is

A. A "confidential" memo from Handgun Control, Incorporated.

HANDGUN CONTROL

ONE MILLION STRONG . . . working to keep handguns out of the wrong hands.

40. Logo and slogan of Handgun Control, Incorporated.

When/where:

In a memo dated December 30, 1993 from Handgun Control Inc. National Headquarters, 1225 Eye Street, NW, Suite 1100, Washington, D.C. 20005, discussing the notes and minutes from a meeting December 17, 1993.

Source:

America's Judgements, What Lies Ahead? documentation supporting the Militia of Montana video, page 82.

Comments:

In an article titled "Gun Report" in *The New American,* reference is made to "Kennesaw, Georgia's ordinance requiring heads of households (with certain exceptions) to keep at least one firearm in their homes. Since the ordinance was enacted, there have been only two murders (one each in 1984 and 1989), both with knives. After the law went into effect in 1982, crimes against persons plummeted 74 percent compared to 1981, and fell another 45 percent in 1983 compared to 1982."[222]

The evidence in Kennesaw and elsewhere indicates that when civilians are armed, the crime rate goes down.

One study found that concealed handgun laws reduced murder by 8.5% and severe assault by 7% from 1977 to 1992. If "right-to-carry" laws had been enacted across the country during that period, 1,600 murder victims would be alive today and 60,000 assaults would have been thwarted.[223]

Let's say you're a crook. Where would you wish to practice your craft? In a neighborhood where all your potential victims have guns, or in a neighborhood where the government has taken all the weapons away?

41. GUN CONTROL

Who said this?

> *I am one who believes that as a first step the U.S. should move expeditiously to disarm the civilian population, other than police and security officers, of all handguns, pistols, and revolvers . . . . [N]o one should have a right to anonymous ownership or use of a gun.*

Was it:

A. A "confidential" memo from Handgun Control, Incorporated.

B. **Edward Fouhy.** Former ABC and CBS executive. Now heading the Pew Center for Civic Journalism.

C. **Albert R. (Al) Hunt.** Columnist. Former president of the Dow Jones Newspaper Fund. Regular participant, NBC's Meet the Press and CNN's Capital Gang. Former Washington Bureau Chief for the *Wall Street Journal.* Husband of Judy Woodruff.[224]

D. **Dean Morris.** Professor. Director, Law Enforcement Assistance Administration.

E. The Preamble to the Handgun Registration Act of 1997.

The answer is

D. **Dean Morris.**

When/where:

In testimony before Congress.

Source:

Operation Vampire Killer 2000, revised 1996, published by Police Against the New World Order, page 50.

41. If indeed, as so many seem to believe, we can stop crime with gun control, why don't we stop fires with match control, stop marijuana and cocaine with drug control, stop drunken driving with alcohol control, etcetera, etcetera, etcetera?

Comments:

A friend of mine was caught in Miami traffic some years ago. A car pulled directly in front of her car as another sandwiched her from the back. The two occupants jumped out of their vehicles and approached my friend, who was driving alone except for her small son.

You can imagine the outcome of that incident, except in this case it didn't happen. My friend reached down and produced a large pistol, which she displayed prominently for the would-be thugs to see. They decided to return with haste to their vehicles and transfer their efforts to easier, more cooperative, more vulnerable prey.

Surely, had she not brandished a revolver, she would have been robbed, assaulted, maybe both. Maybe worse. That the government appears anxious to disarm honest, law-abiding citizens is curious. What about the assailants? Who will take away *their* weapons?

Don McAlvany points out that "on average, over 2,700 Americans each day use a handgun, or a rifle, or a shotgun, to resist a criminal attack."[225]

So if protecting the public isn't what's motivating our liberal friends to ban guns, what is? Perhaps Handgun Control Incorporated chair Sarah Brady has the answer: "Our task of creating a socialist America can only succeed when those who would resist us have been totally disarmed."[226]

42. GUN CONTROL

Who said this?

> *46. The U.S. government declares a ban on the possession, sale, transportation, and transfer of all non-sporting firearms. A thirty day amnesty period is permitted for these firearms to be turned over to local authorities. At the end of this period, a number of citizen groups refuse to turn over their firearms. Consider the following statement: I would fire upon U.S. citizens who resist confiscation of firearms banned by the U.S. government.*
>
> *☐-Strongly disagree, ☐-Disagree, ☐-Agree, ☐-Strongly agree, ☐-No opinion.*

Was it:

A. A question on a BATF (Bureau of Alcohol, Tobacco, and Firearms) questionnaire.
B. A question on a CIA questionnaire.
C. A question on an FBI questionnaire.
D. A question on a UN questionnaire.
E. A question on a U.S. Armed Forces questionnaire.

The answer is

E. A question on a U.S. Armed Forces questionnaire.

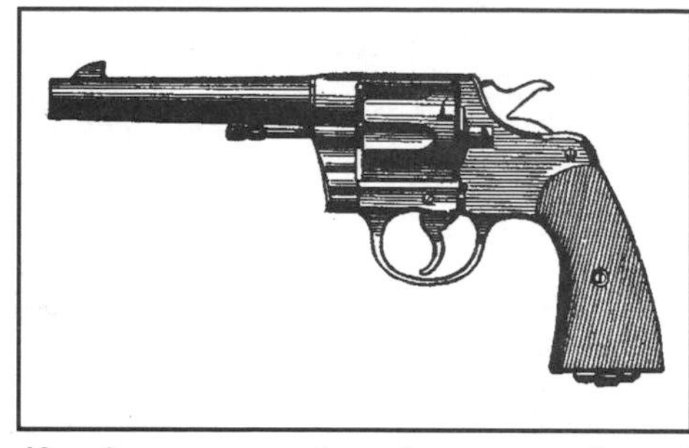

42. Once upon a time there was a Second Amendment to the U.S. Constitution. It said in part, "the right of the people to keep and bear arms shall not be infringed."

When/where:

One of a series of questions in a Joint Services Training Combat Arms Survey (Part A; DD Form 3208, revised 2-96, 70m) given to U.S. Navy SEAL platoons and U.S. Marine combat veterans.
The questionnaire was first administered September 15, 1993.

Source:

America's Judgments, What Lies Ahead?, documentation in support of the Militia of Montana video, pages 76-78, quoting from the article "New World Order Combat Arms Survey," which appeared in *The Resister, The Official Publication of the Special Forces Underground,* Volume I, Number 2, Autumn 1994.[227]

Comments:

The Source states that among new recruits almost 90% gave the response: "If it's the law and they order me to do it, I guess it's okay." However, of those with more than 15 years service, 87% replied that they "disagree" or "strongly disagree" with the statement.

Some of the other questions on the questionnaire:

36. U.S. Combat troops should be commanded by UN officers and noncommissioned officers at battalion and company levels while performing UN missions.
☐-Strongly disagree, ☐-Disagree, ☐-Agree,
☐-Strongly agree, ☐-No opinion.

37. It would make no difference to me to have UN soldiers as members of my team (e.g., fire team, squad, platoon).
☐-Strongly disagree, ☐-Disagree, ☐-Agree,
☐-Strongly agree, ☐-No opinion.

38. It would make no difference to me to take orders from a UN company commander.
    ☐-Strongly disagree, ☐-Disagree, ☐-Agree,
    ☐-Strongly agree, ☐-No opinion.

39. I feel the President of the United States has the authority to pass his responsibilities as Commander-in-Chief to the UN Secretary General.
    ☐-Strongly disagree, ☐-Disagree, ☐-Agree,
    ☐-Strongly agree, ☐-No opinion.

40. I feel there is no conflict between my oath of office and serving as a UN soldier.
    ☐-Strongly disagree, ☐-Disagree, ☐-Agree,
    ☐-Strongly agree, ☐-No opinion.

41. I feel my unit's combat effectiveness would not be affected by performing humanitarian missions for the UN.
    ☐-Strongly disagree, ☐-Disagree, ☐-Agree,
    ☐-Strongly agree, ☐-No opinion.

42. I feel a designated unit of U.S. combat soldiers should be permanently assigned to the command and control of the United Nations.
    ☐-Strongly disagree, ☐-Disagree, ☐-Agree,
    ☐-Strongly agree, ☐-No opinion.

43. I would be willing to volunteer for assignment to a U.S. combat unit under a UN commander.
    ☐-Strongly disagree, ☐-Disagree, ☐-Agree,
    ☐-Strongly agree, ☐-No opinion.

44. I would like UN member countries, including the U.S., to give the UN all the soldiers necessary to maintain world peace.
    ☐-Strongly disagree, ☐-Disagree, ☐-Agree,
    ☐-Strongly agree, ☐-No opinion.

45. I would swear to the following code: "I am a United Nations fighting person. I serve in the forces which maintain world

peace and every nation's way of life. I am prepared to give my life in their defense."

☐-Strongly disagree, ☐-Disagree, ☐-Agree,
☐-Strongly agree, ☐-No opinion.

The Source adds this interesting note: "Our civilian readers [may] be wondering why the Combat Arms Survey was circulated so heavily within the Department of the Navy. The reason is simple: the Navy is not subject to USC Title 10 Posse Comitatus prohibitions against using federal military forces for domestic law enforcement. This includes the U.S. Marine Corps."

I'm wondering why the questionnaire was circulated at all!

And what will they come for after they've come for your guns?

43. MEDIA

Who said this?

> *Our job is to give people not what they want, but what we decide they ought to have.*

Was it:

A. **Richard M. Cohan.** Senior producer of CBS political news.
B. **Rick Davis.** Executive producer, CNN.
C. **Robert Murphy.** ABC vice president for News Policy.
D. **Richard Salant.** Former president of CBS News.
E. **Bill Wheatley.** Vice president, NBC News.

The answer is

D. **Richard Salant.**

43. Richard Salant, president of CBS News, at a Boston University School of Public Communication ceremony April 28, 1971 during which he received a citation for the documentary, "The Selling of the Pentagon."

When/where:

Not specified by Source.

Source:

"But Surely, If this World Conspiracy Were True I Would Have Heard about It in the Daily News!" *Free American Newsmagazine,* February 1998, page 53.[228]

Comments:

The Source also quotes John Swinton, highly respected former chief of staff for the *New York Times,* who announced in a 1953 toast before the New York Press Club: "There is no such thing, at this date of the world's history in America, as an independent press. You know it and I know it. There is not one of you who dares to write your honest opinions, and if you did, you know beforehand that it [sic] would never appear in print . . . . The business of the journalists is to destroy the truth; to lie outright; to pervert; to vilify; to fawn at the feet of mammon, and to sell his [sic] country and his [sic] race for his [sic] daily bread. You know it and I know it and what folly is this toasting an independent press? We are the tools and vassals of rich men behind the scenes. We are the jumping jacks; they pull the strings and we dance. Our talents, our possibilities, and our lives are all the property of other men. We are intellectual prostitutes."[229]

Before World War II, when the press in England censored news about Nazi Germany's arms buildup, Winston Churchill was outraged. Said he, "The worst crime is not to tell the truth to the public."[230]

The crime endures. It flourishes. It overwhelms.

44. MEDIA

Who said this?

> *We in the press like to say we're honest brokers of information, and it's just not true. The press does have an agenda.*

Was it:

A. **Bernard Baruch** (1870-1965). Millionaire by the age of 30. U.S. representative to the UN Atomic Energy Commission.
B. **Bernard Goldberg.** Commentator on the CBS 48 Hours television program.
C. **Bernard Kalb.** Coauthor with Marvin Kalb of the book *Kissinger,* 1974.
D. **Bernard (Bernie) Shaw.** Winner, Cable Ace Award for Best Newscaster, 1994. Commentator, CNN.
E. **Prince Bernhard** of the Netherlands. Largely responsible for the first Bilderberger Group meeting of 100 "global thinkers" at the Hotel Bilderberg, Oosterbeek, The Netherlands, in 1954.[231]

The answer is

B. **Bernard Goldberg.** (By espousing such a view perhaps Mr. Goldberg disqualifies himself from membership in the "liberal" elite.)

44. Bernard Goldberg, 1988.

When/where:

As quoted by Harry Stein in the article "The Media's Middle Name is Not Objectivity," *TV Guide,* June 13-19, 1992.

Source:

Environmental Overkill, by Dixy Lee Ray with Lou Guzzo, copyright © 1993 by Regnery Publishing, page 171. All rights reserved. Reprinted by special permission of Regnery Publishing, Incorporated.[232]

Comments:

In a *Wall Street Journal* op-ed piece Goldberg said "The old argument that the networks and other 'media elites' have a liberal bias is so blatantly true that it's hardly worth discussing anymore. No, we don't sit around in dark corners and plan strategies on how we're going to slant the news. We don't have to. It comes naturally to most reporters."[233]

Not only reporters. The Source quotes Paul Watson, cofounder of Greenpeace: "It doesn't matter what is true; it only matters what people believe is true . . . . You are what the media define you to be. [Greenpeace] became a myth and a myth-generating machine."[234]

Dianne Dumanoski of the *Boston Globe:* "There is no such thing as objective reporting . . . . I've become even more crafty about finding the voices to say the things I think are true . . . ."[235]

Barbara Walters of 20/20 fame: "The news media in general are liberals."[236]

Walter Cronkite, highly respected former news commentator: "News reporters are certainly liberal and left of center."[237]

Richard Cohan, senior producer of CBS political news: "We are going to impose our agenda on the coverage by dealing with issues and subjects that *we* choose to deal with."[238]

45. MEDIA

Who said this?

To hell with the news. I'm no longer interested in news. I'm interested in causes. We don't print the truth. We don't pretend to print the truth . . . .

Was it:

A. **Benjamin Crowninshield (Ben) Bradlee.** Former executive editor, *The Washington Post.* Author of *That Special Grace* (1964), *Conversations with Kennedy* (1975), and *A Good Life - Newspapering and Other Adventures* (1995).[239]
B. **Mary McGrory.** Columnist, *Washington Post.*
C. **Maynard Parker.** Editor, *Newsweek* Magazine.
D. **Matthew Victor Storin.** Former editor and senior vice president, *Chicago Sun-Times.* Former managing editor, *New York Daily News.* Editor and executive editor, *The Boston Globe.* Recipient, Distinguished Political Reporting Award (American Association of Political Science).[240]
E. **Arthur Ochs Sutzberger, Jr.** Publisher, *The New York Times.*

The answer is

A. **Ben Bradlee.**

When/where:

At a recent symposium sponsored by the Smithsonian Institution.

Source:

The News Manipulators, by Reed Irvine, Joseph Goulden, and Cliff Kincaid, Book Distributors, Incorporated, 1993, page 179. (Comments below from pages 300-303.)[241]

45. Ben Bradlee, New York City, 1997.

Comments:

The News Manipulators asserts: "Advocacy journalism by definition suppresses or distorts the true facts. The advocates are so convinced of the correctness of their goal that the facts that get in the way are dismissed as irrelevant . . . ."

Retired Judge Robert Bork, according to the same source, quotes an unnamed journalist as saying: "when a reporter wants to express his opinion in a news story, he goes to a source who agrees with him for a statement."

The News Manipulators also references Stephen Hess, of the liberal think tank Brookings Institute in Washington, D.C., who describes the process of television news production as "the gathering of quotes to fit a hypothesis." Citizens who watch television, he says, should realize that sound bites are chosen to reinforce a preconceived message and not to give a rounded story.[242]

Bryant Gumbel, former co-host of the NBC Today Show declared: "when the truth collides with a legend, print the legend."[243]

Referring to *New York Times* articles concerning "global warming", Alan Caruba, founder of the National Anxiety Center said, "This isn't journalism. It's pure propaganda."[244]

Referring to the mainstream media of his day, Thomas Jefferson said, "Nothing can now be believed which is seen in a newspaper. Truth itself becomes suspicious by being put into that polluted vehicle."[245]

46. NATIONAL EMERGENCY

Who said this?

> *[B]y Executive Order Number 12938, I declared a national emergency with respect to the unusual and extraordinary threat to the national security, foreign policy, and economy of the United States posed by the proliferation of nuclear, biological, and chemical weapons ("weapons of mass destruction") and the means of delivering such weapons . . . . I am continuing the national emergency declared in Executive Order Number 12938.*

Was it:

A. **President Jimmy Carter.** Elected in 1976 with 50% of the popular vote.

B. **President Bill Clinton.** Elected in 1992 with 43% of the popular vote. Reelected in 1996 with 49% of the popular vote.

C. **President Lyndon Johnson.** Elected in 1964 with 62% of the popular vote.

D. **President John Kennedy.** Elected in 1960 with 50% of the popular vote.

E. **President Harry Truman.** Elected in 1948 with 50% of the popular vote.

The answer is

B. **Bill Clinton.**

When/where:

Press Release from the White House Office of the Press Secretary, November 9, 1995.

Source:

American Leadership Magazine, Volume 1, Number 1, Second Quarter 1996, page 57.

46. Bill Clinton smiles to the crowd after addressing the Concord Coalition at the University of New Mexico in Albuquerque, July 27, 1998.

Comments:

According to the Source: "The only so-called 'emergency power' of the Constitution reads as follows: 'The privilege of the Writ of Habeas Corpus shall not be suspended, unless when in Cases of Rebellion or Invasion the public safety may require it.' (Article I, Section 9, Cl. 2.)"

The Source continues: "Since the clause in question resides in Article I, it was obviously intended that only the *legislature* should make such a declaration. Any President who would assume 'commander in chief' powers, 'war powers,' declare 'emergencies' to assume powers not delegated by the Constitution, etc., *should be laughed at as a buffoon."*

In his book, *Constitution: Fact or Fiction,* Dr. Gene Schroder informs us: "Through the insidious, yet steady encroachment of 'emergency powers,' the government has now achieved the ability to rule the people by statute or decree, without the vote or consent of the ruled . . . . [Since 1933] America has continued under the 'unconstitutional dictatorship' of war and emergency powers . . . ."[246]

Don McAlvany reports: "Executive Order 12919, released by President Clinton on June 6, 1994, spells out some of the powers that the president assumes under a national emergency. In it he assumes the power to control *all* transportation, . . . *all* forms of energy, *all* farm equipment, *all* fertilizer, *all* food resources, . . . *all* health resources, *all* metals and minerals, and *all* water resources."[247]

47. PLEDGE of ALLEGIANCE

Who said this?

> *I pledge allegiance to Planet Earth, mother of all nations; and to the Infinite Universe in which she stands; our planet, among millions, expressing truth and unlimited possibilities for all!*

Was it:

A. A comic skit on "Saturday Night Live."
B. An environmentalist anxious to replace the existing pledge.
C. A leader at the Temple of Understanding (New York City) for use in temple services.
D. A portion of the ritual practiced by an earth-worshiping tribe of Indians in Melrose, New Mexico.
E. A spoof by **Mark Russell** during his PBS political satire television show.

The answer is

B. **Yvonne Alden.**

47. Pledge to the flag: *I pledge allegiance to the flag of the United States of America and to the Republic for which it stands, one Nation under God, indivisible, with liberty and justice for all.*

When/where:

This pledge was distributed and read during morning announcements in schools across the country.

Source:

Insider's Report, newsletter of The American Policy Center, September/October 1995, page 3.

Comments:

Our pledge to the flag, written by Francis Bellamy (1855-1931) and adopted by Congress in 1942 as part of the code for flag use, is, according to the Source, "no longer good enough for proponents of the 'new world order' who see national boundaries getting in the way of their wealth redistribution schemes."

According to Colonel James "Bo" Gritz, "State laws are now being passed that make it illegal to say the Pledge of Allegiance in school because of the reference to God and our nation."[248]

Many large corporations, too, are rejecting the pledge and refusing to use it at corporate functions. Why? "We need to maintain a global perspective." "It's not productive." "It's inappropriate." These are a few of the excuses given.[249]

The Greens have their own version of the Pledge: "I pledge allegiance to the Earth, and to the flora, fauna, and human life that it supports, one planet, indivisible, with safe air, water, and soil, economic justice, equal rights, and peace for all." One flag company suggests we should not burn a worn-out American flag, just replace it with the Earth Flag.[250]

Another "Earth Pledge" was prepared by Global Education Associates: "I pledge allegiance to the Earth and all its sacred parts, its water, land and living things and all its human hearts."[251]

Why is it liberals appear so anxious to dump our traditional Pledge of Allegiance?

48. PRIVATE PROPERTY

Who said this?

> *I think [all private property] should be in the public domain. We should get it all. Be unreasonable. You can do it. Yesterday's heresy is today's common wisdom. So I would say, let's take it back, let's take it all back.*

Was it:

A. **Carol M. Browner.** Director, Environmental Protection Agency (EPA). Active in Ralph Nader's Citizen Action Program. Top legislative aide to Senator Albert Gore. Identified by the *Wall Street Journal* as "the most troubling Clinton pick to date."[252] (Browner wants to ban backyard barbecues, restrict boating, and curtail the use of off-road utility vehicles.)[253]

B. **Darrell Christian.** Managing editor, Associated Press Knight-Ridder/Tribune.

C. **Brock Evans.** Vice president, National Audubon Society.

D. **Ashish Kotharie.** Indian Institute of Public Administration.

E. **Kurt Waldheim.** Former Secretary General of the United Nations.

The answer is

C. **Brock Evans.**

When/where:

During a "Growth Management Forum" at the New England Environmental Network at Tufts University, November 1990.

Source:

Environmental Overkill, by Dixy Lee Ray with Lou Guzzo, copyright © 1993 by Regnery Publishing, page 131. All rights reserved. Reprinted by special permission of Regnery Publishing, Incorporated.[254]

48. Brock Evans meets reporters in Washington July 2, 1992 to discuss timber land proposals.

Comments:

Dixy Lee Ray says the government is taking Brock Evans' advice and is adding "more and more land to its holdings."[255] How? With a "plethora of new laws, beginning with the Wilderness Act of 1964 . . . ." Now there's the Wilderness Act, the Wild and Scenic Rivers Act, the Surface Management Control and Reclamation Act, the National Forest Management Act, the Federal Land Policy Management Act, the National Environmental Policy Act, the Endangered Species Act, the Clean Water and Clean Air Acts, "and a variety of others . . . ."

I'm sure almost everyone favors setting aside some land for natural wilderness areas - the Grand Canyon, Yellowstone, and the Florida Everglades come to mind - but today the federal government via dozens of agencies and countless faceless bureaucrats can seize your property and mine *without just compensation,* blatantly violating the Fifth Amendment to the U.S. Constitution.

Spoke John Adams: "The moment the idea is admitted into society that property is not as sacred as the laws of God, and that there is not a force of law and public justice to protect it, anarchy and tyranny commence. Property must be sacred or liberty cannot exist."[256] Attorney Joe Gughemetti adds: "[I]n the battle over property rights, it's not enough to be right. You also have to win."[257]

49. PRIVATE PROPERTY

Who said this?

> *We reject the idea of private property.*

Was it:

A. **Peter Berle.** Former president, National Audubon Society. Board member, Sierra Club.

B. **Bryant Charles Gumbel.** Former sports host for NBC Sports. Former co-host of the NBC-TV Today Show. Recipient of many awards including Emmies, the Golden Mike Award, and the Edward R. Murrow Award.[258]

C. **Alger Hiss.** State Department official who passed secret U.S. documents to the Communists.

D. **Patricia Ireland.** Former flight attendant for Pan American World Airlines. Legal counsel, Dade County, Florida. Contributor to the law review at the University of Miami Law School. President, National Organization for Women (NOW).[259] A woman "who abandoned her marriage vows and her family to move in with a willing woman."[260]

E. **Nelson Mandela.** Johannesburg lawyer. Sentenced to life imprisonment in 1964. Released in 1990. President, South Africa. Recipient of the Nobel Peace Prize (1993).[261]

The answer is

A. **Peter Berle.**

When/where:

Not specified by Source.

Source:

Quoted in a solicitation letter from the Concerned Women for America Legislative Action Committee, 370 L'Enfant Promenade, SW, Suite 800, Washington, D.C. 20042-4025.[262]

49. Peter Berle, acting commissioner of New York State's Department of Conservation, April 30, 1976.

Comments:

"The theory of Communism," wrote Karl Marx, "may be summed up in a single sentence: Abolition of private property."[263] So now perhaps we have a context for Mr. Berle's statement.

In his book, *The Road to Serfdom,* F. A. Hayek says: "What our generation has forgotten is that the system of private property is the most important guaranty of freedom, not only for those who own property, but scarcely less for those who do not . . . ."[264]

The Concise Conservative Encyclopedia defines "private property" as "One of the few, certain natural rights." It goes on to say, "A person has a right to possess that which he justly acquires. 'If historical experience could teach us anything,' [Ludwig Von] Mises wrote (1949): 'it would be that private property is inextricably linked to civilization.'"[265]

Theodore Roosevelt is quoted as saying, "In every civilized society, property rights must be carefully safeguarded; ordinarily and in the great majority of cases, human rights and property rights are fundamentally and in the long run, identical."[266]

Yet documentation from the 1976 UN Conference on Human Settlements states a policy dramatically at odds with the wisdom of Hayek, Mises, and Roosevelt: "Land . . . cannot be treated as an ordinary asset, controlled by individuals and subject to the pressures and inefficiencies of the market. Private land ownership is also a principal instrument of accumulation and concentration of wealth and therefore contributes to social injustice. Public control of land is therefore indispensable."[267]

Henry Lamb, executive vice president, Environmental Conservation Organization (ECO), reacts to these assertions: "The idea of having to justify the use of private property to any government, especially the United Nations, is an idea that has no place in America."[268]

Sierra Club member Debbie Sease joins the debate by declaring, "We're going to take on these phony property rights advocates and kick their butts,"[269]

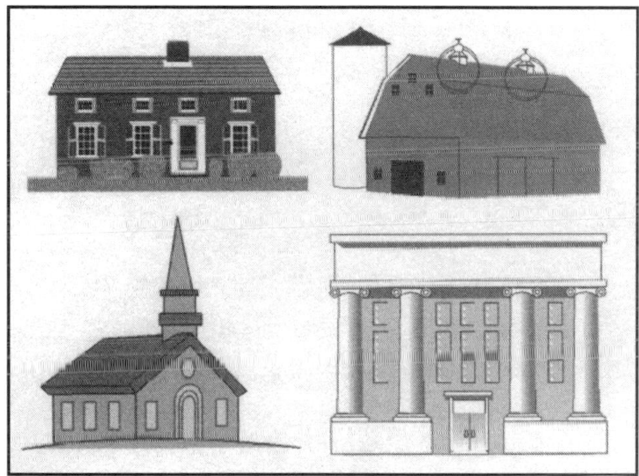

With implementation of Mr. Berle's vision we can look forward to (clockwise from top left): Standardized, Government-Approved Housing Unit. National Food-Production Storage Facility. Federal Life-Long Learning Center. Gaia-Praise Assembly Hall. Thank you, Mr. Berle.

Well, it seems Ms. Sease has some rather honorable butts to kick, because according to Richard Pombo and Joseph Farah, "the Founding Fathers recognized when they drafted the Constitution [that] property rights are the foundation for all other civil rights guaranteed to us by that document. Without the freedom to acquire, possess, and defend property, all other guaranteed rights are merely words on a page."[270]

They continue: "It has been the practice of tyrants throughout history to seize the property and goods of an enemy. By taking away a person's property, you take away his rights and his ability to oppose you. Today, the government rarely sends soldiers armed with rifles to seize private property; it sends bureaucrats armed with regulations and environmental impact statements. But the result is the same."

Arthur Lee of Virginia tells us: "The right of property is the guardian of every other right, and to deprive the people of this, is in fact to deprive them of their liberty."[271]

Thus, when liberals advocate abolishing private property, they advocate the termination of liberty. What kind of "compassion," pray tell, is that?

Don McAlvany suggests that the liberal takeover of property rights is already upon us: "[W]e must understand that the state has abandoned individual property rights in favor of state sovereignty. The state claims absolute ownership of all property through eminent domain, through its ability to seize property, and through its ability to tax property (real estate taxes, estate taxes) and cause it to be forfeited if the tax is not paid. In effect, real estate is owned by the state, and leased to tenants for rent (property taxes)."[272]

This idea of abandoning private property is right out of the pages of the *Communist Manifesto.* That document specifically calls for "the abolition of private property." The *Manifesto* also calls for abolition of the family, abolition of countries and nationalities, and abolition of religion. William Norman Grigg comments: "Under Communism, the state supplants both God and the family and does not tolerate competing loyalties."[273]

50. REDISTRIBUTION

Who said this?

> *We are going to try to take all the money that we think is unnecessarily being spent and take it from the "haves" and give it to the "have nots" that need it so much.*

Was it:

A. **Jimmy Carter.** U.S. President, 1977-1981.
B. **Thomas Daschle.** U.S. Senator (D, South Dakota).
C. **Lyndon Johnson.** U.S. President, 1963-1969.
D. **Karl Marx.** Founder of modern communism and author of the *Communist Manifesto.*
E. **Joseph Stalin.** Dictator of the Soviet Union, 1928-1953.

The answer is

C. **Lyndon Johnson.**

50. Lyndon Johnson, April 1, 1968, during a radio/television broadcast in which he announced, "I will not seek and I will not accept the nomination of my party for the Presidency."

When/where:

In a speech at the White House, January 15, 1964.

Source:

A World Without Heroes: The Modern Tragedy, by George Roche, published by the Hillsdale College Press, 1987, page 173.[274]

Comments:

The Source continues: "Any civilized community would have run him [Johnson] out of town on the spot, wearing tar and feathers. This was nothing more or less than a promise of grand larceny and massive injustice - both of which, as it happens, followed on a grand scale."

"Government is like a big baby," said Ronald Reagan, "an alimentary canal with a big appetite at one end and no responsibility at the other."[275]

And isn't that the liberals' mind set: *they* know better than you do what's good for you, how much of your money you should be allowed to keep, and how everybody should run his or her life. They are the ones with boundless appetites to tax and spend. They are the ones who ignore the disasters of their irresponsible spending and propose as remedies even more massive spending.

By the way, as a bonus for every "compassionate" liberal lawmaker, government handouts tend to "buy" the votes of those who receive redistribution money, as the recipients become dependent upon the politician who doles it out to them.

51. RESTRUCTURING SOCIETY

Who said this?

> *Children and women can be our Trojan Horse for attacking the citadel of poverty, for undergirding democracy, dramatically slowing population growth and for accelerating economic development.*

Was it:

A. **David Brock.** Author of *The Real Anita Hill* and *The Seduction of Hillary Rodham Clinton.* Fired from *The American Spectator* magazine November 13, 1997. Stated on the NBC Today Show: "I'm gay, and my sexuality was even used to discredit what I was saying . . . ."[276]

B. **Judith Espinosa.** Secretary of Environment, State of New Mexico.

C. **Matthew Fox.** Advocate of Gaia.

D. **James P. Grant.** Past executive director, UNICEF (United Nations International Children's Emergency Fund, commonly known as the United Nations Children's Fund).

E. **Laura D'Andrea Tyson.** Formerly professor at the University of California at Berkeley. Chair, Council of Economic Advisors.

The answer is

D. **James P. Grant.**

51. James Grant, executive director of UNICEF, in Mexico City, May 22, 1979.

When/where:

In a speech at the International Development Conference, 1993.

Source:

"Rome Summit Speeds UN Agenda," *ēco•logic,* November/December 1996, page 18.

Comments:

The Source states: "Globalist leaders know that only a new set of beliefs and values will prepare the Western world to accept what Al Gore calls 'sacrifice, struggle and a wrenching transformation of society.'"[277]

Those who treasure the "old" beliefs of truth, family, patriotism, and God, may wonder why "a new set of beliefs and values" is necessary. Indeed, are liberals expecting us to both discard the values that made this country great, and also to "sacrifice, struggle," and suffer "a wrenching transformation of society?"

The Source continues: "Resident UN coordinators would guide and monitor 'the allocation and use of financial and human resources while nations with representative governments would yield their sovereignty to a monstrous multilevel global bureaucracy controlled by socialist UN rulers.'"

Further: "According to UN guidelines, all people and all places would be monitored - schools, homes, workplaces . . . . All who violate the new standards for tolerance, gender equality, or sustainable living at home or at work would be tracked through the vast UN-controlled data system."

So, tell me: If you should become just such a violator and you're tracked down, then what?

52. SEXUAL PREFERENCE

Who said this?

> *Is it possible heterosexuality is a phase you will grow out of? Is it possible you are heterosexual because you fear the same sex? If you have never slept with anyone of the same sex, how do you know you wouldn't prefer that? Is it possible you merely need a good gay experience?*

Was it:

A. **Dr. Joycelyn Elders.** Former U.S. Surgeon General. Comments made during an interview on CNN.
B. **Barney Frank.** U.S. Representative (D, Massachusetts). In remarks made during a speech from the floor of the U.S. House of Representatives.
C. Navy SEALS socialization test questions given to new recruits.
D. Questions posed in a 1994 article in the *Lamda Book Report,* A Review of Contemporary Gay and Lesbian Literature.
E. Questions used in a test administered at a Framingham, Massachusetts highschool.

The answer is

E. Questions 3, 4, and 5 contained in a Framingham, Massachusetts highschool quiz.

52. Your school-tax dollars at work.

When/where:

English professor Eugene Narrett, Framingham State College, described this quiz in an article in the October 1996 issue of *Chronicles.*

Source:

The Homosexual Agenda: How the Gay Lobby is Targeting America's Children, by the staff of Americans for Truth about Homosexuality, 1997, pages 36, 37.[278]

Comments:

The Source reveals other interesting questions contained in the high school's sensitivity-training test:

8. "Most child molesters are heterosexual men. Do you consider it safe to expose your children to heterosexual males? Heterosexual male teachers particularly?"
9. "How can you have a truly satisfying relationship with someone of the opposite sex, given the obvious physical and emotional differences?"
10. "Why are there so few successful heterosexual relationships?"
11. "Given the problems men and women face, would you want your child to be heterosexual? If they [sic] were, would you consider aversion therapy?"

"We're here, we're queer, we're in the classroom," declared lesbian activist Donna Red Wing at a regional conference of the Gay, Lesbian, and Straight Teachers Network in 1995.[279] That cry of the gay and lesbian community is both frightening and accurate.

When Elizabeth Birch, executive director of the Human Rights Campaign, appeared on the CNN Crossfire program December 4, 1996, she was asked if she wanted to use the schools to promote the notion that homosexual love is the moral equivalent of heterosexual love. She sidestepped the question, but was then asked again "[D]o you think in a public school, same sex marriages should be taught as normative?" Her answer: "Yes." [280]

In his book, *Shadow in the Land,* Congressman William Dannemeyer (R, California) says: "Homosexuals are now insisting that young people be taught how to perform homosexual acts as well as heterosexual acts. They demand that such instruction be mandatory in our public schools and that the courses also teach that homosexuality is a normal and desirable appetite. Many schools have instituted such sex education."[281]

This is lockstep in accord with the communist strategy: "Present homosexuality, degeneracy, and promiscuity as 'normal, natural, healthy,'" as described in *The Naked Communist,* by W. Cleon Skousen.[282]

Sharon Earls of Toccoa, Georgia tells of her two daughters, ages 13 and 15, who were taken by the school "counselor" to the county health clinic "for the express purpose of giving them birth control pills and colored condoms." They were also forced to undergo Pap smears and tests for the AIDS virus. Sharon and her husband did not give permission for this visit and the "counselor" told them the test results were none of their business.[283]

In Massachusetts at the Chelmsford High School, the students were treated to a special "Hot, Sexy and Safer" program presented by Suzanne Landolphi.[284] Parents were not notified of this program and had no opportunity to object to it . . . until after the fact. Landolphi simulated masturbation and explicitly talked about ejaculation, breast size, penis size, sexual intercourse, nudity, urination, oral-genital contact, erections, sodomy, testicles, the homosexual lifestyle, and premarital heterosexual conduct by minors. Hot and sexy indeed!

Then with students from the audience Ms. Landolphi made them participate in a little skit she called a "group sexual experience." She used four-letter words throughout her presentation and employed lewd language to describe body parts and excretory functions. She made extensive use of the "F" word and encouraged students and teachers alike to repeatedly chant the word with her. She encouraged oral sex, masturbation, mutual masturbation, homosexuality, and condom use. She got a male student to lick an oversized condom with her, then had a female student pull it over the male student's head.

One child who asked to be excused from this ordeal was denied his request and threatened with three-day detention.

Is this how you wish your school tax dollars to be spent?

Shocked by such a disgusting program, the Rutherford Institute filed a lawsuit to stop it. The case was appealed all the way to the U.S. Supreme Court, which refused to hear it. So Ms. Landolphi may be appearing in a high school near you. Don't look for any notification, however; there won't be any.

Berit Kjos reports in *Media Bypass* magazine: "When 15-year-old Kevin walked into his American History class at Cupertino High School in California, he was given a handout. The title: 'Heterosexuality: Can it be Cured?' Weird, he thought . . . . He read on: 'Whatever the cause of this phenomenon, we can state without doubt that there are many problems associated with heterosexuality, both for the individual and society at large . . . .' The suggested treatments included psychotherapy and widespread sterilization of the heterosexual population."[285]

Now if these examples aren't enough to curl your toes, cross your eyes, and burn out a few cerebrum fuses, wait 'til you hear what happened at the Montpelier High School in Vermont.[286] Yes, we're talking about a school in the lovely, picturesque Green Mountain State, which, at least at one time had the lowest percentage of city dwellers of any state in the union. But everything's up to date at the Montpelier High School in the state capital . . . when it comes to sex education, that is.

The parents of a teenager attending the school made a little discovery while paging through their daughter's "confidential journal," which each student in the Psychology/Sociology class is required to maintain.

It seems the teacher had carefully instructed the students "not to tell their parents about or allow them to read" this secret journal, but one student refused to allow school orders to supersede the relationship she had with her parents.

What the parents found in Units Seven and Eight (Sexuality and Relationships) was a collection of materials, many of which were copied from a book titled *The Teen Body Book.* Now, if you'd say you've led a somewhat sheltered life, you may wish to skip the next few paragraphs. Many who have *not* led sheltered lives may likewise find what's being taught at Montpelier High School disgusting, disgraceful, and totally unacceptable.

Here are a few quotations from *The Teen Body Book*:

"The couple may kiss and stroke one another all over . . . especially sensitive areas like the woman's clitoris or the head and underside of the man's penis . . . . When a woman kisses, licks, or sucks a man's penis, this is called fellatio. When a man does the same with a woman's clitoris, vulva, and the opening of the vagina, this is called cunnilingus . . . ."

"You can have sex with anyone. It can be fun." Virgins may have their hymens "stretched or removed via medical methods . . . before you have sex."

"Testing your ability to function sexually . . . may be . . . less threatening with your own sex, if you happen to be quite young and/or still a bit uncomfortable with the opposite sex."

"I put Vaseline on my **** and [also] in a roll of toilet paper to make it like a vagina. I like to thrust my **** in and out of this roll . . . . It's the only way I can come. My hand isn't enough."

"Against the standard set by lesbians, heterosexual couples do not fare so well in distributing responsibility for rational health."

"Billy, come in the kitchen and tell Mommy what you learned in kindergarten today."

The daughter of Joel and Felicity Bachman attends high school in Montpelier. "Our daughter tells us that the *in* thing at her high school now, if you're a girl, is to 'be' a lesbian," they say. "She . . . read that 'two lesbians make a more nurturing relationship than a heterosexual couple' because women are naturally more nurturing."[287]

Now, let's all tell each other once again how much we approve of Goals 2000 and how much we endorse Outcome-Based Education. Let's all put our full and complete trust in the Federal Government, the National Education Association,[288] the school administration, and the teachers. Let's all celebrate the grand and glorious success of America's public schools.[289]

You may think sex programs don't affect the kids. Well, too bad you missed the art exhibit in a Ft. Lauderdale, Florida library:[290] A 12th grader drew a man leaning on a ladder with his penis pointing up. A ninth grader drew a woman with bare breasts and pubic hair. This is but a sample of the "art" shown.

What in heaven's name is going on in the schools? What are they teaching our children? What's being taught *your* child today, *right now*? And have you ever wondered about what the long-term objectives might be of such training? What's the agenda? What will be the likely results?

"Parents need to beware," cautions Carmen Pate, vice president, Concerned Women for America, "to ask their children what they learned in school today and to make sure they tell them the other side of the story."[291]

The NARTH (National Association for Reparative Therapy for Homosexuality) Bulletin has the answer: "Today more than ever, homosexual activists with perhaps only a 1-3% American presence are successfully dumbing down and desensitizing our moral landscape through their growing influence in government, business, the media, even the church. An important part of that agenda has included widespread acceptance of the redefinition of important concepts central to the preservation of a healthy social fabric: family values, sexual fulfillment, religious bigotry, human rights, even the basic definitions of right and wrong."[292]

In an article in *Gay Community News,* author Michael Swift displays the contempt some liberals harbor for traditional values: "The family unit - spawning ground of lies, betrayals, mediocrity, hypocrisy, and violence - will be abolished. The family unit, which only dampens imagination and curbs free will, must be eliminated."[293]

"In no area of human life has the diabolical influence of liberalism been more evident and more calamitous than in sexuality," says Father James Thornton. "Militant homosexuality is a huge wrecking ball designed to demolish the foundations of our religion and families, and of our nation and civilization."[294]

53. TRUTH

Who said this?

> *I'd say, "Gee, I just don't remember what happened back then," and they won't be able to indict me for perjury and that, maybe that's the principal thing that I've learned in four years . . . . I just intend to rely on that failure of memory.*

Was it:

A. **Mark Gearan.** Director, White House Communications.
B. **Abner Joseph Mikva.** Former judge, U.S. Circuit Court of Appeals (Washington, D.C.). Author. Member, American Bar Association. Former White House Counsel.
C. **Bernard Nussbaum.** Former White House Counsel.
D. **Charles Oglevtree Ruff.** Counsel for Anita Hill (administered her polygraph test). Clinton Administration White House Counsel.
E. **Margaret Williams.** Assistant to President Clinton. Chief of staff to Hillary Rodham Clinton.[295]

The answer is

D. **Charles Ruff.**

When/where:

In a conversation with Bob Woodward in Ruff's office, 1977.

Source:

"The White House Plays Ruff," by Byron York, *The American Spectator,* June 1997, page 30.

53. Charles Ruff, outside the Senate Judiciary Committee hearing room, speaking to reporters October 31, 1991 about a polygraph test he had administered to Anita Hill.

Comments:

This quotation came at a time when Ruff feared Congress might reopen the Nixon Watergate inquiry. He was concerned that tough questions might be asked about the actions of the original Watergate prosecutors, one of whom was Ruff himself. His scheme, clearly not original, has been used by dozens (thousands?) of liberals over the years. Probably some conservatives, too! Its effectiveness can't be argued!

In his *AIM Report* Reed Irvine concludes: "No one in high position seems the least bit concerned about committing perjury to cover up wrongdoing."[296]

Concludes Thomas Jefferson: "The whole art of government consists in the art of being honest."[297]

One might think liberals have learned well the lesson of Vladimir Lenin, who in 1921 advised: "Telling the truth is a bourgeois prejudice. Deception, on the other hand, is often justified by the goal."[298]

54. TRUTH

Who said this?

I just don't have any memory of that.

Was it:

A. **Hillary Rodham Clinton.**
B. **William Jefferson Clinton.**
C. **Albert Arnold (Al) Gore, Jr.**
D. **Webster Hubbell.** Former U.S. Associate Attorney General. Sentenced to 21 months in prison. Recipient of as much as a million dollars or more in what many suspect was "hush money."
E. **Craig Livingstone.** Former bouncer. Former Clinton White House director of security, despite the fact that no one seems to claim responsibility for hiring him. (Gary Aldrich, in his book *Unlimited Access,* seems to solve the mystery when he quotes associate counsel William Kennedy as saying, "It's a done deal. Hillary wants him."[299])

The answer is

A. **Hillary Rodham Clinton** (but clearly, it could have been any one of the bunch).

54. Hillary Rodham Clinton, outside U.S. District Court January 26, 1996, after answering grand jury questions for over 4 hours. She said she "did not know how [Rose Law Firm] billing records came to be found where they were found."

When/where:

Commenting on a 1993 David Watkins' memo in which it was revealed Mrs. Clinton was the one who ordered the firing of the White House travel office staff.

Source:

"Stupid Quotes," *The Limbaugh Letter,* February 1996, page 6, quoting from *Newsweek.*

Comments:

You don't suppose Mrs. Clinton ever met with Mr. Ruff (see Quote 53) to discuss such weighty matters as memory recall and the wondrous advantages of the loss thereof.

In the Clinton White House a code of lying was apparently well established. White House director of security, the now infamous Craig Livingstone, told FBI special agent Dennis Sculimbrene, after Sculimbrene had testified at the trial of Billy Dale (who had headed the White House Telegraph and Travel Office): "The truth, Dennis? Don't you know the truth is relative? Your testimony was *your* version of the truth. Truth is whatever you want it to be."[300]

What's tragic is *not* that weak men and women lie. What's tragic is that the American people tolerate lies and deception from their leaders. Why is it we don't *demand* honesty, integrity, and morality from those we elect?

Dick Morris, close political consultant to Bill Clinton, quoted him as saying: "what I think I'll say is I never used illegal drugs . . . . I did, but it was in England, and it was legal there."[301]

Ah, the lawyer's lie is a work of art.

55. UNITING THE WORLD

Who said this?

> *[W]ithout exception, we operated under directives issued by the White House. We are continuing to be guided by just such directives, the substance of which was to the effect that we should make every effort to so alter life in the United States as to make possible a comfortable merger with the Soviet Union.*

Was it:

A. **Thomas R. Donahue.** Former president, AFL-CIO.
B. **H. Rowan Gaither.** President, Ford Foundation.
C. **Aurelio Peccei.** President and founder, Club of Rome.
D. **Peter Roth.** President, Fox Broadcasting.
E. **Marc Tucker.** President, National Center on Education and the Economy (NCEE).

The answer is

B. **H. Rowan Gaither.**

When/where:

At a 1953 meeting at the New York City headquarters of the Ford Foundation to which Norman Dodd, director of research for the Reese Committee (a congressional committee investigating foundations), had been invited.

55. H. Rowan Gaither, chairman of the board of the Ford Foundation, puffs on his pipe at his farm near Upper Black Eddy, Pennsylvania, December 24, 1957.

Source:

The World Order - Our Secret Rulers, by Eustace Mullins, Second Edition, Ezra Pound Institute of Civilization, 1992, page 258.[302]

Comments:

Norman Dodd, director or research for the Reese Committee, asked Gaither if the American people would be informed about this U.S./Soviet Union merger plan. Gaither replied, "We wouldn't think of doing that, Mr. Dodd."[303]

Now, let's look briefly at the foundation Gaither headed. In his book (Source) Eustace Mullins' says: "*The National Guardian* (January 13, 1968), pointed out that 'The Ford Foundation plays a key part in financing and influencing almost all major civil rights groups including Congress of Racial Equality, Southern Christian Leadership, National Urban League, and NAACP.'"

Mullins continues, "The Ford Foundation has spent many millions to promote racial agitation and possible civil war in America, completely polarizing the races . . . . It takes money to promote a civil war. Ford Foundation entered the Hispanic field by giving $600,000 to the openly revolutionary Southwest Council of La Raza in 1968, and an additional $545,717 in 1969 . . . ."

It seems "philanthropy" has an agenda.[304]

56. UNITING THE WORLD

Who said this?

> *We are on the verge of a global transformation. All we need is the right major crisis and the nation will accept the New World Order.*

Was it:

A. **Zbigniew Brzezinski.** Member, Council on Foreign Relations. Co-founder and first director, Trilateral Commission.[305]

B. **Walter Mondale.** Member, Council on Foreign Relations. Member, Trilateral Commission.

C. **David Rockefeller.** Founder and honorary chairman, Council of the Americas. Chairman, Americas Society. Founder, Forum of the Americas. Chairman emeritus, Council on Foreign Relations. Founder and honorary chairman, Trilateral Commission.[306]

D. **James Schlesinger.** Member, Council on Foreign Relations.

E. **Cyrus Roberts Vance.** Member of the board of directors, Federal Reserve Bank of New York City. Trustee, Rockefeller Foundation. Recipient of the Medal of Freedom. Recipient of Grand Cordon of Order of the Rising Sun (Government of Japan), and other honors. Member of the American Bankers Association. Member, Council on Foreign Relations.[307]

The answer is

C. **David Rockefeller.**

When/where:

Not specified by Source.

Source:

America's Judgments, What Lies Ahead? documentation in support of the Militia of Montana video, page 139.

56. David Rockefeller, president, Chase National Bank.

Comments:

Bill Clinton's mentor, the late Carroll Quigley, professor of history at Georgetown University and also a member of the Council on Foreign Relations described it thus: "The CFR is the American branch of a society which originated in England . . . [and] . . . believes national boundaries should be obliterated and one-world rule established."[308]

[Note: Formation of the CFR can be traced to the work and vision of one Mr. Cecil John Rhodes, whose simple desire was, according to Rhodes biographer Sara G. Millin, a "government of the world." This is the same Rhodes who gave us the Rhodes Scholarships, opportunities for "chosen" students to study and become committed to the idea of one-world government.[309]]

Writing in the *Washington Post,* Richard Harwood said the CFR is "the nearest thing we have to a ruling establishment in the United States."[310]

That's clear enough, but in her booklet, *Why a Bankrupt America,* Devvy Kidd is a little more forceful on the subject: "In other words, the CFR's activities are treasonous to our U.S. Constitution. They mean to put an end to the United States of America and make our nation part of their global government scheme."[311]

"The Constitution may not be perfect," somebody said, "but it's a lot better than what the government's using these days."[312]

But we need to talk about this idea of uniting the world, creating a new world order, establishing a single global governance. The United Nations has been hot on this trail for decades. The UN octopus of power, the liberals' dream, has been extending its tentacles and tightening its hold on every facet of life around the planet.

"Global government is not just a pipe dream of starry-eyed dreamers," says Phyllis Schlafly. "It is the world view and goal of the Clinton Administration. Its advocates are all around us."[313]

She continues, "Global treaties and conferences are a direct threat to every American citizen. They are an assault on our right to raise and educate our children as we see fit. They are an attack on our ownership of our private property and on American ownership of our national treasures. They are an attack on our pocketbooks because, if the UN ever gets taxing power, there is no limit to how much of our money it can grab. They are an attack on the American standard of living because their goal is to steal American wealth and give it to the rest of the world."

There is a UN-funded Commission on Global Governance which has completed a three-year study on the subject and has publicly announced plans to implement global governance by the year 2000. Toward that end, a World Conference on Global Governance is planned for 1998 with the objective of preparing treaties and agreements for submission to the world so ratification *and implementation* can be achieved by the year 2000.[314]

This is not news. That the mainstream media have not chosen to display headlines about it should come as no surprise. They're all on board with the idea and don't want to rock the boat with the public.

Way back in 1953 Public Law 495 (Title 1, Section 112) stated that "None of the funds appropriated in this title shall be used for the promotion, direct or indirect, of the principle or doctrine of one world government or one world citizenship." However, when the Appropriations bill of 1987 came along, some 34 years later, presto, that language was deleted. The State Department explained, with a straight face I'm sure, it was just trying to "get rid of the dead wood" in the legislation.[315]

Heck, even the Pope has the message, for he has proclaimed: "By the end of this decade (A.D. 2000) we will live under the first one-world government that has ever existed in the society of nations. One world government is inevitable."[316]

The United States Day Committee is a little bolder in its timetable projections: "World government is here, Americans[.] [W]hether we like it or not, we are living right now under world government, with foreign policy and economic decisions being made under United Nations Charter Law, not the Constitution! Senate Document 87, 'Review of the United Nations Charter,' p. 289, January 7, 1954 states: 'The Charter (of the United Nations) has become the *supreme law of the land;* and the judges in every state shall be bound thereby, anything in the Constitution or laws of any state to the contrary notwithstanding.'"[317]

What's important is that the liberals' plans intend to place the UN in control of the world and at the same time to diffuse, dismantle, and disintegrate national boundaries, laws, and traditions. Whereas the U.S. Constitution provides an umbrella of government on a federal level while reserving major power for the States and the people, the UN tips upside down the power structure. It reserves *all* power for the UN.

Barry Goldwater had it figured out way back in 1971. Said then-Senator Goldwater: "[T]he time has come to recognize the United Nations for the anti-American, anti-freedom organization that it has become. The time has come for us to cut off all financial help, withdraw as a member, and ask the United Nations to find a headquarters location outside the United States that is more in keeping with the philosophy of the majority of voting members, someplace like Moscow or Peking."[318]

The *DeWeese Report* sums up: "The UN is an open and direct threat to the sovereignty and constitutional rights of all Americans.[319] The UN has chosen to set the agenda. The UN has chosen to make itself more than an international debating society. The UN has decided that it wants more power. These are the real reasons why those who oppose the UN's agenda and its infringement on American sovereignty believe this nation has little choice but to get completely out of the UN - a world body out of control."[320]

We must learn anew the lesson Thomas Jefferson taught almost 200 years ago: "I do verily believe that . . . a single, consolidated government would become the most corrupt government on the earth."[321]

57. WORLD GOVERNMENT

Who said this?

> *We shall have World Government whether or not you like it. The only question is whether World Government will be achieved by conquest or consent.*

Was it:

A. **Henry Kissinger.** Former U.S. Secretary of State. Director, special studies project for the Rockefeller Brothers Fund. Author. Recipient of the Nobel Peace Prize (1973), President's Medal of Freedom (1977), Medal of Liberty, and other awards. Member, American Academy of Arts and Sciences. Member, Bilderbergers. Member, Council on Foreign Relations. Member, Trilateral Commission.[322]

B. **Alice Rivlin.** Member, Council on Foreign Relations.

C. **Robert Rubin.** Member, Council on Foreign Relations.

D. **James Tobin.** Economist. Winner of a Nobel Prize in 1981. Author of the proposed "Tobin Tax", which would tax all international currency transactions and deliver the revenue to the UN.[323]

E. **James Paul Warburg.** Member, Council on Foreign Relations. Foreign agent of the Rothschild Dynasty. Major player in the Federal Reserve Act scam.[324]

The answer is

E. **James Warburg.**

When/where:

In a boast before the U.S. Senate, February 17, 1950.

Source:

Why a Bankrupt America? by Devvy Kidd, Project Liberty, 1994, page 20.[325]

57. James Paul Warburg speaks to the Senate Foreign Relations committee, March 28, 1952.

Comments:

According to Devvy Kidd (Source): "The final nail in the economic coffin of America is NAFTA [North American Free Trade Agreement]. The North American 'Fraud and Theft' Agreement is not about improving the standard of living for our neighbors south of our border . . . ."

"Every time you hear NAFTA, the IMF, the World Court, or the UN, think New World Order and think Civil War II," cautions author Thomas Chittum.[326]

While many economists endorse free trade because it will equalize access to products, income, and life styles around the world, Americans ought to be concerned because we'll be the losers. Our incomes will drop and our life styles will deteriorate to reach a balance with levels in present Third-World countries.

Don McAlvany reminds us that for years globalist leaders have been telling us of the wonders of the global economy, but, says he, "contrarians have been warning that China and Asia would more likely be a source of supply than demand."[327]

Says former GM executive Gus Stelzer: "Free trade has evolved into a corrupt, double-dealing scheme to evade U.S. laws, not only contrary to moral principles, but also in violation of the Equal Protection Clause of . . . the U.S. Constitution . . . ."[328]

In 1848 Karl Marx observed, "Free trade breaks up old nationalities . . . in a word, the free trade system hastens social revolution [i.e., socialism]."[329]

A "SUSTAINABLE" WORLD

A DECLARATION OF WAR: Killing People to Save Animals and the Environment.

- Title and subtitle of an activist's handbook written by Screaming Wolf and produced by the Animal Liberation Front[330]

What do you do when you see an endangered animal eating an endangered plant?

- Posting on the Internet; author unknown

58. ENVIRONMENT

Who said this?

> *In searching for a new enemy to unite us, we came up with the idea that pollution, the threat of global warming, water shortages, famine and the like would fit the bill . . . . All these dangers are caused by human intervention . . . . The real enemy, then, is humanity itself.*

Was it:

A. The Bilderberger Group.
B. The Council of the Club of Rome.
C. The Council on Foreign Relations (CFR).
D. **Alvin Toffler.** Author of the bestseller book *Future Shock,* published in 1980. Key advisor to House Speaker Newt Gingrich.[331]
E. The Trilateral Commission, condemned by Barry Goldwater as "A skillful, coordinated effort to seize control [leading to] the creation of a worldwide economic power superior to the political governments of the nation states. . . ."[332]

The answer is

B. **The Council of the Club of Rome** (100 globalist leaders).

58. Club of Rome symbol.

When/where:

As described in *The First Global Revolution,* by Alexander King (president of the Club of Rome[333]) and Bertrand Schneider, 1991, Pantheon Books, New York, page 115.

Source:

Brave New Schools, by Berit Kjos, Harvest House Publishers, 1995, page 105.[334]

Comments:

Don McAlvany describes the Club of Rome as "one of the most powerful and influential of the elitist one-world groups. The Club states: 'Only a revolution, the substitution of a new world economic order can save us.' The COR intends to control international trade, world food, world minerals, and ocean management."[335]

In an article in *Dispatches,* Patrick Moore, founding member and former director of Greenpeace, is quoted from his testimony before the U.S. House Resources subcommittee on forests and forest health: "Much of the environmental movement has been hijacked by extremist activists who use the language of the environment for a movement that has more to do with class struggle and anti-corporatism."[336] It would seem Mr. Moore is a "reformed" environmentalist.

But the spite and hatred for humanity lives on in many a liberal heart. For example, you'd think the Unabomber would be universally condemned. But no, many on the left, like *Boston Globe* columnist Alex Bearn, seem to endorse his antisocial agenda: "I can't bring myself to hate the Unabomber. Quite the opposite," says he.[337]

59. ENVIRONMENT

Who said this?

> ***I got the impression that instead of going out to shoot birds, I should go out and shoot the kids who shoot birds.***

Was it:

A. **Sara Brady.** Chair of Handgun Control, Incorporated. One who endorses mandating that trigger locks must be provided whenever handguns are sold. (President Clinton urged approval of national trigger-lock legislation during his 1997 State of the Union address.)[338]

B. **Paul Ehrlich.** Butterfly specialist and biologist, Stanford University.

C. **William Reilly.** Administrator of the EPA.

D. **Jonathan Schell.** Author of *Our Fragile Earth* and *The Fate of the Earth.*

E. **Paul Watson.** Co-founder of Greenpeace.

The answer is

E. **Paul Watson.**

When/where:

In *Access to Energy,* Volume 10, Number 4, December 1982.

Source:

Trashing the Planet, by Dixy Lee Ray with Lou Guzzo, copyright © 1990 by Regnery Publishing, page 166. All rights reserved. Reprinted by special permission of Regnery Publishing, Incorporated.

59. Canadian Paul Watson operates the anchor winch on deck the icebound protest vessel *Sea Shepherd* in the Gulf of St. Lawrence, March 23, 1979. The purpose of the voyage: to disrupt the killing of baby harp seals.

Comments:

Dixy Lee Ray (Source) states: "Environmentalism . . . goes far beyond the traditional conservation movement - be kind to animals, support good stewardship of the earth, and so on - a philosophy of nature that we have known from the past. It is complex in that it incorporates a strongly negative element of anti-development, anti-progress, anti-technology, anti-business, anti-established institutions and above all, anti-capitalism . . . ."

Dixy Lee Ray continues: "As a movement, it is activist, adversarial, punitive, and coercive. It is quick to resort to force, generally through the courts or through legislation, although some of its more zealous adherents engage in physical violence (Earth First! and Greenpeace, for example). Finally, the environmentalist movement today has an agenda that goes far beyond a mere concern for nature, as shown by its links to and common cause with other leftist radical movements . . . ."

"The radical environmental movement is destroying America," says writer John Meredith. "It is turning our society, once based on individual freedom and responsibility, into little more than mindless followers of regulations established at the whim of unelected special-interest groups."[339]

Don't overlook the sage words of Nikita Khrushchev: "The environmental crisis is the cornerstone of the New World Order."[340]

60. ENVIRONMENT

Who said this?

> *We routinely wrote scare stories about the hazards of chemicals, employing words like "cancer," and "birth defects" to splash a little cold water in reporters' faces . . . . Our press reports were more or less true . . . . Few handouts, however, can be completely honest, and ours were no exception . . . . We were out to whip the public into a frenzy about the environment.*

Was it:

A. **John H. Adams.** Executive director, Natural Resources Defense Council.

B. **Mike Demaree McCurry.** Former director of communications, Democratic National Committee. Former spokesman for the U.S. Department of State. White House press secretary.[341]

C. **Rafe Pomerance.** Deputy assistant Secretary of State for Environment, Health and Natural Resources. Former senior associate for policy affairs, World Resources Institute.

D. **William Ruckelshaus.** Former EPA Administrator. Chairman, Browing-Ferris Industries, Incorporated.

E. **Jim Sibbison.** Former EPA (Environmental Protection Agency) press officer.

The answer is

E. **Jim Sibbison.**

When/where:

In an article in the March 1984 issue of *The Washington Monthly.*

Source:

Environmental Overkill, by Dixy Lee Ray with Lou Guzzo, copyright © 1993 by Regnery Publishing, page 165. All rights reserved. Reprinted by special permission of Regnery Publishing, Incorporated.

60. Frightened citizens will more readily relinquish their freedoms.

Comments:

The Source reports that Sibbison boasted about how easy it was to use "gullible reporters to spread scare messages." He wrote: "In those days the idea was to get the media to help turn the EPA into an enforcer that struck fear into the heart of polluters." And into the hearts of the American public as well.

By the EPA's own estimate, the cost to the American people resulting from environmental regulations since the EPA was founded in 1970 exceeds $1.4 trillion.[342] (When you write out all the zeros, that's $1,400,000,000,000!)

You know what a wetland is? Any area so designated is fair game for big-time regulation by the Federal Government. Robert J. Pierce of the Army Corps of Engineers gives us the definition: "[F]or regulatory purposes, a wetland is whatever we decide it is." He added that the definition "has changed virtually every year for the last decade . . . ."[343]

Pat Buchanan cautions: "While much good has been done in the name of 'preserving the environment', a wing of that movement has become a radical cult, its adherents intolerant zealots who believe themselves possessed of some great truth denied to the rest of us. Their goal is power; their ambition is to take control of the destiny of nations in the name of preserving and exalting their goddess; Mother Earth . . . . [T]hese people must be resisted at all costs, for their victory is inconsistent with the preservation of a free and self-governing republic."[344]

61. ENVIRONMENT

Who said this?

> *I think if we don't overthrow capitalism, we don't have a chance of saving the world ecologically. I think it is possible to have an ecologically sound society under socialism. I don't think it's possible under capitalism.*

Was it:

A. **Judi Bari.** Earth First!
B. **Katherine (Katie) Couric.** Broadcast journalist. Co-anchor of NBC's Today Show.
C. **Dianne Dillon-Ridgeley.** Co-chair, Citizens Network for Sustainable Development.
D. **Charles Grodin.** Motion pictures actor. Television talk show host.
E. **Jane Pauley.** Television journalist. Writer/reporter for NBC Nightly News. Co-anchor for Dateline NBC.[345]

The answer is

A. **Judi Bari.**

When/where:

As quoted by William Williams, in *State Journal-Register,* June 25, 1992.

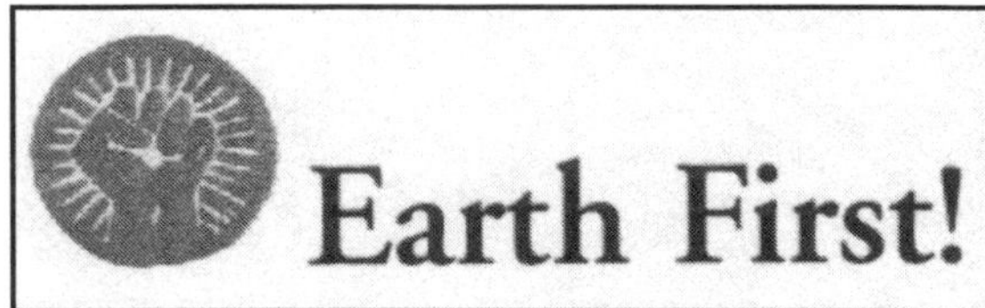

61. Environmentalism *über alles!* The Earth First! logo as displayed in the organization's website (www.imaja.com/imaja/change/environment/ef/earthfirst.html). The fist (in green) seems to make a defiant statement.

Source:

Environmental Overkill, by Dixy Lee Ray with Lou Guzzo, copyright © 1993 by Regnery Publishing, page 203. All rights reserved. Reprinted by special permission of Regnery Publishing, Incorporation.

Comments:

Who cares about wacko Earth First! fanatics, such as our friend Ms. Bari? Well, we all should, because as Tom DeWeese reports: "The worldwide green movement, clear to the United Nations, is now using the Earth First! agenda. The UN's Biodiversity Treaty which calls for the 'wilding of 50 percent of all the territory in every state' is taken directly from the Earth First! blueprint, 'The Wilding of American,' as published in its journal, *Wild Earth.* Bruce Babbitt's federal Department of the Interior has already started implementation of the plan, as homeowners lose their property, businesses are shut down, national parks become off limits to people, and grizzly bears and wolves are brought into communities . . . ."[346]

Ms. Bari's view of things fits nicely with the Unabomber's perspective. In "Unabomb's Leftist Goals Are Mainstream 'Green,'" Llewellyn Rockwell, Jr. says, "Unabomb's years of thinking . . . are fully in tune with the ethics of environmentalism (people are dispensable; nature is not), the long-run goal of environmentalism (to destroy prosperity and capitalism), and the tactics of the environmental movement (using violence, whether through the central state of more private means)."[347]

Alan Caruba, founder, National Anxiety Center, observes: "Since 1970, fully one third of all federal laws and regulations represent environmental mandates, many of which represent an attack on property rights, the keystone of our economic system."[348]

62. ENVIRONMENT

Who said this?

> *[We need] a coordinated global program to accomplish the strategic goal of completely eliminating the internal combustion engine over, say, a twenty-five year period.*

Was it:

A. **Helen Caldicott.** Union of Concerned Scientists.

B. **Dr. Paul Ehrlich.** Harvard professor. A statement in his book, *Population Explosion.*

C. **Al Gore.** Author. A statement in his book *Earth in the Balance.*

D. **The Very Reverend James Parks Mort.** Dean of the Cathedral of St. John the Divine.

E. **Otter Zell.** A statement in *Green Egg,* a publication that describes itself as "The official journal of the Church of All Worlds . . . ."

The answer is

C. **Al Gore.**

When/where:

In his book *Earth in the Balance,* published by Penguin Books, 1992, pages 325-326.

Source:

"The War on Energy," *ēco•logic,* November/December 1996, page 7.

62. Al Gore in Pretoria, South Africa, December 5, 1995.

Comments:

Quoting the Source: "The coordinated global program [attacking automobiles] is well underway." A report following the second Preparatory Committee meeting for the International Car Summit in Geneva, Switzerland in July 1996, states that in America, automobiles account for half of all carbon dioxide emissions and more than 25 percent of all greenhouse gas emissions. The Source's conclusion: "The attack on automobiles is worldwide, but focused primarily on the United States and other developed countries."

You think it would never happen here? Take a look at what appears in the *Governor's Commission on a Sustainable South Florida.* Among the recommendations: "[D]o away with cars; encourage people to walk to work; build bike paths so they could ride bikes to their jobs; remove all people out of the rural areas; stop authorizing single family homes and encourage apartment or community living."[349] The wheels are in motion to remove motorized wheels from our landscape. The UN Biodiversity Assessment specifies that we assume "a peasant level of subsistence."[350]

Says Holly Swanson in her book *Set Up & Sold Out*: "The American people are making the same mistake about the Green Movement the German people made about the Nazi movement. Americans are buying into the Green Movement based on emotional ploys, political fanfare, clever propaganda, hate, lies, terrorism and the promise of all things."[351]

63. ENVIRONMENT

Who said this?

> *We've got to ride the global-warming issue. Even if the theory of global warming is wrong, we will be doing the right thing in terms of economic policy and environmental policy.*

Was it:

A. **Bruce Babbitt.** Former head of the League of Conservation Voters. Registered professional engineer. Professor. Author. Mensa. U.S. Secretary of the Interior. The only other geologist to run for U.S. President besides Herbert Hoover.[352]

B. **Jacques Cousteau.** French oceanographer.

C. **Penny Patterson.** President, the Gorilla Foundation.

D. **William Julius Wilson.** Professor, sociologist, Harvard University.

E. **Timothy Wirth.** U.S. Under Secretary of State for Global Affairs, and one of a number of politicians (including Barbara Boxer, Barney Frank, Al Gore, John Kerry, Daniel Moynihan, Christopher Shays, and others) who have been identified as "Green Leadership for the '90s."[353]

The answer is

E. **Timothy Wirth.**

63. Timothy Wirth, at a briefing at the State Department, August 31, 1994.

When/where:

Spoken to a reporter in 1990, when Wirth was a U.S. Senator.

Source:

"The Week," *National Review,* January 27, 1997, page 8.[354]

Comments:

The Source observes: "It is interesting to know that the Administration's top Green doesn't really care whether the theory of global warming is correct. It's a good scare, and that's enough."

Let's look at what Greens were predicting as published January 30, 1970 in the *Life* magazine article, "Ecology: A Cause as Movement": "[S]cientists have solid experimental and theoretical evidence to support each of the following predictions: In a decade [the 1980s], urban dwellers will have to wear gas masks to survive air pollution. In the early 1980s air pollution combined with a temperature inversion will kill thousands in some U.S. city. By 1985 air pollution will have reduced the amount of sunlight reaching earth by one half. Increased carbon dioxide in the atmosphere will affect the earth's temperature, leading to mass flooding or a new ice age."[355]

So that's the kind of track record Greens have achieved with their insightful, dire predictions. And now they want us to believe their new, wild, and wacky predictions?

But of course. And many liberals are only too willing to spread the word. And too many Americans appear only too willing to join the con game.

Walter Williams sharpens the focus: "While the Soviet Union has collapsed, communism is not dead. It has [been] repackaged under a new name: environmentalism. Communism is about extensive government regulation and control by elites, and so is environmentalism."[356]

64. ENVIRONMENT

Who said this?

> *[W]e have to offer up scary scenarios [about global warming and destruction of the environment], make simplified, dramatic statements, and make little mention of any doubts one might have . . . . Each of us has to decide what the right balance is between being effective and being honest.*

Was it:

A. A Comedy Channel humorist and satirist.
B. A National Weather Center scientist.
C. A *New York Times* journalist.
D. A Stanford University environmentalist.
E. A University of Michigan educator.

The answer is

D. **Stephen Schneider,** who, 13 years after endorsing Lowell Ponte's book *The Cooling,* wrote the book *Global Warming* in 1989.

64. Stephen Schneider.

When/where:

In the article "Our Fragile Earth," by Jonathan Schell, *Discover,* October 1989, page 44.[357]

Source:

The News Manipulators, by Reed Irvine, Joseph Goulden, and Cliff Kincaid, Book Distributors, Incorporated, 1993, pages 296-297.[358]

Comments:

Dear me, dear me! The sky is falling! The globe is warming! The ice is melting! The seas are rising! You'll recall the old story in which Foxy-Loxy's "sky is falling" deception frightened Ducky-Lucky, Goosey-Loosey, and Turkey-Lurky, straight into the fox's den to their speedy demise. How many turkey-lurkys are there, I wonder, eager to swallow Mr. Schneider's line and leap into *his* lair?

The News Manipulators contains an editorial comment from the *Detroit News*: "The next time you hear about some scary environmental horror on the nightly news, keep that [Schneider] quote in mind. It goes far to explain the debasement of American environmental science into cheap political theater. Apparently *being honest* is no longer the test of a good scientist."

William Norman Grigg in *The New American* pulls no punches: "The 'global warming' hoax may be the largest and most brazen . . . falsehood ever perpetrated."[359]

Dixy Lee Ray speaks up: "[W]e must recognize that the environmental movement is not about facts or logic. More and more it is becoming clear that those who support the so-called 'New World Order' or World Government under the United Nations have adopted global environmentalism as a basis for the dissolution of independent nations and the international realignment of power . . . ."[360]

65. LIFESTYLES

Who said this?

> *It is clear that current lifestyles and consumption patterns of the affluent middle class - involving high meat intake, consumption of large amounts of frozen and convenience foods, use of fossil fuels, ownership of motor vehicles and small electrical appliances, home and work-place air conditioning, and suburban housing - are not sustainable.*

Was it:

A. **Woody Allen.** Film actor. Writer. Director.

B. **Dr. Shirley McGreal.** Chairwoman, International Primate Protection League.

C. **Maurice Strong.** UN radical who speculated that a worldwide economic collapse might be necessary to "punish" rich countries like the U.S. for harming the planet.[361]

D. **Ted Turner.** Promoter of belief in Gaia via his "Captain Planet" television cartoon for kids. Outspoken CNN chairman who has described Christianity as a religion "for losers."[362] He also said, "Communism is fine with me."[363] He described the Ten Commandments as "obsolete."[364]

E. **Max Yasgur.** Owner of the farm which was the site of the August 1969 Woodstock Festival.

The answer is

C. **Maurice Strong,** secretary general, UN Earth Summit, and senior advisor to Kofi Annan, UN Secretary General.

65. Maurice Strong (left) shakes hands with Xavante's chief Aniceto Tsudzavere and thanks him for the feathered headdress during the Global Forum in Rio de Janeiro, June 10, 1992.

When/where:

In an address at the opening session of the UN Earth Summit in Rio de Janeiro, June 1992.

Source:

Environmental Overkill, by Dixy Lee Ray with Lou Guzzo, copyright © 1993 by Regnery Publishing, page 4. All rights reserved. Reprinted by special permission of Regnery Publishing, Incorporated.[365]

Comments:

The overall goal of the Earth Summit, attended by government representatives of 178 nations and numerous non-governmental organizations (NGOs), was to "Save the Planet." Dixy Lee Ray inquires: "Save the planet from what?" She has the answer: "From human beings, of course."

Are the omniscient liberals concealing their plans to turn our world into a world dictatorship? Oh, no. Their designs are right out in the open, available for inspection, if only the Propaganda Machine would choose to look and report. Here's what the UN bureaucracy recommends, as contained in its own publication:

"The Global Biodiversity Assessment suggests an answer: simply cut the world population by about 80% - or return to a feudal lifestyle (no cars, planes, air conditioners . . .)."[366]

Read the 1993 book *Goddess Earth,* by Samantha Smith: "World socialism is the primary goal of the Environmental movement. To get there, independent Americans have to be scared, as well as shamed into conforming to an international agenda calling for earth stewardship, simple lifestyle, and the redistribution of the world's wealth."[367]

66. MAN VERSUS THE ENVIRONMENT

Who said this?

> *Human happiness and certainly human fecundity [productivity] are not as important as a wild and healthy planet. I know social scientists who remind me that people are part of nature, but it isn't true. Somewhere along the line - at about a billion years ago and maybe half that - we quit the contract and became a cancer. We have become a plague upon ourselves and upon the earth . . . .*
>
> *Until such time as Homo sapiens should decide to rejoin nature, some of us can only hope for the right virus to come along.*

Was it:

A. A mid-level bureaucrat in the Interior Department.
B. A representative of the National Wildlife Service.
C. A research biologist at the National Park Service.
D. A researcher at the National Institutes of Health.
E. A senior officer of the Sierra Club.

The answer is

C. **David Graber.**

When/where:

As quoted in the *Los Angeles Times Book Review,* October 22, 1989, page 9.

Source:

This Land Is Our Land, by Richard Pombo and Joseph Farah, St. Martin's Press, 1996, page 98.[368]

66. Three cheers for all the living creatures that *do* belong here on Earth.

Comments:

These "eco-maniacs", as I call all environmental extremists, appear intent to cede this planet to all the creepy-crawly forms of life at the expense of Mr. and Mrs. Homo Sapien. Hey, humans, get out of the way of the snails, kangaroo rats, and spotted owls.

Thanks to eco-maniacs we now have the Earth Charter,[369] Agenda 21,[370] the Wildlands Project,[371] the American Heritage Rivers Initiative,[372] the Border XXI Program,[373] Sustainable Development,[374] and a host of other ventures all designed to marginally aid the environment while pirating land from the citizens and abridging their freedoms.

One of the founders of the eco-maniac's environmental movement, a Mr. John Muir, summed things up when, according to the Source, he said . . . to *alligators:* "May you enjoy your lily pads and your aquatic grasses, secure in your undisturbed habitat. And may you occasionally enjoy a mouthful of terror-stricken man . . . ."[375]

I wonder if Mr. Muir would be willing to be the first to volunteer, in the name of environmentalism of course, to submit an arm or leg, or something even more juicy, to his alligator friends.

67. MAN VERSUS THE ENVIRONMENT

Who said this?

> *The collective needs of non-human species must take precedence over the needs and desires of humans.*

Was it:

A. Director, African Wildlife Foundation.
B. Director, People for the Ethical Treatment of Animals (PETA).
C. Director, Philadelphia Symphony Orchestra.
D. Director, Wildlands Project.
E. Director, World Wildlife Fund.

The answer is

D. **Dr. Reed F. Noss.**

67. *"All human beings to the back of the bus!"*

When/where:

In his article "The Wildlands Project," *Wild Earth, Special Report,* 1993, page 13.

Source:

"Rewilding America," *ēco•logic,* November/December 1995, page 20. ALSO: "Rome Summit Speeds UN Agenda," in the November/December 1996 issue, page 19.[376]

Comments:

The Source says: "The Wildlands Project seeks to return 'at least 50 percent' of the land area in America to 'core wilderness areas' where human activity is barred. Core wilderness areas are to be connected by corridors that may be 'several miles wide.' Core areas, including corridors are to be surrounded by 'buffer zones' in which there may be managed human activity providing that biodiversity protection is the first priority."

Inside the core areas all evidence of mankind will be eradicated: homes, roads, power lines, all things man-made.[377]

But these protected areas are not being safeguarded as *American* treasures. My goodness, no. They're being protected under the watchful eye of the UN. An article titled "Congressional Opposition to UN Land Grab Grows as 'Sovereignty Protection Act' is Reintroduced," states: "UN Biosphere Reserves and World Heritage Sites . . . are now in place on 68% of our National Parklands, Preserves, and Monuments. UN Biosphere Reserves alone cover an area about the size of Colorado, our eighth-largest state. Local communities did not consent to these designations. Neither did state governments. Not even Congress was allowed to participate in the designation process . . . ."[378]

68. MAN VERSUS THE ENVIRONMENT

Who said this?

1. *While the death of young men in war is unfortunate, it is no more serious than the touching of mountains and wilderness areas by humankind.*

2. *Loggers losing their jobs because of Spotted Owl legislation is, in my eyes, no different than people being out of work after the furnaces of Dachau shut down.*

Was it:

A. **Carl Bloice.** Communist leader in the U.S.
B. **David Brower.** Director, Sierra Club. Founder, Friends of the Earth.
C. **Karl Paschke.** UN under-secretary-general for Internal Oversight Services.
D. **Michelle A. Perrault.** International vice president, Sierra Club.
E. **Jonathon Porritt.** Spokesman for Britain's Ecology Party.

The answer is

B. **David Brower.**

68. David Brower, 1979.

When/where:

A. As reported in "Building on Unlimited Future," by Rudolf Bahro, *Imprimis,* January 1992.

B. Spoken to a travel group in Whisler, British Columbia, September 23, 1992.

Source:

Environmental Overkill, by Dixy Lee Ray with Lou Guzzo, copyright © 1993 by Regnery Publishing, page 204. All rights reserved. Reprinted by special permission of Regnery Publishing, Incorporated.[379]

Comments:

Dixy Lee Ray quotes Carl Amery, spokesman for the Green Party in West Germany as saying: "We in the Green Movement aspire to a cultural model in which the killing of a forest will be considered more contemptible and more criminal than the sale of 6-year-old children to Asian brothels."[380]

So the liberal's true colors do occasionally show through the facade of compassion and caring which masks their secret agenda.

The Seattle Audubon Society's Havel Wolf said: "The Communist Party USA's environmental program 'presents a viable plan to carry out on the long march to socialism.'"[381]

It has been suggested that such passionate environmentalists ought to be labeled "watermelons." They're green on the outside, but red on the inside where it matters.

Dr. Walter E. Williams notes: "Since Communism has lost respectability, its ideas of control and coercion must be relabeled into more respectable titles, such as environmentalism and care for endangered species. Americans had better wise up while we still have the freedom to act."[382]

69. MAN VERSUS THE ENVIRONMENT

Who said this?

> *[Do the] "Wild Earth" and the "Wildlands Project" advocate the end of industrial civilization? Most assuredly. Everything civilized must go!*

Was it:

A. **John Davis.** Editor of *Wild Earth* and the *Earth First Journal.*
B. **Joan Downs.** Editor of *Wildlife Conservation Magazine.*
C. **Jeffrey Klein.** Editor of *Mother Jones.*
D. **Owen Lipstein.** Managing editor of *Mother Earth News.*
E. **Doug Moss.** Editor of *The Environmental Magazine,*

The answer is

A. **John Davis.**

When/where:

In the *Wild Earth Magazine,* 1992. (This is the journal in which "The Wildlands Project" was published.)

69. When Mr. Davis tells us "Everything civilized must go," do you suppose he really means *everything* civilized?

Source:

ēco•logic Special Report - The Convention on Biological Diversity: Cornerstone of the New World Order, prepared by the Environmental Conservation Organization, November 4, 1994, page 13.[383]

Comments:

John Davis once said "eradicating smallpox was wrong." Why? Because smallpox "played an important part in balancing ecosystems."[384]

The communist mind set runs deep throughout the Green Movement. According to Dixy Lee Ray, "[O]ne of the founders of the German Green Movement, Rudolf Bahro, recommends that people should live in socialist communities of no more than 3,000, consuming only what they produce, and that they should be restricted from trading with other communities . . . ."[385]

Hilary F. French, coauthor of the Worldwatch Institute's *Annual Report,* asserts: "What is needed is a transfer of financial and technological support from the North to South, from wealthy developed countries to debt-ridden, trade-starved developing countries."[386]

Notice how anxious liberals are to impose their will on others and how little regard they have for the idea of freedom. Notice, too, how their will and ways appear to be slowly prevailing.

70. MAN VERSUS THE ENVIRONMENT

Who said this?

> *But now we know that if we're going to have [mountain lions] around, maybe they're going to eat us every now and then. I'm comfortable with that . . . .*

Was it:

A. **Dr. Paul Beier.** Wildlife ecologist. Associate professor, Northern Arizona University.

B. **Jay Hair.** President, International Union for Conservation of Nature. President emeritus, the National Wildlife Federation. Member, the President's Council on Sustainable Development. One who has proposed "an environmental revolution [which] will be socially disruptive, potentially violent - but will receive massive support."[387]

C. **Max Nicholson.** Cofounder of the World Wildlife Fund.

D. **Charles Robert Redford.** Actor. Director. Film superstar. Sundance ski resort owner. Recipient of the Audubon Medal (1989).[388]

E. **Russell Errol Train.** Environmentalist. Former president and chairman of the board of the Conservation Foundation. Head U.S. delegate to the UN Conference on the Human Environment. Chairman of the National Council, World Wildlife Foundation. Trustee emeritus, African Wildlife Fund. President of World Wildlife Fund - USA.[389] President, World Resources Institute.

The answer is

A. **Dr. Paul Beier.**

When/where:

While commenting to the *New York Times* about a California ballot proposition which would lift the strict protection of the state's mountain lions. (The proposition failed.)

Source:

"Quote of the Week," *Human Events,* April 19, 1996, page 1.

70. Dr. Beier received his Ph. D. from the University of California at Berkeley in 1988.

Comments:

Item: *Sun-Sentinel,* July 19, 1997, Associated Press: "Grand Lake, Colorado - A 10-year-old boy was dragged away by a mountain lion that attacked and killed him in front of his family as the group returned from a hike in a national park."[390]

Compassionate Dr. Paul Beier is comfortable with that.

Near Idaho Springs in 1991 an 18-year-old runner was killed by a mountain lion. In California a couple of years ago a woman jogger was likewise dispatched. A compassionate liberal California environmentalist observed: "It's too bad for the woman, but we can always get more people. We can't replace the mountain lion."[391]

Don McAlvany comments: "The insane anti-business, anti-private property, people-controlling Gestapo-like behavior of the EPA and our environmental bureaucracy begins to make sense if one can see the larger picture of the environmental movement being used for the abolition of U.S. sovereignty, the U.S. Constitution, and private property, and the subjugation of America into a one-world socialist government."[392]

Nevertheless, the American public is demanding even more action from agencies such as the EPA. One poll indicated that about half of the citizens think current environment protection laws don't go far enough; only 15% say they go too far.[393]

71. MAN VERSUS THE ENVIRONMENT

Who said this?

> *If you haven't given voluntary human extinction much thought before, the idea of a world with no people in it may seem strange. But if you give it a chance, I think you might agree that the extinction of Homo sapiens would mean survival for millions, if not billions, of earth-dwelling species. Phasing out the human race will solve every problem on earth, social and environmental.*

Was it:

A. An animal rights fruitcake.
B. An outspoken member of the Green Movement.
C. Someone believed to be suffering from a deep and troubling inferiority complex.
D. Someone who may not like animals at all.
E. All of the above.

The answer is

E. All of the above. (This one is just too easy!)

When/where:

In *Wild Earth,* a newsletter for Green extremists.

Source:

"Animal Rights 101," by Kathleen Marquardt, *Insider's Report,* September 1996, page 3.

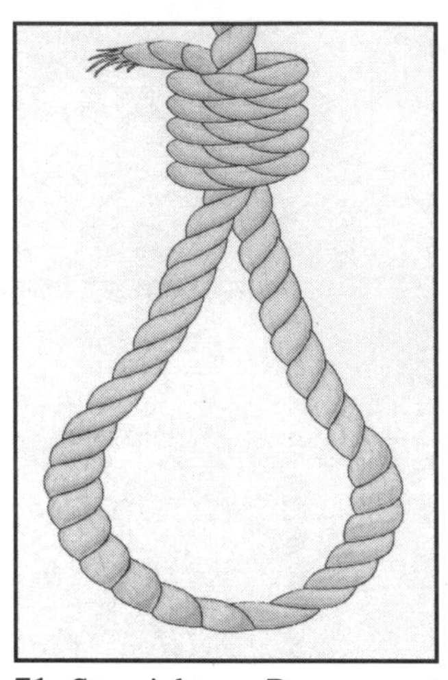

71. Step right up. Do your part to save the world.

Comments:

Ah, yes, anything we can do to keep all those fauna and flora happy will be much appreciated. Can we count on you to do your part?

"The message I hope you will take from this short lesson on Animal Rights 101," says Marquardt in the source article, "is this: More than anything, the 'animal rights' movement is a smoke screen to attack humanity - plain and simple. This warped movement is simply a means for another group of extremists to gain political power. What makes them so dangerous is that their message is hidden behind the cuddly image of animals and pets we all love."

Marquardt continues, "Animal rights is like worms - expose them to the light of day and they dry up and go away. Their points of view cannot stand up to scrutiny. We must strive to expose them for what they truly are. When the public sees beyond the cuddly image to the fanaticism and anti-humanism of animal rights, they will reject this nonsense outright."

72. POPULATION CONTROL

Who said this?

> *If I were reincarnated, I would wish to be returned to Earth as a killer virus to lower human population levels.*

Was it:

A. **"Prince."** Stage name of Prince Roger Nelson (named after Prince Roger Trio). Singer and composer who achieved international success with the release of *Purple Rain* in 1984.[394]
B. **Prince Bernhard** of the Netherlands, who founded the 1001 Club (which was formed to fund the World Wildlife Fund), but resigned his position and quit the World Wildlife Fund-International after he was caught taking a million-dollar bribe from the Lockheed Corporation in 1976.[395]
C. **Prince Charles.** Eldest son of Queen Elizabeth II.
D. **Prince Edward.** Third son of Queen Elizabeth II.
E. **Prince Phillip.** Husband of Queen Elizabeth II. Founder, World Wildlife Fund.

The answer is

E. **Prince Phillip.**

72. The Duke of Edinburgh, Prince Phillip, in London, November 1986.

When/where:

As quoted in Rep. Claudine Schneider's "The Greenhouse Effect Hoax: Legislation in Washington," Special Report, *Executive Intelligence Review,* 1989, pages 28-29 and 127. This quotation appeared in the *Deuntsche Press Agentur* in 1988.

Source:

Trashing the Planet, by Dixy Lee Ray with Lou Guzzo, copyright © 1990 by Regnery Publishing, page 169. [396]

Comments:

Echoing Prince Phillip's "compassion," the respected London weekly *The Economist,* editorialized, according to the Source: "The extinction of the human species may not only be inevitable, but a good thing . . . ."

Says Earth First! founder, Dave Foreman: "AIDS is not a malediction, but the welcome and natural remedy to reduce the population of the planet . . . . [S]hould human beings disappear, I surely wouldn't mind." "[M]y three main goals would be to reduce human population to about 100 million worldwide, destroy the industrial infrastructure, and see wilderness with its full complement of species returning throughout the world."[397]

Dixy Lee Ray sums up: "[H]umans cannot live on earth without altering it and without using natural resources. Our responsibility is to be good stewards of the environment and to remember that a well-tended garden is better than a neglected woodlot. It is demeaning beyond belief to consider mankind simply another species of animal, no better and no worse than wild beasts."[398]

73. POPULATION CONTROL

Who said this?

> *Our society is turning toward more and more needless consumption. It is a vicious circle that I compare to cancer . . . . Should we eliminate suffering, diseases? The idea is beautiful, but perhaps not a benefit for the long term. We should not allow our dread of diseases to endanger the future of our species . . . . In order to stabilize world population, we need to eliminate 350,000 people a day. It is a horrible thing to say, but it's just as bad not to say it.*

Was it:

A. **Jimmy Breslin.** Columnist. Author of *World Without End, Amen* (1973), *Forsaking All Others* (1982), and other books. Recipient of several writing awards.[399]

B. **Jacques Cousteau.** Navel officer. Underwater explorer.

C. **Walter Cronkite.** Journalist and broadcaster. Former anchorman, *CBS Evening News.* Internationalist who once said, "The proud nations someday will see the light and . . . yield up their precious sovereignty . . . ."[400]

D. **George Frampton.** Clinton Administration Assistant Secretary of the Interior for Fish, Wildlife, and Parks.

E. **Fred Krupp.** Executive director, Environmental Defense Fund. Member, President's Council on Sustainable Development.

The answer is

B. **Jacques Cousteau.**

When/where:

In an interview published in the *UNESCO Courier,* November 1991.

Source:

The McAlvany Intelligence Advisor, Don McAlvany, editor, October 1997, pages 6, 7.[401]

73. Jacques Cousteau, at the "World of Silence" Gala, January 8, 1956.

Comments:

Let's stray from the question of consumption to discuss some of the phenomena which have excited so many "scientists," like Cousteau. Let's see what all their scientific "methods" have achieved and let's also see how compassionate these liberals are, and how honorable and ethical as well. Then, let's consider their apparent objectives.

First, the ozone-depletion scare: Scientists (other than the eco-maniac fear mongers) have calculated that banning chlorofluorocarbons (CFCs) will result in starvation and disease which will wipe out millions of people in Third World countries. The ban prohibits Freon, curtailing much-needed refrigeration. The effect on the ozone hole from not banning Freon is considered minor by many knowledgeable scientists.[402]

The *Geophysical Research Letters* indicate that the ozone layer is in fine shape. Recent reductions were caused by the eruption of Mount Pinatubo in the Philippines, but chemicals from that disturbance have now settled out of the air.[403]

"The likely cost of a worldwide CFC ban would total $5 trillion within a dozen years, accompanied by 20 to 40 million deaths annually," says Robert W. Lee in *The New American.*[404]

Next, the question of global warming: Direct satellite measurements suggest that instead of global warming, a slight *cooling* of the planet is presently underway, despite all the "sky is falling" calls from the alarmists.[405] But how could that be? We've been told incessantly on television and in magazines and newspapers that because of all the carbon dioxide we humans dump into the air, the polar icecaps are melting, ocean levels are rising, and in no time at all Florida will be but a memory.

No less than President Clinton himself said: "Scientists warn[406] that if the trend continues, the seas will rise two feet or more in the next century. In America that means 9,000 square miles of Florida, Louisiana, and other coastal areas will be flooded . . . . We can expect more deaths from heat stress."[407]

But as Walter Williams tells us, "According to the November 1992 issue of *Science,* termites generate more than twice as much carbon dioxide as mankind does burning fossil fuels . . . . Humans contribute only 5% of atmospheric carbon dioxide; nature does the rest."[408]

Moreover, CO_2 is only one of the "greenhouse gasses," and it's by no means the one in greatest abundance. Which is? Which gas constitutes 95% of the atmospheric materials that contribute to "global warming"? It's water vapor! Yes, the dreaded gas H_2O![409] So the only effect man has on the "greenhouse effect" is about 5% of 5% - about one quarter of 1%!

Let's say the UN imposes a worldwide law prohibiting use of *all* fossil fuels. That would leave 99+% of the "global warming problem" completely unaddressed. It therefore seems clear that both the "problem" and the "solution" advanced by environmentalists are factually fatally flawed.

According to scientists at the Oregon Institute of Science and Medicine, temperatures today are still lower than the average temperature for the last 3,000 years![410]

State Department employee Richard Benedick proclaimed: "A global climate treaty must be implemented even if there is no scientific evidence to back the greenhouse effect."[411] So the policy appears to be: Implement draconian measures even if there's no reason to do so.

"The simple fact is," according to American Policy Center president Tom DeWeese, "the proponents of global warming are part of a radical *putsch* that intends to turn back American technology and redistribute American wealth and power. They don't have the science to back up their claims, so through the use of smoke and mirrors they work to scare us out of our liberties."[412]

"The 'Global Warming' hypothesis is wrong," states Dr. Arthur B. Robinson, publisher of *Access to Energy,* "That is the end to that. It is time that we all moved on toward more promising ideas."[413]

But we're *not* moving on toward more promising ideas. "The Environmental Protection Agency wants Congress to give it sweeping powers," says *The Washington Times,* "to start carrying out the global-warming treaty even before the treaty has been ratified by the Senate."[414]

Just for the sake of argument, let's say the amount of CO_2 is *indeed* increasing, significantly increasing. Let's say it *doubles!* Do all the plants in the world shrivel up and die? Well, not exactly. Early in the evolution of plant life on Earth, CO_2 was in much greater abundance.[415] Studies show that if CO_2 levels doubled, plant productivity would actually *improve* an average of 32% across all species![416] Tomato yields would improve up to 50%, grains up to 64%, corn and sugar cane up to 55%, potatoes up to 75% . . . . You get the idea.

Says Phyllis Schlafly: "The only warming we are experiencing is the hot air manufactured by politicians who seek higher taxes and more regulations, wacko environmentalists who want to make humans serve the Earth instead of vice versa, and envious Third World regimes that seek to transfer U.S. wealth to themselves."[417]

Richard Kerr, writing in *Science Magazine* has the answer: "Climate modelers have been 'cheating' for so long it's almost become respectable. The problem has been that no computer model could reliably simulate the present climate . . . . So climate modelers have gotten in the habit of fiddling with fudge factors, so-called 'flux adjustments', until the model gets it right."[418]

However, "right" for some scientists isn't based on fact, it's based on agenda. When racist scientists wanted to prove whites were more intelligent than blacks, they fudged their figures dealing with brain-size measurements. Likewise, when liberal scientists wish to advance their cause, they see all sorts of danger ahead and actually manufacture it if none can actually be found. Take for example the dichloro-diphenyl-trichlorothane (DDT) ban.

The DDT ban has had absolutely disastrous effects. "[T]here are now approximately 60 to 100 million people who are dying each year as the direct or indirect result of anti-pesticide campaigns that have caused restrictions or bans on the products that could have prevented such deaths," says Dixy Lee Ray.[419] Well, we're told, DDT is a dangerous pesticide. Our pristine environment would have collapsed if we didn't ban the stuff. However, despite constant messages of fear, no harmful effects of DDT on humans have been shown.

"DDT was the safest pesticide ever known to mankind," states Dr. Stanley K. Monteith, M.D. "[W]e have probably lost well over 600 million human lives during the past twenty-five years since . . . outlawing DDT."[420]

Adds Dr. Arthur Robinson: The act of banning DDT was "probably the largest act of genocide in human history."[421]

Dr. Charles Wurster, a major opponent of DDT, was once asked about the possibility that banning DDT would necessitate use of far more toxic and dangerous pesticides. The good doctor was quoted as responding: "So what? People are the cause of all the problems. We have too many of them. We need to get rid of some of them and this is as good a way as any."[422]

A new pollution-control campaign to save the environment.

The endangered spotted owl: What about that noble bird? How could we be so cruel as to tolerate the destruction of this friendly, feathered critter? Well, it turns out the critter never has been endangered. It doesn't need old-growth forests any more than you need to live in your grandmother's farmhouse.[423] Working in an area east of the Redwood area in California, wildlife biologist Steve Self reports: "we have not found any areas where we do *not* have owls."[424]

And so goes the story with global warming, the ozone hole, acid rain, Alar, endangered species, asbestos, radon, PCBs, the rain forest, wetlands, and on and on. When you only hear one side of a story, how can you make balanced, wise judgements?

So what, you may say. So what if we indulge our compassion and care for the creatures of nature. What harm can come of that? Writing in *Insider's Report,* Alan Caruba answers the question: "Fully one-third of all federal laws and regulations are currently devoted to environmental mandates that impose billions of dollars of cost to every aspect of life in America."[425] So I guess if you find pleasure in dumping hundreds and thousands of your hard-earned dollars down a rat hole, you, too, will wish to join the green march.

Jay Colvin and his Eden, Arizona neighbors took action to protect the home of a wheelchair-bound resident as flood waters threatened her life and property. Turning to the Corps of Engineers for help to avert future flooding, Mr. Colvin and his neighbors were dumbfounded when a Corp representative said, "Sir, you don't understand. I am from the green side of the corps. We are not here to help, but to stop you from doing anything. In fact, we may charge you with a felony for your actions."[426]

"Today environmental policy is not about safety, or survivability, or sustainability," says William Perry Pendley, author of *War on the West,* "but about achieving power and control over people's lives."[427]

Marshall Wittmann, head of the Heritage Foundation's Government Integrity Project calculates that $39 billion in taxpayer money is dispersed annually to "organizations which may use the money to advance their political agendas."[428] He reports that in 1993 Friends of the Earth received $35,000 from the taxpayers. The World Wildlife Fund received $790,000. The Environmental Defense Fund got $341,000. This is but a small sampling.

Who is funding the organizations that present contrary views? How will the American people ever hear them?

Have you received an impassioned plea lately from the Natural Resources Defense Council, the National Parks and Conservation Association, the National Wildlife Federation, Defenders of Wildlife, the Wilderness Society, the African Wildlife Foundation, the Fund for Animals, or any of dozens of others? How much did you contribute to help the compassionate help our fine, furry friends? (Don't be embarrassed; I used to donate to many of these organizations, too.) How do you suppose that money is being used?

The more cynical among us might conclude that when scientists like Dr. Cousteau tell us we must curb our appetites, compromise our lifestyles, and curtail our freedoms, their scientific "thought" has more to do with an effort to *reduce* the population than to *sustain* it.

74. POPULATION CONTROL

Who said this?

> 1. *Right now, there are just way too many people on the planet.*
>
> 2. *A total world population of 250-300 million people, a 95% decline from present levels, would be ideal.*

Was it:

A. **Truman Capote.** Author of *Breakfast at Tiffany's,* and other works.
B. **Don Imus.** Radio talk show host.
C. **Robert Edward (Ted) Turner.** Chairman of the board, Turner Broadcasting. Chairman of the board, Better World Society. Director, Martin Luther King Center. Winner of the America's Cup in his yacht *Courageous* (1977). Recipient of dozens of awards. Inducted into several Halls of Fame. Owner of CNN.[429]
D. **Andy Warhol.** Printmaker and filmmaker.
E. **Frank Zappa.** Rock musician.

The answer is

C. **Ted Turner.**

74. Ted Turner during a news conference September 20, 1993.

When/where:

1,2. In an interview with *Audubon* magazine.

Sources:

A. *Environmental Overkill,* by Dixy Lee Ray with Lou Guzzo, copyright © 1993 by Regnery Publishing, page 80. All rights reserved. Reprinted by special permission of Regnery Publishing, Incorporated.

B. *Facts, Truth, Evidence that Will Affect All Americans,* support material for David Wegener's video *Barbed Wire on America,* page 11.

Comments:

Dixy Lee Ray notes that in the same *Audubon* interview, Ted Turner scolded: "[W]hen you look at us, we are a bunch of pigs . . . and losers . . . . The indigenous people were the ones who were right. I mean they had their own religion, their ethics, their own technology. We just went down the wrong road."[430]

So, with Ten Turner at the helm, I suppose it would be, as Dixy Lee Ray suggests: back to loin cloths, spears, bon fires, and human sacrifice. Oh, what fun!

At Mikhail Gorbachev's September 1995 State of the World Forum in San Francisco, attended by such notables as James Baker, George Bush, Alan Cranston, Jane Fonda, Bill Gates, Al Gore, Ted Koppel, Shirley McLaine, Rupert Murdoch, Colin Powell, Carl Sagan, Maurice Strong, Margaret Thatcher, Alvin Toffler, Ted Turner, Desmond Tutu, and many others, New-Age guru Sam Keen said to enthusiastic applause: "The ecological crisis, in short, is the population crisis. Cut the population by 90%, and there aren't enough people left to do a great deal of ecological damage."[431]

Also at the forum were representatives from the Bilderbergers, Club of Rome, Council on Foreign Relations (CFR), Trilateral Commission, and the World Economic Forum.[432]

75. POPULATION CONTROL

Who said this?

> *To feed a starving child is to exacerbate the world overpopulation problem.*

Was it:

A. A Columbia University theologian.
B. A New York University philosopher.
C. A quotation from *The Population Bomb,* by Paul R. Ehrlich, Ballantine Books, 1968.
D. A representative from UNICEF (United Nations International Children's Emergency Fund).
E. A Yale University environmentalist.

The answer is

E. **Dr. LaMont Cole.**

When/where:

Not specified by the Source.

Source:

Environmental Overkill, by Dixy Lee Ray with Lou Guzzo, copyright © 1993 by Regnery Publishing, page 77. All rights preserved. Reprinted by special permission of Regnery Publishing, Incorporated.[433]

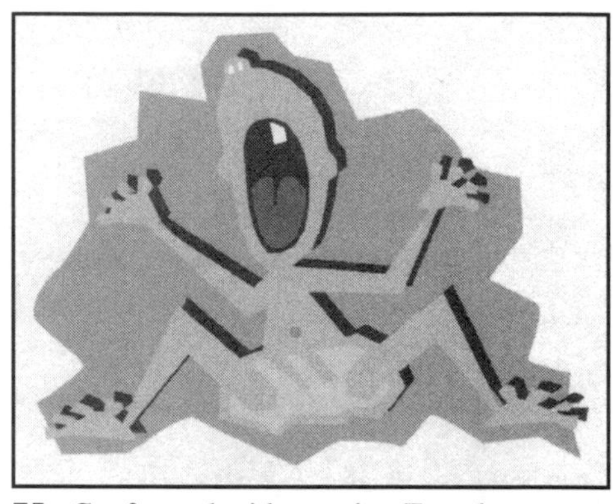

75. Confronted with starving French peasants in 1770, Marie Antoinette is said to have remarked, "Let them eat cake." Confronted with the world's starving children today, Dr. Cole seems to be saying, "Let them eat nothing."

Comments:

The premise of our friend, Dr. Cole, appears to be that we are about to exhaust the world's resources. We must therefore take immediate, draconian steps to control population levels so the planet can sustain itself.

Richard Pombo and Joseph Farah dispute that premise in their book, *This Land Is Our Land.* "Are we running out of food? No. Enough food could be raised to provide an American-type diet for 35.1 billion people, more than seven times the present world population . . . . Are we running out of space? No. Only three-tenths of 1 percent of the earth's land surface are used for human settlements. Are we running out of arable land? No. We use less than one-ninth of the earth's ice-free land area to raise all agriculture products."[434]

More and more it seems, these deeply "compassionate" liberals reveal themselves to be suffering from, I guess we'll call it CDS, Compassion Deficit Syndrome. Perhaps more correctly: their rhetoric more and more exposes the sham of their "compassionate" talk and reputation. They use feigned "feelings" as a net to snare caring individuals for their cause.

But their cause is not compassion. It is statism, control, socialism, communism.

76. PROTECTING THE ENVIRONMENT

Who said this?

> *The Precautionary Principle:*
>
> *In order to protect the environment, the precautionary approach shall be widely applied by States according to their capabilities. Where there are threats of serious or irreversible damage, lack of full scientific certainty shall not be used as a reason for postponing cost-effective measures to prevent environmental degradation.*

Was it:

A. **Al Gore.** In his book, *Earth in the Balance.*
B. Green Cross International (founded by Mikhail Gorbachev).
C. Sierra Club.
D. UN Conference on Environment and Development.
E. U.S. Environmental Protection Agency (EPA).

The answer is

D. UN Conference on Environment and Development.

76. The United Nations: UN-accountable, UN-representative, UN-American. UN-stoppable?

When/where:

Principle 15 in the Rio Declaration, 1992.

Source:

Global Governance: Why? How? When?, in a section titled "The Rise of Global Green Religion," by Henry Lamb, copyright 1996 by National Review, Incorporated, reprinted by Murchison Chair of Free Enterprise, University of Texas at Austin, 1997, page 89.

Comments:

What's the UN saying? It's saying fact and scientifically proven principles will not necessarily be used in the formulation of world policy. Then what will? Ah, there's the rub. If reason, truth, and scientific certainty are cast aside, then the door is swung open for whatever the elite power brokers of the world would wish. The "Precautionary Principle," says William Norman Grigg, is, in short, "a license to lie."[435] If we swallow the concept (and it seems we have), then the Bill Clintons, Jane Fondas, Al Gores, Reed Nosses, David Rockefellers, Maurice Strongs, Ted Turners, Timothy Wirths et al. have the green light (pun intended) to transform our world into their playground, where they can establish a pagan-Gaia belief system as the world's religion, socialism as the single economic and political system, and serfdom as the proletariat lifestyle.

In the name of protecting the environment, look what the UN has already produced:[436]

- The UN Convention on Biological Diversity, which directs half of North America to be converted into core wilderness areas off limits to human beings.
- The UN Vienna Convention on Ozone Depleting Substances (plus the Montreal Protocol) which bans CFCs (Freon and halons) in the U.S.

- The UN Framework Convention on Climate Change, which increases the cost of all fossil-fuel-based energy and reduces its availability.
- The UN Convention on the Law of the Seas, which declares all nonterritorial Seas of the world to be under UN authority, and establishes authority to impose global taxes on use of the waters.

But the UN's agenda is far broader than merely environmental matters. This meddling body has also produced:

- The UN Convention on the Rights of the Child, which delineates children's rights which must be guaranteed by the state. This treaty tramples upon parents' rights, allows the state (i.e., the UN) to interfere with family matters, and decimates rights guaranteed by the U.S. Constitution.
- The UN Convention on the Elimination of All Forms of Discrimination Against Women, which, among other things grants to every woman in the world the "right" to housing.
- The UN Convention on Food Security, which grants to every human being on earth (even white males) the "right" to a full stomach.
- The UN Covenant on Human Rights, which states, in Article 13: "Freedom to manifest one's religion or beliefs may be subject only to such limitations as are prescribed by law . . . ."[437] Ergo: whenever the government wishes, it may limit, restrict, or even prescribe your religion in any way it chooses.

"The UN is an avid enemy of Christianity . . . . [I]n fact to take the place of Christian culture, the UN seeks to install pagan religion based on worship of 'mother earth' - as represented in the occult goddess 'Gaia,'" says Father Paul Marx, founder of Human Life International.[438]

All these UN conventions are a little overreaching, don't you think? Indeed, but they are only a few of *hundreds* of treaties and international agreements presently in force or patiently waiting in the wings for ratification. The World Trade Organization (WTO) that we heard so much about in conjunction with GATT (General Agreement on Tariffs and Trade) provides for the first time the legal mechanism necessary for the UN to enforce all these onerous treaties and agreements.

Comments David Russell: "The UN has laid claim to all the 'global commons:' the air, the oceans, the skies, natural resources outside the boundaries of nations. . . . They have even proposed to tax coal, oil, gas, gold, silver, iron, and other minerals extracted from the earth . . . . They want to tax air and ocean travel, place a tax on the electronic airways by which we transmit our radio, television and other signals, even taxing sites for our satellites in the sky."[439]

In his book, *Earth in the Balance,* author Al Gore says "I have come to believe that we must take bold and unequivocal action: we must make the rescue of the environment the central organizing principle for civilization . . . ."[440] This rescue, he adds will require "sacrifice, struggle, and a wrenching transformation of society."

Comments Henry Lamb: "Al Gore's passionate plea to reorganize civilization around the principle of 'environmental protection' is well underway. And while he suggests that the 'wrenching transformation' should be voluntarily agreed to, he is advancing regulations, laws, and international agreements to force behavior modification, often without prior knowledge by the individuals affected, and certainly without their voluntary agreement."[441]

At the UN Building February 1, 1992, former President George Bush proclaimed: "It is the sacred principles enshrined in the UN Charter to which we will henceforth pledge our allegiance."[442] Really? I wonder if Mr. Bush is simply speaking for himself, or did he unilaterally dump the U.S. Constitution sometime during his administration when no one was watching?

The UN publication *Our Global Neighborhood* states: "[I]t is necessary to assert . . . the rights and interests of the international community in situations within individual states . . . ."[443]

"In other words," says Henry Lamb, "the Commission on Global Governance believes the world is now ready to grant to the UN the authority to enter the sovereign borders of any nation to guarantee the 'security of people' as defined by the 'rights' expressed in the various international treaties and agreements." This, he says, "is the essence of global governance."

This, say I, is the shredding of the U.S. Constitution and the irrevocable collapse of this great country of ours.

SCORING THIS TEST

[The teacher's job is] not to judge the rightness and wrongness of each student's answer.[444]

- Guide to Teaching Mathematics in California, as quoted in *Investor's Business Daily*

The philosophy of the classroom today will be the philosophy of the government tomorrow.

- Abraham Lincoln[445]

To educate a man in mind and not in morals is to educate a menace to society.

- Theodore Roosevelt[446]

All right, students, at this time I want you to go back through the liberal quotations in this book and review your answers. Then, take a freshly sharpened number 2 pencil from your book bag along with a pad of lined paper and write a brief essay in response to each of the these questions:

1. How do you think liberals *feel* when they denigrate Christians (Quotation #1), Republicans (Quotation #14), and conservatives (Quotation #7), and reveal themselves to be anything but compassionate?

2. How did you *feel* when you found that liberals are anti-religion (Quotation #26), anti-family (Quotation #18), anti-truth (Quotation #45), anti-freedom (Quotation #20), and anti-civilization (Quotation #69)?

3. Knowing the mainstream media aren't interested in reporting the truth (Quotation #45), do you *feel* angry, foolish, deceived, frustrated, or resentful?

4. Would you disagree with environmentalists who claim (falsely) that man created global warming (Quotation #73) if you knew it would hurt their *feelings?*

5. Would you *feel* better about teaching children homosexuality in the public schools (Quotation #52) if it made homosexuals *feel* better about themselves?

[Allow 10 minutes for writing the essays.] All right, time's up! But if you haven't finished writing your responses, take as much additional time as you need. I want to be fair to you students who write slowly. Let me know when you're ready to go on.

We certainly don't want to bruise anyone's self-esteem, so everybody gets a perfect score!

Now then, let's score your work. But before we do, you should understand we don't take off points for bad spelling, grammar, or punctuation. That wouldn't be fair to those of you who haven't learned anything. We don't take off points for incomplete sentences, unclear thought, or unintelligible scribbles. That wouldn't be fair to those of you who are sloppy or careless, or perhaps have just had a bad day. And finally, we don't take off points if you didn't answer some of the questions, or for that matter if you didn't answer any of the questions. It wouldn't be fair to students thinking of more important things. Or, I suppose, for students thinking of less important things.

So, class, I'm happy to announce you all did very well on this test. You should feel real proud of yourselves. I'd like to give each and every one of you A+ grades, but of course we don't give out grades any more.

Class dismissed.

If it's OK with you.

CONCLUSION

[T]he great majority of mankind [is] satisfied with ***appearances*** *as though they were* ***realities*** *. . . and are often more influenced by the things that* ***seem,*** *than by those that* ***are.***

- Machiavelli[447]

Matters are not hopeless, just worse than most citizens have grasped.

- George E. Lee[448]
October 7, 1994

ou may be thinking to yourself: I wonder why I didn't read those quotations by prominent liberals in my local newspaper or see them reported on television. You can imagine the attention they would have received had they been uttered or written by conservatives! The Propaganda Machine would have risen up in righteous indignation, to give glaring publicity to such outrages. The ranting and raving would last for weeks. Maybe months.

But when foolish or unreasonable thought originates with liberals, the Propaganda Machine concludes such utterances are wholly unnewsworthy. Apparently liberal nonsense is "protected" speech, while conservative nonsense is heralded and harangued with hoots of horror!

But what's worse, far worse: Suppose when a liberal makes an assertion as offensive as many of those reproduced here, suppose he or she really means it! Suppose liberals are indeed in favor of expanded government and contracted freedom. Suppose they favor giving preference to bugs, swamps, and weeds over the needs, even *lives* of human beings. Suppose they consider property rights dispensable. Suppose these people willingly, eagerly embrace socialism and communism as replacements for capitalism.

If you listen closely to their rhetoric, I'm afraid you'll find many of our liberal friends are indeed willing, often anxious, to relinquish our freedom, the most precious gift ever bestowed upon a people, to an omnipotent government, and to allow this nation's proud and honorable citizens to be transformed into servitude.

John Locke cautioned: "I have no reason to suppose, that he, who would take away my Liberty, would not when he had me in his Power, take away everything else."

The second president of the U.S. advised us: "You have rights antecedent to all earthly governments; rights that cannot be repealed or restrained by human laws; rights derived from the Great Legislator of the Universe."

If we as a people trade in our God-given rights, which we inherited from our inspired Founding Fathers and their sacrifices, for a set of *state*-given rights, dispensed by the government in accord with governmental convenience, then we the people will have but ourselves to blame, and the American dream will inexorably become an unimaginable nightmare.

The painful truth is that American liberty is being decayed like an old wooden house attacked by endless armies of carpenter ants. While the destruction from an individual ant is inconsequential, in legions these tiny invaders can inflict massive damage, to the point of total devastation.

If we allow our liberty to be traded away, then what of any real value will remain?

Political satirist H.L. Mencken warned: "The whole aim of practical politics is to keep the populace alarmed, and hence clamorous to be led to safety, by menacing it with an endless series of hobgoblins, all of them imaginary."[449]

In an article titled "Truth: Our Only Weapon," author Father James Thornton reminds us: "An uneducated people is afflicted with historical amnesia. Remaining unaware of the struggles and sacrifices of its ancestors and of the mistakes and triumphs of past cultures, it fecklessly sells its heritage in exchange for platitudes and promises. Lacking any connection to its history, such a people becomes an amorphous mass, a rabble ruled by swindlers and hoodwinked by hucksters, a money-obsessed herd without past, without future, without faith, without morality, without dignity, without will."[450]

Back in 1849 Frederick Douglas warned us about the dangers of an unbridled government. "The limits of tyrants are prescribed by the endurance of those whom they suppress," he said. Thus, it is we the people who empower the tyrants when we *allow* them to inflict their agenda of tyranny upon us.

"Why didn't the people stop Adolf Hitler," asks Holly Swanson, in her book, *Set Up and Sold Out.* "History reminds us, the fate of a nation depends on the strength and will of its people."

"The Holocaust is not only the result of Hitler's ideas," she observes, "it is [also] the result of the people who followed his ideas."[451]

A Russian by the name of Iosif Vissarionovich Djugashvili, better known as Joseph Stalin, used the phrase "useful idiots" to describe concerned Russian citizens who were helping him advance the cause of Communism. These "patriotic" people thought they were advancing freedom when in fact they were consolidating Stalin's power and strengthening his regime. How would the Communist leader reward all those "useful idiots" when their work was completed? His command: "Eliminate them!"[452]

"The end will not come when the commissars finally haul 60 million hopelessly diseased, capitalistic 'animals' off to liquidation centers," predicts John Stormer in *None Dare Call It Treason.* "The battle will be lost, not when freedom of speech is finally taken away, but when Americans become so 'adjusted' or 'conditioned' to 'getting along with the group' that when they finally see the threat, they say, 'I can't afford to be controversial.'"[453]

The State's dedication to the best interests of its citizens is proportional to the people's power and their passion for freedom.

We the people, by inaction, permit powerful politicians and institutions in and out of government to define the government's reach into our lives, to decide policy which will accrue for the politicians' own advantage, and to impose ever-increasing limitations on our freedom. We the people prove Dante's wisdom: "The hottest places in hell are reserved for those, who in times of moral crisis, do nothing."[454]

"Americans have imposed the tyranny of Washington upon ourselves," says Jack Wheeler, columnist with the *Strategic Investment* financial newsletter. "No longer innocently oppressed, America has become a nation of belligerent beggars, demanding with insufferable arrogance an endless cornucopia of government handouts, subsidies, and entitlements. Refusing to pay for them themselves, they demand that others pick up the multi-trillion-dollar tab - most especially and contemptibly, their children and grandchildren."[455] Richard M. Ebeling, Ludwig von Mises professor of economics at Hillsdale College, adds: "When individuals began to ask government to do things for them, rather than merely to secure rights and property, they began asking government to violate other's rights and property for their benefit. Their demands on government have been rationalized by intellectuals and social engineers who have persuaded them that what they wanted but didn't have was due to the greed, exploitation, and immorality of others. Basic morality and justice have been transcended in the political arena in order to take from the 'haves' and give to the 'have nots'."[456]

"A government that is anxious to give alms to as many people as possible is even more anxious to commandeer their earnings," notes journalist and policy analyst James Bovard.[457]

Ebeling continues: "When the state becomes the violator of liberty and property rather than its guarantor, it debases respect for all law. People in society develop an increasing disrespect and disregard for what the law demands. They view the law as the agent for immorality in the form of legalized plunder for the benefit of some at the expense of others. And this same disrespect and disregard sooner or later starts to creep into dealings between individuals. Society verges on the brink of lawlessness."[458]

Jack Wheeler observes: "One of the reasons America is moving toward fascism today is because it has lost its constitutional moorings. We're supposed to believe in limited government in the United States. The federal powers are enumerated in the Constitution. But, in recent years, Washington has far exceeded its authority. And very few politicians - Democrats or Republicans - seem to give a darn. Even worse, most Americans don't even seem to be aware of the problem."[459]

"Strange, but I didn't notice they were gradually taking away my freedoms, until all of a sudden, here I am."

"Rights were not the language of government action," said Philip K. Howard, author of *The Death of Common Sense*. "Rights were the protection that prevented government and others from telling us what we could say, where we could travel, or who our friends could be. 'Rights,' said Oliver Wendell Holmes, 'mark the limits of interference with individual freedom.'"[460]

There are those who say no honorable American would oppose the actions and policies of the U.S. government. We've heard President Clinton so admonish us any number of times. But Teddy Roosevelt saw through this deception: "Patriotism means to stand by the country. It does not mean to stand by the president or any other public official save exactly to the degree in which he himself stands by the country. It is patriotic to support him insofar as he efficiently serves the country. It is unpatriotic not to oppose him to the exact extent that by inefficiency or otherwise he fails in his duty to stand by the country."[461]

"In questions of power let no more be heard of confidence in man," spoke Thomas Jefferson, "but bind him down from mischief by the chains of the Constitution."[462]

President John F. Kennedy said it thus: "If we are to give the leadership the world requires of us, we must rededicate ourselves to the great principles of our Constitution .... [O]ur nation needs the services of organizations who will remain vigilant in the defense of our principles."[463]

U.S. Supreme Court Justice Robert Houghwout Jackson put it simply enough: "It is not the function of our government to keep the citizen from falling into error; it is the function of the citizen to keep the government from falling into error."[464] "We the People are the rightful master of both congress and the courts," said Abraham Lincoln, "not to overthrow the Constitution, but to overthrow the men who pervert the Constitution."[465]

Those who speak for the government always present us with a crisis: a health care crisis, crime crisis, terrorism crisis, smoking crisis, etc. The choices presented are always but two: To be consumed by the crisis, or to let the government "solve" the threat of the day by limiting, constraining, or removing freedoms.

"The first goal of a tyranny," cautions Bo Gritz, "is to create fear in the population, fear so paralyzing that the public will accept any measure to allay it."[466] Make the threat onerous enough and the people will relinquish everything.

"Those who are willing to sacrifice their freedoms for a measure of security," warned Benjamin Franklin, "deserve neither."[467] "If a nation values anything more than freedom," wrote William Somerset Maughm, "it will lose its freedom; and the irony of it is that if it is comfort or money that it values more, it will lose that too."[468]

Remember the old Aesop fable about the horse tormented by a boar. Exasperated, Horse asked Man for help. "Certainly," said Man, "I shall help you, but first you must let me saddle you up." Agreeing to the terms, Horse found his problem quickly resolved, but found, too, the price extracted was weighty: Horse's freedom. And the moral of this little fable may apply directly to a frightened and tormented people willing to horse trade away its fundamental freedoms.[469]

Dixy Lee Ray notes that throughout history the world's great democratic nations endure roughly 200 years before their fall from power and their subsequent disintegration. In every case there appears to be a clear-cut sequence of stages:

> From bondage to spiritual faith.
> From faith to great courage.
> From courage to liberty.
> From liberty to abundance.
> From abundance to complacency.
> From complacency to selfishness.
> From selfishness to apathy.
> From apathy to dependency.
> And from dependency back again into bondage.[470]

Granted, we're a constitutional republic, not a democracy, but do you see the U.S. somewhere in this sequence? Has our great country been so compromised and corrupted that we're now willing to march in lock step to our doom in the footsteps of other fallen nations?

Alexander Tyler, British historian, warned: "Democracies cannot exist as a permanent form of government; they will only exist until the people find that they can vote money for themselves from the treasury and until the politicians find that they can distribute that money in order to buy votes and perpetuate themselves in power. Hence, democracies always collapse over weak fiscal policy to be followed by a dictatorship."[471]

"A country which leads the world in homosexuality, promiscuity, pornography, divorce, abortion, violent crime, drug usage, alcoholism, and child abuse; a country which embraces its enemies while betraying its friends; and a country which turns its back on its spiritual, Christ-centered heritage while believing itself to still be the greatest - is ready for a major fall," says Don McAlvany. "It happened to Rome, Babylon, Persia, Assyria, and Greece - it could happen to America in the 1990s."[472]

Do you fear the government? Do you fear the IRS? Do you have confidence in the FBI? Are you satisfied with the job being done by the BATF, CIA, CPSC, DEA, EEOC, EPA, FCC, FDA, FDIC, FERC, FTC, NLRB, OSHA, and SEC?[*] What about the ATBCB, CFTC, FCA, FEC, FHFB, FMC, NCUA, NMB, NTSB, NRC, PBGC, PRC, SBA, SSA, USITC, and USPS?[**] And what about all the others?[473] Do you even know what all those jumbles of letters stand for? What kind of a job is each agency, commission, board, or corporation doing? Who's checking up on them? Who's looking for corruption? If (when) corruption is found, who's prosecuting? Who's assuring justice will be served?

Did you know that for every law passed by Congress, unelected bureaucrats in government agencies pump out on average 18 new regulations, each with the force of law?[474] I suggest you check the U.S. Constitution to see if that sort of run amuck federalism is allowed. (Of course it isn't.)

And when these powerful governmental organizations go astray (as surely they have in the past and will in the future) and *your* freedoms are at odds with the powerful central government, whose side will win? Is there any

---

[*] Bureau of Alcohol, Tobacco, and Firearms; Central Intelligence Agency; Consumer Product Safety Commission; Drug Enforcement Administration; Equal Employment Opportunity Commission; Environmental Protection Agency; Federal Communication Commission; Food & Drug Administration; Federal Deposit Insurance Corporation; Federal Energy Regulatory Commission; Federal Trade Commission; National Labor Relations Board; Occupational Safety & Health Administration; Security & Exchange Commission.

[**] Architectural and Transportation Barriers Compliance Board, Commodity Futures Trading Commission, Farm Credit Administration, Federal Election Commission, Federal Housing Finance Board, Federal Maritime Commission, National Credit Union Administration, National Mediation Board, National Transportation Safety Board, Nuclear Regulatory Commission, Pension Benefit Guaranty Corporation, Postal Rate Commission, Small Business Administration, Social Security Administration, United States International Trade Commission, United States Postal Service.

doubt? Voltaire noted: "It is dangerous to be right when your country [i.e., your government] is wrong."[475]

The wisdom of Thomas Jefferson bears repeating: "When the government fears the people, there is liberty," he opined. "When the people fear the government, there is tyranny."[476]

Who is to blame the people for their fear of the government today? When it's revealed, for example, that the U.S. Army director of Resource Management has confirmed discussions about establishing a civilian inmate labor program, is it unreasonable for the people to be concerned? An Army memo states: "Enclosed . . . is the draft Army regulation on civilian inmate labor utilization and establishing prison camps on Army installations . . . ." "The new regulation will provide . . . procedures for preparing request to establish civilian inmate labor programs [and] civilian prison camps . . . ." [477]

Congressman Henry Gonzales (D, Texas) provides further substantiation: "[Y]es . . . the plans are here . . . whereby you could, in the name of stopping terrorism . . . evoke the military and arrest Americans and put them in detention camps."[478]

The U.S. Senate has revealed the existence of a "Master Search Warrant" and "Master Arrest Warrant," the latter of which (authorized by the Attorney General) directs the head of the FBI to: "Arrest persons whom I deem dangerous to the public peace and safety. These persons are to be detained and confined until further order."[479]

"Mr. Crawford, we're from the BATF and our records show you still have a handgun that hasn't been turned in."

Would you please explain to me what happened to the Bill of Rights in the derivation of these onerous laws and directives. Who stole Articles IV, V, and VI?

There are reports of large movements within the U.S. of foreign military equipment, much of it Russian made, including SAM-13 (surface-to-air) missile platforms, fire-control systems, armored personnel carriers, and fully armed tanks.[480] There are reports of massive foreign-troop movements within our borders.[481] It has been reported that the Holloman Air Force Base in Alamogordo, New Mexico has been turned over to the Germans lock, stock, and runway, and is now exclusively occupied by German troops engaged in flight training exercises over our sovereign air space.[482] There are also reports that in times of national emergency, according to Bill Clinton's Presidential Decision Directive #25 (the detailed contents of which remain classified), command and control of the entire U.S. Military will be relinquished by the President and transferred to the Secretary General of the UN.[483]

Perhaps there are simple explanations that would quickly dispel the fear these reports generate, but I haven't heard any explanations. And on what basis would we suppose explanations from our government could be believed anyway? It's a "Catch 22" dilemma.

The trouble with government is that those who administer it - Democrats, Republicans, and Independents alike - operate within the context of "centralized governmental control". Politicians argue endlessly about the minutia of the legislation they propose. The debate always hinges on the question: in which direction should *extended* control be legislated. This circumvents a fundamental conservative concern: how can centralized control be *curtailed?* Sadly, such a perspective is rarely advanced.

To use a sports metaphor, both major basketball teams (the Republicans and the Democrats), though bumping, pushing, and dodging one another, appear intent upon scoring points in the same hoop, the hoop of intrusive, powerful government control!

Republicans and Democrats pummel one another mercilessly when it comes to elections, but become very friendly when it comes to passing liberal legislation.

Another disquieting factor in play in today's politics is the "my team" mentality. The game of politics seems to have become transformed into some kind of entertaining sport. Too many citizens with Republican pennants cheer on the Republicans regardless of their stand on the issues. Too many of those with Democrat banners root blindly for "their team." Citizens (all too few in number) with flags and placards proclaiming "Protect the Constitution" seem to have no team to root for at all, and are left to shout their encouragement to but a few scattered individual players.

Reducing the government's hold on the people will not be an easy task. Where are the leaders to set the charge? Clearly, no Democrat is qualified for such a role. Regrettably, many (most?) Republicans also appear only too eager to adopt big-government solutions for society's ills, and are therefore also ineligible. So the cause of true conservatism flounders in the absence of energetic and aggressive leadership.

But nobody said safeguarding America's freedom would be a piece of cake. Quite to the contrary. "We are not to expect to be translated from despotism to liberty in a featherbed," advised Thomas Jefferson.[484]

So the challenge is clear: we must reclaim our God-given rights, reclaim a lion's share of the power we (in many cases unknowingly) relinquished to federal jurisdiction, and reclaim our fundamental freedoms as laid out in the U.S. Constitution.

But rights alone are worthless if they are not asserted, prized, and protected. "Give me liberty or give me death," spoke Patrick Henry, who clearly perceived that without liberty all is lost.

Ralph Waldo Emerson was more poetic: "For what avail the plow or sail, Or land or life, if freedom fail?"[485]

SUMMARY

Politicians and diapers need to be changed periodically . . . usually for the same reason.
- (Source unknown)[486]

Here richly, with ridiculous display,
The Politician's corpse was laid away.
While all of his acquaintance sneered and slanged,
I wept; for I longed to see him hanged.
- Hilaire Belloc[487] (1870-1953)
Epitaph on the Politician Himself

Let me summarize not with my own words but with the impassioned words of Tom DeWeese as written in an open letter to the Republican Majority: "Why the Right Mistrusts You." This essay, published March 1998 in *The DeWeese Report,*[488] eloquently reviews many of the points I've covered herein and effectively summarizes the frustration, anger, and disgust so many Americans are now experiencing. I'm indebted to Tom DeWeese for letting me use major portions of his letter here.

In the Spring of 1970 I found myself standing in front of the ROTC building on the Ohio State University campus. Inside, graduation exercises were taking place. Also, just inside the front door, was a group of grim-looking police officers, dressed in full riot gear. Outside with me, wearing no such equipment, was a ragtag band of about one hundred students. Most, like me, were members of Young Americans for Freedom (YAF). Others were members of the College Republicans along with an assortment of fraternity brothers from around campus. We were spread out in a thin line, running the length of the long glass front of the ROTC building.

We were there because the violent Students for a Democratic Society (SDS) had vowed to disrupt and stop the ROTC graduation exercises. My colleagues and I had vowed they would never get inside. And so there we stood, barehanded, as the SDS, led by the soon-to-be Weatherman terrorist, Bernadine Dohrn, came over the hill, several hundred strong, Viet Cong flag flying. They charged, throwing rocks, bottles, and eggs. Hand-to-hand combat ensued. We drove them back. The cops never had to get into the battle.

That's how I spent my early days in the political arena; locked in a titanic battle against those who sought to destroy the very core of the nation I loved. They were called radicals, revolutionaries, the counter culture, the underground or, sometimes, just the movement.

They advocated rebellion, resistance, and revolution against the foundations of America. They opposed free enterprise, blaming technology for oppressing the poor. They demanded universal health and child care, women's liberation and confiscation of wealth - for the common good. They denounced private property, national defense, and morality. They denounced national boundaries, calling for a worldwide "class struggle".

They used every means possible, from rhetoric to violence, to force their vision of society onto the rest of us. They demonstrated, marched, rioted, burned buildings, organized strikes, sit-ins, and school evacuations to disrupt our daily routines. They were the SDS, the Black Panthers, the Yippies, the Young Lords, and the Weathermen. And they sought to change America into the vision of Mao and [Ernesto] Che [Guevara].

I fought for what was called the "establishment". I believed in what our Founding Fathers had created. I believed government's job was to remain as small and unobtrusive as possible while protecting our liberties, as outlined in the Constitution. I believed that Americans had the right to be free to carry out commerce as they saw fit, without intrusion or regulation from the government - so long as they did not infringe upon those same rights of others. I believed that an individual's private property was his to use, develop, enjoy, and protect in any manner he chose - without government intervention - and it was the duty of the government to uphold that right. I believed that "volunteerism" was a personal choice, not (as is now the case) a "mandatory" requirement for high school graduation.

I believed that only individuals, not groups, had rights - and that only individuals created human progress. I believed in absolutes and that certain things were indisputable, such as 2 plus 2 equals 4. I believed that American science and technology worked hand in hand to create the greatest standard of living the world had ever known. I loved the United States of America because it was the only nation on Earth that was founded on the idea that individuals had the right to "pursue happiness." And I spoke out against the tyranny being proposed by the street thugs in their drive to destroy my beloved nation. I supported my government, my elected officials, and my nation's institutions. Even in disagreement, I treated them with respect.

That was 30 years ago. Times have changed. The nation has changed. The paradigm has swung. Today, as I continue to take exactly the same positions as 30 years ago, I find I no longer want to be considered part of the "establishment". I find I now stand on the outside, opposed to the actions of most of the nation's once-respected institutions. I find it increasingly difficult to feel respect for elected officials. As a result, I am now considered by many in the "establishment" to be "unreasonable" and "uncompromising". I find that my views (mainstream 30 years ago) are now considered radical. I have now been labeled an "extremist".

I have never been bothered by name-calling from the Left. It's to be expected. After all, I oppose the very core of their ideas. But in the past 3 years a very painful reality has set in. As I continue to fight for my unchanged belief in the limited role of government, the accusation of "extremist" has been most often thrown at me by the new majority Republican leadership of the Congress. How can that be?

It was a glorious day in 1994 when the Republicans finally became the majority in Congress. Now those of us who had been fighting in the cold thought we had friends on the inside. Now those friends would control the committees and the flow of legislation. Hearings could be held, and the good guys would be called to testify. The true damage of the Democrats' social revolution would finally get a hearing.

No more would we need to fear the creation of massive legislative initiatives of social change. There would be no more Hillary Clinton socialized-medicine proposals. Property rights would be protected. The federal invasion of the schools could be stopped. At the very least, we would have sympathetic allies in possession of voices of reason and a sense of honor, bent on reestablishing the principles of limited government intrusion in business, schools, and private lives. Americans finally had hope that the out-of-control government created by the Democrats could now be tamed to again serve the people instead of the other way around.

Frankly, since Waco and Ruby Ridge, a great many Americans have been growing afraid of their own government. Every aspect of our lives has become subject to federal regulation. The massive data banks of the various federal agencies have become a source of near panic as citizens try to come to grips with a growing invasion of personal privacy.

Use of the military has changed. Suddenly, unannounced, in the middle of the night, tanks roll through the streets of unsuspecting neighborhoods as helicopter gun ships rumble over head, troops rappelling to the streets, in unannounced "urban training missions". Such reports of in-city maneuvers have come from Pittsburgh, Memphis, New Orleans, Houston, Dallas, small communities in the Adirondacks, and Los Angeles. On some occasions the troops have actually been using live ammunition. Unlawful joint maneuvers are being held between military and local police. Americans are becoming afraid of their own protectors.

Occasionally we hear reports that an American base has been transformed into a German, Russian, or UN training center. Americans have never experienced foreign troops on our soil - so this is a cause for alarm. But no explanations are received. Instead, those asking questions are simply put down as "nuts". Under the silence, Americans, who are used to a free and open society, are becoming suspicious of the purpose of such activities.

Vast areas of American land are being placed off-limits, many times taken from land owners by gun-toting federal agents in the name of some environmental regulation. Americans who try to comply with the ever-growing number of green regulations are often told conflicting stories by the same agency. And in the end, some Americans find themselves in jail for a violation - even after permits had been issued. As development is banned, retirement nest eggs have been destroyed and families have faced ruin.

Property owners are becoming little more than government-sanctioned tenants on their own land as property rights disappear. Some Americans have begun to fear once-benevolent agencies such as the Park Service and the Forest Service. Smokey the Bear is becoming a feared killer Grizzly.

Parents who question school policies find themselves on the "troublemaker" list. They are barred from seeing tests their children are forced to take. They are told not to help with homework. They are refused permission to see text books and class material. Parents who home-school find themselves harassed by public-school officials.

Meanwhile, federal programs engorge schools with more money and more regulations, assuring the education establishment more power and more arrogance over parents, as kids grow steadily dumber.

School-to-Work is a federally funded nightmare that represents a complete transformation of public schools into job-training centers. Some Americans have begun to fear the day their children reach school age and liberally become "wards of the state".

Under the guise of fighting drugs, new laws have given police unprecedented powers to invade private homes. Private confiscation laws, under the anti-drug statutes, now give local and federal police agencies the power to take property, sell it, and buy more equipment.

Consequently, we find local police units equipped like a modern-day army. How long can civil liberties last in such an atmosphere? People are terrified as more and more stories emerge of police violently breaking down doors of innocent homeowners, forcing the occupants to the floor as the officers destroy the home's contents, in some cases killing pets, only to find they've come to the wrong address. No compensation, not even an "I'm sorry" is offered by this new breed of brutes.

In 1996 the federal government had 45,366 law enforcement investigative personnel at 13 agencies. All have the power to arrest. All are armed. And Americans are afraid.

Black helicopters, the Chinese in Longbeach, election fraud, UN land grabs, the New World Order - these are the reasons Americans have grown to fear their own government and its elected officials who don't seem to take notice of these threats.

Certainly some of these things are just rumors, misunderstandings, or just plain, unfounded fears. But enough have proven to be true to give credibility to much of the rest. People are paranoid - with good reason. But their fears have been met with silence and ridicule by intolerant, arrogant, power-hungry federal, state, and local agents who admit to having a great disregard for Constitutional rights that get in the way of their desired policies. That was all supposed to begin to end with the Republican victory of 1994. Unfortunately, for many, these hopes were soon dashed.

The Republicans stormed out of the gate of the 104th Congress, armed with the *Contract with America* and Republican ideas for cutting costs and regulations and limiting government infringement in the personal lives of Americans. The Democrats were on the ropes. But almost overnight things changed. All the Democrats had to do, it seemed, was challenge Republican ideas, pinning the usual label of "mean-spiritedness" on Republican attempts to roll back or eliminate government programs.

To the dismay of their most loyal supporters, the Republicans failed to even try to counter the attack. So the charges stuck and the fight seemed to be drained out of the leadership. Rather than fighting to reduce government, Republicans began to use Democrat rhetoric about "helping the poor", "saving the environment", and assuring that our children receive a "world-class education". Worse, the Republicans began to introduce and support "recycled" Democrat legislation - sold to the American people as "Republican" ideas.

And as they began to lose the support of their most loyal grassroots activists, Republican leadership responded by calling those with whom they had once fought side-by-side in the trenches, "misguided", "uncompromising", "impatient", and "extremist". Sound too harsh? Consider the following examples of Republican bait and switch:

Grassroots activists across the nation unified like never before to stop Hillary Clinton's socialized health-care scheme. Yet, step by step, during the 104th and the 105th Congresses, Republicans have allowed the passage of so-called education legislation creating in-school health clinics and the expansion of Medicaid/Medicare programs to increase federal intrusion into health care. Hillary's hated, discredited program is being implemented one step at a time - on the Republican watch.

Republicans are now going through a great hand-wringing exercise as they attempt to decide whether to use predicted federal budget surpluses for a tax cut or to reduce the deficit that has accumulated over 40 years of Democrat rule. Yet, the decision would be much easier if Republicans would have listened to their own rhetoric when they were creating the 1998 fiscal year budget. Incredibly, the Republicans produced a bigger budget than Bill Clinton asked for.

In trying to play favor to the radical, property-hating, anticapitalist Sierra Club, the Republicans actually gave the Interior Department $206 million to rip more private lands out from under their owners. Republicans upped the foreign aid bill, raised appropriations to the Export-Import Bank, [and] increased the budgets for subsidized housing, Head Start, refugee assistance, and even the hated Food and Drug Administration. And the pork was flying higher and faster than in the days of Dan Rostenkowski. In fact, the Republicans spent almost $5 billion more on domestic programs than Bill Clinton had even requested.

Even worse, without firing a shot, the once-fierce Republican attack dog instantly put its tail between its legs and surrendered on the raising of the minimum wage. There is no stronger economic principle held by Republicans than the fact that a federally dictated minimum wage is intrusive to private enterprise and harmful to the very people it's supposed to help. Yet, there it was, with a Republican majority in power, a minimum wage enacted with little opposition. And as a result, the emboldened Democrats have decided to seek another increase this year. What do they have to lose?

But as the Republican leadership gives us the rhetoric of tax cuts, reform and elimination of the IRS, and family values, they have actually succeeded in perpetuating federal power. American education is a mess. It is the issue parents are most concerned about. Kids are stupid. Employers can't find suitable employees. Test scores are plummeting. Parents are beginning to yank their kids out of public schools in droves. And the Republicans see this issue as one that can drive them to new majorities.

That would be true if they would only spend an afternoon researching the real problem, listening to parents, reading a text book, and finding that children can't read, write, or add and subtract because the psychology-driven, behavior-modification curriculum is doing it deliberately. But instead, somewhere along the way Republicans grabbed hold of the socialists' concept of combining education and job training. Rather than understanding that a political agenda is driving our kids to the stupid farm, Republicans have decided to throw the baby out with the bath water and rework the whole education system. And no matter how much evidence of its failure is presented, they are determined to push on.

The Republicans promised to get rid of the Department of Education, Goals 2000, and School-to-Work. But instead, they have strengthened all of these with more money and more power. That department and these programs have brought about an unprecedented revolution in public schools that, if left unchecked, will change the very foundation of this nation. It will result in a nation driven by the dictates of the federal government. The economy will become a planned socialist nightmare, with goods and services controlled by unelected goons and the future of the children determined by national need instead of personal choice. Is that the kind of reform the Republicans now support?

If just once Trent Lott and Newt Gingrich would take a look at what is going on in the classroom, instead of listening to the glorious rhetoric about computers for every student, national guidelines for excellence, and a "world-class education", they would see very quickly why children can't read and write. Trent, Newt, just ask yourselves these question: If children aren't taught to spell, can they do well on spelling tests? If children aren't taught multiplication tables or the process of creating math equations, can they learn math? Do you know who is creating the software for all of the computers you are helping to put in every classroom? Could it be possible that the software is not value neutral? Is someone's political agenda involved?

No matter how much money you throw at the classroom, no matter how many tests you call for, no matter how many teachers you hire, or school buildings you provide, education will not improve until you replace the psychologists with real teachers and the behavior-modification and self-esteem programs with basic academics. It is not the purpose of education to provide workers to employers. Schools exist to teach children the basics so they can make their own decisions.

How is it possible that Republicans have failed to understand the origins of today's education restructuring? It's written, plain as day, in Marc Tucker's report, *A Human Resources Development Plan for the United States,* written for the Clinton White House shortly after the 1992 election. Have the Republicans ever read it?

That report clearly shows the purpose of School-to-Work, Goals 2000, and the CAREERS Act. It outlines in great detail, in a report written by an avowed leftist, that the Clinton White House intends to have the Federal Government take over schools; control the curriculum; engage in behavior modification programs to change the attitudes, values, and beliefs of the children; implement cradle-to-grave control over the development of children; interfere with parental rights; reeducate parents; build massive data banks on every child; control employment and career choices; interfere with home-schooling; use the schools to implement socialized medicine; and expand the welfare system. Yet, this is what the Republican majority has embraced as its own agenda.

In the 103rd Congress, Ted Kennedy first introduced the CAREERS Act with language almost verbatim to the Tucker Report. In the 104th Congress, Republican Buck McKeon, with the blessing of Bill Goodling, introduced an almost identical bill as a Republican measure. They sold the bill as simply a cost- and bureaucracy-cutting plan.

In spite of the fact the back-to-basics activists have proven time and again that the bill not only did not cut costs, but actually built federal power through new bureaucracy, the Republican leadership pushes on in its efforts to pass this legislation. Why? Why do Republicans fail to hold hearings on the education crisis? Why do they refuse to hear from parents about the true crisis in the classrooms? Why do they rarely listen to anyone but the National Governors Association, the Chamber of Commerce, and the American Federation of Teachers when it comes to education issues? Each of these groups stands to gain power and control from this legislation.

Republican support for charter schools and vouchers sounds good. It sounds voluntary and "Republican". But the truth is each of these initiatives comes with federal strings attached. Each will only serve to entangle private schools in the big government web and increase federal power. Charter schools have become the Trojan Horse to suck in the remaining holdouts to the education restructuring revolution. And Republicans have become the Judas Goat to lead the lambs to the slaughter.

Worse, the Republicans' favorite block-grants have become the fuel to perpetuate the system on the state level, where the same type of bureaucrats with the same Hillary Clinton/NEA pedigree wait to implement the programs so faithfully supplied by the Republicans. Republicans naively believe the block-grants are returning power to the states. Yet that's not possible as long as federal programs and the Department of Education continue to call the shots from Washington.

Goals 2000 is due for reauthorization. Here is the chance for Republicans to take the first step toward actually rolling back the education crisis by removing a massive part of the federal intrusion. But will Republicans lead the charge so hoped for by the core of the party faithful? Apparently not. According to my sources on the House education committee, Republicans plan to take a page from the Democrats on this one. They intend to keep appropriating money to Goals 2000 without trying to reauthorize it. Again, an opportunity is lost as the Left's agenda goes on with Republican help.

Do Republicans simply fail to understand the true motives behind those pushing the education restructuring agenda or have they now joined in lock step with Marc Tucker and Hillary Clinton? There's only one answer to the education crisis. Get the federal government completely out of the education business, block grants and all.

Hand in hand with the education restructuring agenda is the radical environmental agenda that is usurping private property rights nationwide. Once considered a western states' battle, the assault on property rights is now invading cities nationwide, through a monster called Sustainable Development.

Americans all want clean water and air. They all want polluters stopped and endangered species protected. And Americans have proven that they are willing to sacrifice [some of] their liberties, alter their property rights, even their way of life, to save the planet. But if the American people were told the truth about the land grabs, the deceit and the utter lack of scientific reasons for it all, their support for the warm and fuzzy-sounding agenda would be shaken.

It is the most cynical hoax ever perpetrated on the American people. The majority of Americans, who get their news from the networks and CNN, have not been told that there is no scientific consensus in support of the theories of global warming. They have not been told that the Endangered Species Act not only has never been credited with saving a single species, it is actually hazardous to the existence of most. They have not been told that the idea of a "Biosphere Reserve" has absolutely no scientific basis whatsoever.

A simple study of the environmentalist movement will show an agenda that literally places people in a category below other animals and plants. Here is an agenda driven by earth-worshiping pagans who reject all of the tenets of Western Civilization, including private property rights, free enterprise, and individual liberty. Just by reading their reports, attending their conferences, and reading their quotes, informed Americans could learn of the true agenda of the radical environmental movement.

By reading the *Wildlands Project,* authored by Earth First!'s Dave Foreman and Reed Noss, Americans could learn that the environmental movement intends to head Americans into "human habitat" areas while converting the rest of the nation to wild, uninhabited areas. They could learn that Sustainable Development and Biosphere Reserves and wetland regulations are just some of the tools already in place to implement such a radical assault on America's way of life. Don't Members of Congress have some staffers who could research all of that, as I have?

Here is an opportunity for Republicans to rush to the forefront with truth and with genuine American solutions. Here, Republicans are finally in a place of power to stop and turn around the assault that has been in the works for almost three decades. Here Republicans could expose the lies and deceit used by the radical environmental movement to steal our liberties, simply by holding hearings and bringing in a wide array of scientists and property-rights experts to testify.

But instead, except for a few courageous Republican members of the House (Helen Chenoweth, Don Young, Ron Paul, John Shadegg, to name a few), the Republican leadership is doing exactly the opposite. House Speaker Newt Gingrich has called for an "International Biodiversity Year" where scientists would be encouraged to "think big about biodiversity." They would call for millions of federal dollars to dally in a folly dreamed up by radical environmentalism as a tool to stop human development.

But it's not the first time the Speaker has helped those who seek to destroy property rights and American liberties. In the 104th Congress, Gingrich deliberately derailed all attempts to pass property rights protection legislation.

Congressman John Kasich, with eyes on the White House, along with Congressman Rob Portman, have announced a "Debt for Nature Swap". According to news reports, Kasich and Portman are trying to "shake off their anti-green image." In the scheme, the U.S. would forgive 400 million dollars of debt owed by developing countries if the money is used to save the rain forest. The World Wildlife Fund, Conservation International, and the Nature Conservancy are "pleased".

During the 104th Congress the grassroots activists politely stood on the sidelines to allow the Republicans to rewrite the Endangered Species Act (ESA). These activists, who faced losing their homes and jobs to a bad law, based on bad science, believed in Newt Gingrich's words about a new Republican revolution. They believed their long fight was about over, until suddenly Gingrich betrayed them by refusing to allow the Congress to act on any of the ESA reform bills offered.

Today in the 105th Congress, the activists are being rewarded for their silence and cooperation with a new ESA bill offered by Senator Dirk Kempthorne of Idaho. Turning a deaf ear to their pleas, Kempthorne has refused to add any language for property-rights protection.

But it gets even worse. Under the current ESA, the federal government has been shutting down property and production illegally without compensation to the owners. Kempthorne's legislation, rather than stopping such practices, actually now legalizes them through provisions of the bill. Is it any wonder Bruce Babbitt has endorsed the bill and is actively pushing for its passage?

This is the bill property-rights activists are now being told they must support. And the Republican leadership is upset with activists who openly oppose it. Again, they call us "extremists" for attempting to fight for our homes and our jobs and the American liberties we thought Republicans were elected to protect.

Why have the Republicans joined forces with those who seek to destroy Constitutionally guaranteed property rights, free enterprise, and individual liberty? Why have they abandoned the call for sound science? Why are they not taking the lead for property rights? When did the Republican party decide to abandon individual citizens in favor of large, multinational industries which owe allegiance to no county or party?

In what can only be called a "flimflam", Republicans have taken on the UN in a silly exercise. They puff out their chests and threaten the UN with severe sanctions if it does not "reform" itself. Republicans talk of bloated budgets and huge bureaucracies and unpaid parking tickets in New York City. Speaker Gingrich threatens to support nonpayment of UN dues unless such "reforms" are achieved. But then pushes for payment anyway as our "duty" to the international body.

Republicans stand before cheering crowds and speak with indignation of "American boys being forced to fight under foreign generals while wearing UN uniforms." Maddening, yes, but it's not the real problem with the UN.

International treaties that ignore American property rights and commerce are the real threat. UN plans for "global governance", UN taxation, and a UN standing army threaten America's sovereignty. These are not pipe dreams or "right-winged conspiracy" theories. The information comes from the UN's own documents. Anyone can read them. They're on the Internet, they're for sale in the lobby of UN headquarters in New York. The information is readily available to anyone who wants it.

In the 104th Congress, when UN officials first sent up the trial balloons to check reaction to UN tax schemes, Members were swift in their reaction. There was evidence that the Clinton Administration, through its hand-picked UN Development Program Administrator, James G. Speth, was working hand-in-hand with the UN to implement the idea. Outraged Congressmen called for hearings. Bob Dole introduced a bill to block such an idea. Clearly the schemes were viewed to represent a real threat to the nation. But that was before Republicans lost their will to fight for their principles. The hearings were dropped, no bill was passed, and vocal opposition to the UN by the Republican leadership evaporated, except, perhaps, for the demand of payment for those parking tickets.

But, of course, those of us who have read these documents and are aware of the true UN threat, have been labeled "extremists", not to be taken seriously.

When Secretary of State Madeleine Albright served as Ambassador to the UN she said, "This is not a world government and the people who say that are trying to create a boogeyman . . . it is really a complete figment . . . ." But within 3 weeks of her denial, the UN's Commission on Global Governance released its 3-year study which provides a 400-page blueprint to achieve global governance by the year 2000.

That plan calls for a UN standing army, UN taxation, UN authority over the "global commons" (the world), an International Court of Justice, expanded authority for the Secretary General, and a parliamentary body of non-elected private organizations like the Sierra Club and the Nature Conservancy called NGOs (non-governmental organizations).

These plans are prepared and are being distributed. International agreements like the Biodiversity Treaty set up the NGO power structure. Others, including the Convention on Climate Change, Agenda 21, the UN Rights of the Child, and the Rio Declaration, put in place UN family intervention, internationalized Sustainable Development, and the Wildlands Project.

Why the concern over these UN activities? Because the U.S. is signing these treaties and giving them the power of American law. Shouldn't the mere mention of a UN document entitled "Global Governance" sound alarm bells to the Republican majority that professes to support and defend the Constitution of the U.S.? Where are the hearings? Where is the concern?

There was a time, in the early days of this Republic, when Members of Congress carried a copy of the Constitution in their pocket. Whenever a bill was introduced, they would take out their copy and review it to decide if the bill fit in the framework as outlined by the Founding Fathers.

The Constitution has become a bothersome roadblock to a host of great sounding schemes. Members rarely consult or consider it when drawing up legislation. The main concern now is simply whether they can get the law passed. Opinion polls, rather than the Bill of Rights, are the guide posts for these modern-day legislators. Defend liberty? Relative to what?

Our Founding Fathers (who are now being written out of the history books as nothing more than white slave owners) were scholars and historians. They researched other civilizations and cultures, looking for the best and the worst ideas man had used to govern himself. Their search was part of an intellectual movement in the eighteenth century, called the "Enlightenment", which questioned traditional beliefs and taboos. They sought to achieve absolute scientific fact and reason in their decisions. They questioned the accepted traditions and the old ways of doing things. And they worked to put together a means of existence that recognized natural rights and logic.

The movement was led in England by John Locke, David Hume, and Sir Isaac Newton. In the colonies, students of the "Enlightenment" included Thomas Jefferson, Benjamin Franklin, and James Madison. The result was the creation of an idea for self-government that was based on sound science, free speech, property rights, individual freedom, free enterprise, and freedom of religious expression and choice.

It was no casual remark, then, when Ben Franklin's answer to the question "[W]hat sort of government have you given us" was "a Republic, if you can keep it." It was purely experimental, never attempted before in the world.

That's why we fight so passionately to keep those once-unheard-of liberties from disappearing at the hands of "unenlightened brutes". It's easy to take [away those liberties]. It's each generation's job to see that they aren't. Now they are in the hands of the Republican Congress to defend.

Shortly after one of the failed coup attempts on Newt Gingrich's leadership, Senate Majority Leader Trent Lott stormed into a meeting of House staffers with fire in his eyes. He told them that if their Congressman had been a part of this attack on Newt, then they had better grow-up and learn reality. He said that the leadership in place was the leadership that would stay. Lott went on to attack voters when he said, "[I]f any of your constituents call to complain about Republican leadership, tell them that they are the ones who elected Bill Clinton." Lott admitted that "we can't beat him."

If the current Republican leaders can't positively express and promote Republican ideas, then it would indicate that the current leadership either doesn't understand those ideas or doesn't truly believe in them. Step aside and let someone who does believe take a crack at the Clinton machine.

As I listen to Republicans whine about lack of support, I can't help but think back to our founding fathers and their sacrifice to give birth to the idea of the U.S. I think of poor Caesar Rodney, Delaware delegate to the Continental Congress, who was literally roused from his sick bed to make an emergency trip by carriage over muddy, bumpy roads to Philadelphia. He was urgently needed to sign the Declaration of Independence. Had he whined and refused, independence would not have been possible.

Then there is the story of another signer named Thomas Nelson, Jr. of Virginia. At the final battle of Yorktown, where the outcome meant life or death for the new nation, Nelson noted that American forces were not firing at a certain key section of the British line. When he inquired as to the reason, he was told that his own house was in the way. Nelson quietly urged George Washington to fire on his home, destroying it. As a result, Nelson died bankrupt.

Congress constantly whines that it must offer the toothless legislation and the Democrat-cloned bills it has put forth because otherwise "we can't get it signed by Bill Clinton." Just once, it would be nice to hear the other side complain that it dare not move forward with its agenda because "we'll never get it past the Republican Congress." Then we would know that the Republicans had finally started fighting back. But such an attitude apparently would damage the "spirit of bipartisanship".

Yet most of the grassroots want to remain loyal. It pains them to fight the very ones they helped to put in office. But let it be known to the Republican leadership that these are Americans and parents first, Republicans last. They will fight anyone who represents a threat to their American-guaranteed liberties. They have no choice.

They are ready to charge to the sounds of the guns - the legislative battles Republicans should be leading to restore their freedoms. The trouble is, we hear no guns blazing, only the sound of the clinking of glasses at the Republican's bipartisan party. It's time for the Republican majority to remember who got them their invitation.

AFTERTHOUGHT

You are now the guardians of your own liberties.
- Samuel Adams[489]
1776

The condition upon which God hath given liberty to man is eternal vigilance; which condition if he break, servitude is at once the consequence of his crime and the punishment of his guilt.
- John Philpot Curran[490]
Speech Upon the Right of Election of Lord Mayor of Dublin, July 10, 1790

Liberty is not a means to a higher political end. It is itself the highest political end.
- Lord Acton[491]
The History of Freedom and Other Essays, 1907

s this book nears completion, it occurs to me that the words I've assembled here may not be looked upon with favor or delight by our friendly entrenched liberals. Indeed, these folks may react with mighty indignation to the message I've attempted to convey. So, should this book receive wide distribution, I expect the Propaganda Machine might find it necessary to roll out a few weapons to point and discharge in my direction.

If this book should achieve *real* success (I should be so lucky), I suppose the Propaganda Machine might then feel compelled to launch a few high-tech, high-caliber munitions in defense of their precious liberalism. But when shells begin to whistle overhead and explode, don't look for a serious discussion of the issues. Don't look for an honest, intelligent examination of the points I raise or positions I present. Oh, no! Instead, watch for the smear, the personal discrediting, the personal attack. Watch for the focus on some small error (I'm sure a number of mistakes will slip by the editors in spite of their dedicated efforts). Watch for criticism based on the *liberal's* interpretation of what *they* say I've said. They won't tolerate explanations or reasoning I might offer in defense. For such is the Propaganda Machine's *modus operandi.* Such is their tried and true technique of presenting but one side - their side - of the issues upon which they choose to report.

I will not be the lone target, however, if this book makes liberals squirm and perspire. Many of those I've used as sources will likewise become the object of the media's wrath and attack. If this should happen, I will be greatly distressed to have caused angst upon these prized sources. My voice, even supplemented with a hundred others, cannot outshout the Mighty Propaganda Machine. In the end my reputation will be tarnished and besmirched, perhaps that of others, and that will be the end of it.

Well, no, I'm afraid that won't be the end of it, if the Propaganda Machine is sufficiently roused. If printed words and television commentary cannot extract from me sufficient pain in the collective view of the Propaganda Machine, then a lawsuit or two can be swiftly called into service. Any of a thousand liberal organizations can quickly step forward to apply pain not only to my pride but my wallet as well.

As Congressman J.C. Watts (R, Oklahoma) said, "If liberals can't beat you, if they're losing on the issues, they do one of two things. They either call you a bigot or a racist. Or they sue you."[492] (Just ask Matt Drudge.)

Should the White House be displeased, heaven forbid, a heavy-duty IRS audit can be promptly initiated to properly punish my transgressions. Agents "just doing their jobs" can extract a mighty penalty, if not in actual back taxes (real or imagined) and fines, then at least in tax accountant fees, lawyer fees, and endless exasperation.

As author Tom Chittum notes: "By the use of the IRS and other government bodies, the establishment can financially ruin any individual of modest means without convicting him. It doesn't matter if the charges have an ounce of truth or not . . . . In effect, the government can fine any dissident into bankruptcy at will."[493]

So the point is there's risk in poking at the big giant. It can arise and display a downright nasty temper, in spite of the benevolent, compassionate, loving facade behind which it so carefully hides. If you become a target - I mean a serious target - the toll can be excessive. Ask Robert Bork, Clarence Thomas, or any of dozens of others.

However, when we see an evil cloud building over America's greatness, how can we be still? Edmund Burke admonished us: "He trespasses against his duty who sleeps upon his watch as well as he that goes over to the enemy."[494] So, speaking out is not an option. It's a duty.

For many years the objective of the Propaganda Machine has *not* been the honest pursuit and publication of the truth. It has been the fostering of an agenda, the imposition of a political philosophy upon the masses, the indoctrination of a populace such that it not only thinks in accord with the mighty Propaganda Machine, but actually becomes an extension of it, willingly assisting in the propagation of its world view and its political perspective.

In spite of overwhelming evidence to the contrary, which the Propaganda Machine chooses to ignore or at least to shield from public awareness, many Americans think Lee Harvey Oswald alone killed John F. Kennedy.[495] Many think Vince Foster committed suicide in that quaint little Fort Marcy Park.[496] Many think TWA 800 fell out of the sky because the central fuel tank spontaneously exploded, wholly unprovoked.[497] Many think just Timothy McVeigh and his buddy Terry Nichols (maybe Timothy alone) blew up the Murrah Building in Oklahoma City.[498] Many think the FBI, BATF, and other government forces didn't fire a single shot at the Waco Branch Davidians.[499] (A Department of Justice report states: *"The FBI did not fire a shot during the entire operation."*[500] - Emphasis in the original.) Many still think the UN serves U.S. interests.[501] And many will think the president walks on water if that's what the Propaganda Machine wishes them to think.

In 1955 Vladimir Ilyich Lenin said, "The press should be not only a collective propagandist and a collective agitator, but also a collective organizer of the masses."[502] In contemporary America the press measures up well to Vladimir's expectations.

"Just imagine! Some people still believe this stuff!"

In 1957 Nikita Sergeyevich Khrushchev said, "The press is our chief ideological weapon."[503] Indeed. A more powerful and effective weapon can't be found. It fires unceasingly and the public pays to be indoctrinated. Russian journalist and political thinker Alexander Herzen said, "It is possible to lead astray an entire generation, to strike it blind, to drive it insane, to direct it towards a false goal."[504] Bingo!

Is that what's going on in America today? Are there really agents and powers and influences anxious to subvert, undermine, and derail this nation? Of course. I'm old enough to remember watching television when Khrushchev pounded his shoe on the table at the UN. I remember his proclamation: "We will bury you! And we will never even have to fire a shot."[505] I happen to think he meant it.

Why, for goodness sakes, would we think the whole world has gone soft and now only wishes us good fortune? That's liberal think. That's Pollyanna. That's nonsense!

Too many Americans, I fear, have swallowed the line and are now quite comfortable in their ignorance.

Thomas Jefferson foresaw the result. "If a nation expects to be ignorant and free," he said, "it expects what never was and never will be."[506]

Our Founding Fathers relied heavily on a free press to guarantee an educated, well-informed public, so as to guarantee a *free* people. The framers of the Constitution so revered the role of the press in a free republic, they enshrined its protection in the First Amendment. Not the second or third, mind you, but the *First* Amendment.

Regrettably, this country's massive and powerful Propaganda Machine and liberals in general have disappointed our Founding Fathers, and indeed all who cherish freedom.

ENDNOTES

Good intention will always be pleaded for every assumption of power . . . . It is hardly too strong to say that the Constitution was made to guard the people against the dangers of good intentions. There are men in all ages who mean to govern well, but they mean to govern. They promise to be good masters, but they mean to be masters.

- Daniel Webster[507]

That's what liberalism is. It's spend, spend right now, or do anything that makes you feel good right now, and forget any calculating of how it affects the long term.

- U.S. Representative Dana Rohrabacher (R, California)[508]

The Selected Bibliography provides additional information regarding many of the sources identified here.

1. As quoted in *Bartlett's Familiar Quotations,* 14th edition, by John Bartlett, Little, Brown, and Company, Incorporated, 1968, page 327.
2. Reprinted with permission from *The Quotable Conservative,* compiled by Rod L. Evans and Irwin M. Berent, copyright © 1995, Rod L. Evans and Irwin M. Berent, published by Adams Media Corporation, page 250.
3. As quoted in *The Concise Conservative Encyclopedia,* by Brad Miner, Free Press Paperbooks, division of Simon & Schuster, Incorporated, 1994, pages 43, 44.
4. As quoted in *Are You a Conservative or a Liberal?,* by Bradley O'Learly (conservative) and Victor Kamber (liberal), Boru Publishing, 1996, page 71.
5. Grant Russell, "Inside the Liberal Mind," *Midnight Messenger*, 1995, page 2.
6. *Ibid,* page 3.
7. Bradley O'Learly (conservative) and Victor Kamber (liberal), *Are You a Conservative or a Liberal?,* Boru Publishing, 1996, page 72.
8. *Ibid,* page 70.
9. *Ibid,* pages 71, 72.
10. *Ibid,* page 68.
11. *Ibid,* page 69.
12. Henry Grady Weaver, *The Mainspring of Human Progress,* Foundation for Economic Education, 1997, as quoted by James "Bo" Gritz in his newsletter *Center for Action,* March 1998, page 8.
13. Bradley O'Learly (conservative) and Victor Kamber (liberal), *Are You a Conservative or a Liberal?,* Boru Publishing, 1996, page 74.
14. As quoted in *Bartlett's Familiar Quotations,* 14th edition, by John Bartlett, Little, Brown, and Company, Incorporated, 1968, page 117.
15. *Ibid,* page 49.
16. Additional portions of Codrescu's quotation can be found in "Quotes of the Year," *Human Events,* January 10, 1997, page 13.
17. Dwight L. Kinman, *The World's Last Dictator,* Whitaker House, 1995, page 185.
18. *Who's Who in America - 1996,* Reed Reference Publishing Company (now a Reed Elsevies Company), page 4343.
19. James "Bo" Gritz, *Center for Action* newsletter, December 1997, page 14.
20. *Who's Who in America - 1996,* Reed Reference Publishing Company (now a Reed Elsevies Company), page 1079.
21. *Ibid,* page 3010.
22. ALSO: "Big Media Behind the Curve During Conservative Year," "Damn Those Conservatives Award," *Human Events,* January 20, 1995, page 13.
23. As quoted in a July 7, 1998 solicitation letter signed by U.S. Representative J.C. Watts, Jr. (R, Oklahoma) for the Leadership Institute, Morton C. Blackwell, president.
24. "Quote of the Week," *Human Events,* November 10, 1995, page 1. ALSO: "Stupid Quotes," *The Limbaugh Letter,* November 1996, page 5.

25. Cliff Kincaid, *Global Taxes for World Government,* Huntington House Publishers, 1997, page 90.
26. *Ibid.*
27. As quoted in *The American Sentinel,* February 1998, page 7.
28. Peter LaBarbera, *Clinton's Crazies,* Eagle Publishing, Incorporated, 1994, page 9.
29. "Inside Politics," compiled by Greg Pierce, *Washington Times,* National Weekly Edition, June 22, 1997, page 16.
30. *Who's Who in America - 1996,* Reed Reference Publishing Company (now a Reed Elsevies Company), page 3418.
31. The same quote appeared in the November 1996 issue of the *Limbaugh Letter*, and it was also published in "Quotes of the Year," *Human Events,* January 10, 1997, Page 13.
32. "Quote of the Week," *Human Events,* November 8, 1996, page 1.
33. *Who's Who Among African Americans - 1996/1997,* Gale Research, Incorporated, page 1360.
34. Anne Wortham, *The Other Side of Racism, A Philosophical Study of Black Race Consciousness,* Ohio State University, 1981, as quoted in *The Quotable Conservative,* compiled by Rod L. Evans and Irwin M. Berent, copyright © 1995, Rod L. Evans and Irwin M. Berent, published by Adams Media Corporation, page 254. (Reprinted with permission.)
35. Reprinted with permission from *The Quotable Conservative,* compiled by Rod L. Evans and Irwin M. Berent, copyright © 1995, Rod L. Evans and Irwin M. Berent, published by Adams Media Corporation, page 254.
36. As quoted in *The Death of Common Sense,* by Philip K. Howard, Random House, Incorporated, 1994, page 141.
37. *Who's Who in America - 1996,* Reed Reference Publishing Company (now a Reed Elsevies Company), page 506.
38. *Who's Who of American Women - 1997/1998,* Marquis Who's Who, a Reed Elsevies Company, page 195.
39. *Who's Who in America - 1996,* Reed Reference Publishing Company (now a Reed Elsevies Company), page 952.
40. James "Bo" Gritz, *Center for Action* newsletter, October 1997, page 8.
41. Cliff Kincaid, "Ted 'Turncoat' Boosts UN," *ASAP Report,* August 1997, page 5.
42. Thomas D. DeWeese, in an October 24, 1996 address in Cleveland, Ohio, as reported in *The DeWeese Report,* Tom DeWeese, editor, January 1997, page 6.
43. *Ibid.*
44. Howard Will, "New Age Teaching Spells Trouble in California," *Chicago Tribune,* May 14, 1995, as quoted in *Brave New Schools,* by Berit Kjos, Harvest House Publishers, 1995, page 61.
45. Carol Innerst, "U.S. High School Seniors Rank 19th in 21-Nation Survey," *The Washington Times,* National Weekly Edition, March 8, 1998, page 1.
46. Carol Innerst, "No Challenge for Growing Minds," *The Washington Times,* National Weekly Edition, November 2, 1997, page 1.
47. Jeannie Georges, "Outcome-Based Education," *Media Bypass* magazine, page 3, as quoted in *Brave New Schools,* by Berit Kjos, Harvest House Publishers, 1995, page 64.
48. Rush Limbaugh, "What's Wrong with American Schools?" *The Limbaugh Letter,* March 1997, page 15.
49. *Ibid.*
50. Berit Kjos, *Brave New Schools,* Harvest House Publishers, 1995, page 218.

51. As quoted in the *U.S. Congressional Record,* House of Representatives, October 23, 1989, pages 3517-3519, as reprinted in *Brave New Schools,* by Berit Kjos, Harvest House Publishers, 1995, page 218.
52. *Ibid,* page 211.
53. Benjamin Bloom, *All Our Children Learning,* McGraw Hill, New York, New York, 1981, page 180.
54. Berit Kjos, *Brave New Schools,* Harvest House Publishers, 1995, page 13.
55. Roger Morris, *Partners in Power,* Henry Holt and Company, Incorporated, 1996, page 323.
56. *Who's Who in America - 1996,* Reed Reference Publishing Company, page 1078.
57. *Ibid,* page 4335.
58. Tom Knott, "Where's the Outrage over Rodman's Slur against Mormons?" *The Washington Times,* National Weekly Edition, June 22, 1997, page 13.
59. See endnote 55.
60. See endnote 56.
61. See endnote 57.
62. Roger Morris, *Partners in Power,* Henry Holt and Company, Incorporated, 1996, page 325. ALSO: *None Dare Call It Murder,* a video narrated by Anthony J. Hilder, Mondo Libre Productions, 1996. But Roger Clinton isn't the only one to suggest Bill Clinton has been a heavy user of cocaine. Sharlene Wilson, who allegedly bedded down with Roger, and over the years many of the Dixie Mafia, has testified she once saw Bill Clinton get so high on cocaine he fell into a garbage can. (See Joseph Farah's article "Bring Sharlene Wilson Home for Christmas," *Dispatches,* December 1997, page 2.) Observers suspect Sharlene wouldn't be cooling her heels in an Arkansas prison were it not for her testimony in 1990 that she provided cocaine to then-Governor Bill Clinton. According to *The American Enterprise* ("Scan," November/December 1998, page 11), former Miss Arkansas, Sally Perdue, was warned by a Democratic operative that her "pretty little legs" might be broken if she continued to speak publically about Clinton's dancing around her apartment in her nightgown, playing his saxophone, and snorting cocaine.
63. Balint Vazsonyi, director, Center for the American Founding, "Four Points of the Compass: Restoring America's Sense of Direction," *Imprimis,* November 1997, page 3.
64. *Who's Who in America - 1996,* Reed Reference Publishing Company (now a Reed Elsevies Company), page 2052.
65. During a May 3, 1997 videotaped debate in Los Angeles between Dr. Khallid Abdul Muhammad and Anthony J. Hilder (Free World Alliance), Muhammad spoke eloquently and passionately to the all-black audience: "Why kill the [white man's] babies? They're just little, innocent, blue-eyed babies. Because goddamn it, they're gonna grow up one day to rule *your* babies. Kill 'em now. . . . We kill the men. We kill the women. We kill the children. We kill the babies. I said, goddamn it, we kill 'em all!" The listeners responded with shouts of encouragement. Muhammad's declaration continued: "We kill the blind. We kill the crippled., We kill the crazy. We kill the faggots. We kill the lesbians." Then, as though he wasn't making himself clear, he goaded the excited throng: "After you kill 'em all. . . you go to the goddamn grave and dig 'em up and kill 'em a-goddamn-gain, because they didn't die hard enough. And if you don't have the strength to dig 'em up after you've done all that work, just go to the grave and shoot in the damn grave. Kill 'em again because they didn't die hard enough." The standing-room-only audience that had gathered in the little church to hear the debate cheered wildly. (A video of this debate, "Kill the White Man," a Free World Film Production,

1998, is available for purchase, should you wish to witness the entire spectacle. Call 800-201-7892.)

66. Jay Parker, president, The Lincoln Institute for Research and Education, in a "Dear Concerned American" letter, undated.
67. Arthur M. Schlesinger, Jr., *The Disuniting of America - Reflections on a Multicultural Society,* W.W. Norton & Company, Incorporated, 1991, page 102.
68. *Ibid,* page 118.
69. *Ibid,* page 130.
70. Balint Vazsonyi, director, Center for the American Founding, "Four Points of the Compass: Restoring America's Sense of Direction," *Imprimis,* Hillsdale College, November 1997, page 3.
71. Philip K. Howard, *The Death of Common Sense,* Random House, Incorporated, 1994, page 118.
72. Edward Dent (Washington, D.C.), "Conservative Forum," *Human Events,* August 18, 1995, page 21.
73. Pat Buchanan, *Right from the Beginning,* Regnery Gateway, copyright © 1990 by Regnery Publishing, page 351. All rights reserved. Reprinted by special permission of Regnery Publishing, Incorporated.
74. *Who's Who in America - 1996,* Reed Reference Publishing Company (now a Reed Elsevies Company), page 2085.
75. *Ibid,* page 2257.
76. "Stupid Quotes," *The Limbaugh Letter,* November 1996, page 4, quoting a speech delivered in the U.S. House of Representatives.
77. Mark R. Levin, "Voices of Reason?" *The Washington Times,* National Weekly Edition, August 31, 1997, page 30.
78. Jeff Jacoby, "The Left Spews Hatred with Impunity," *Orange County Register,* January 5, 1998.
79. "Stupid Quotes," *The Limbaugh Letter,* November 1996, page 4, quoting *The Washington Post.*
80. As quoted in *The Informed Christian,* published by the Christian Coalition of Florida, Orlando, July 1997, page 1.
81. As quoted by John Fund, Editorial Board, *Wall Street Journal,* in remarks delivered at the Shavano Institute for National leadership, October 1997.
82. *Who's Who in America - 1996,* Reed Reference Publishing Company (now a Reed Elsevies Company), page 1344.
83. *Ibid,* page 1440.
84. William F. Jasper, *Global Tyranny . . . Step by Step,* Western Islands, 1992, page 47.
85. *Who's Who of American Women - 1997/1998,* Marquis Who's Who, a Reed Elsevies Company, page 195.
86. ALSO: From the website of the National Center for Policy Research: "Talking Points on the Environment," www.nationalcenter.org/tp2.html, accessed 5-23-98. ALSO: *Set Up and Sold Out,* by Holly Swanson, 1995, page 170.
87. See endnote 85.
88. ALSO: "Supplanting Parents," by William Norman Grigg, *The New American,* July 21, 1997, page 44. ALSO: "Is Socialism/Communism at Work in America? You Decide." *Freedom Alert,* Newsletter of the Defenders of Personal Property Rights, Citizens for Constitutional Property Rights, Incorporated, January 5, 1998, insert sheet.

89. *Licensing Parents: Can We Prevent Child Abuse and Neglect?* by Dr. Jack Westman, University of Wisconsin, Madison, 1994, as referenced in William Norman Grigg's article, "Supplanting Parents," *The New American,* July 21, 1997, page 44.
90. William Norman Grigg, "Supplanting Parents," *The New American,* July 21, 1997, page 44, quoting a December 17, 1994 article in the *Minneapolis Star-Tribune.*
91. Peter LaBarbera, *Clinton's Crazies,* Eagle Publishing, Incorporated, 1994, page 26.
92. *AIM Report,* Reed Irvine, editor, Accuracy In Media, Incorporated, September-B 1997 issue, insert, page 2.
93. John W. Whitehead, president of the Rutherford Institute, in a "Dear Friend" letter dated February 1998.
94. Robert W. Lee, "Family Fundamentals," *The New American,* January 5, 1998, page 37.
95. Don McAlvany, "A New Kind of Government: The Elected Dictatorship," *Power & Money - Depression II - The Tragedy Unfolds Before Our Eyes,* published by the McAlvany Intelligence Advisor, Fall 1997.
96. ALSO: *The McAlvany Intelligence Advisor,* Don McAlvany, editor, October 1997, page 24.
97. William Norman Grigg, "Supplanting Parents," *The New American,* July 21, 1997, page 43.
98. *Ibid.* ALSO: "Is Socialism/Communism at Work in America? You Decide." *Freedom Alert,* Newsletter of the Defenders of Personal Property Rights, Citizens for Constitutional Property Rights, Incorporated, January 5, 1998, insert sheet.
99. *Who's Who in America - 1996,* Reed Reference Publishing Company (now a Reed Elsevies Company), page 1604.
100. *Ibid,* page 3445.
101. ALSO: "Times Change, but Collectivist Message Remains Constant," *The New American,* June 9, 1997, pages 24-25.
102. "Stupid Quotes," *The Limbaugh Letter,* August 1995, page 13.
103. *Chicago Tribune,* July 4, 1997, Section 1, page 1.
104. "Stupid Quotes," *The Limbaugh Letter,* January 1997, page 3.
105. Peter LaBarbera, *Clinton's Crazies,* Eagle Publishing, Incorporated, 1994, page 17.
106. Nader once said the solution of America's problems is "socialism or communism of one sort or another." ("Super Patriot Ralph Nader," *The New American,* August 31, 1998, page 8).
107. *Who's Who in America - 1996,* Reed Reference Publishing Company (now a Reed Elsevies Company), page 4427.
108. Quoted in an undated "Stop Socialism - Stop Clinton" letter (a joint project of The American Conservative and the National Conservative Student Review), signed by Leroy Corey, publisher.
109. Wesley J. Smith, "Going Dutch?" *National Review,* October 10, 1994, page 64.
110. *Dispatches,* News Publication of the Western Journalism Center, July 22, 1997, page 8.
111. *Who's Who in America - 1996,* Reed Reference Publishing Company (now a Reed Elsevies Company), page 4509.
112. See the video *Waco - The Rules of Engagement,* a William Gazecki Film, C.O.P.S. Distribution, 1997.
113. ALSO: *The Florida Catholic,* February 14, 1992.
114. David A. Russell, *Who Is Leading the Attack on American Liberty?,* Citizens for Constitutional Property Rights, Incorporated, 1996, page 85.
115. ALSO: *Ibid,* page 86-A.

116. In an article titled "The Pagan Roots of Environmentalism - Update on the Worship of Gaia" (*Insider's Report,* October 1998, page 2), Tom DeWeese writes: "Private property ownership is impossible; free enterprise is exploitation; technology is an abomination against nature; Western Culture is the root of all evil. These are some of the teachings of what is little more than the bastardized products of Eastern mysticism. Now called New Age religion, it culminates in deep ecology, eco-feminism, and the worship of an ancient Greek God called Gaia - Mother Earth. . . . Gaia worship is at the very heart of today's environmental policy. The Endangered Species Act, the United Nation's Biodiversity Treaty, and the President's Council on Sustainable Development are all offspring of the Gaia hypothesis of saving 'Mother Earth. . . .' The Gaia Hypothesis, introduced by James Lovelock and Lynn Margulis (formerly, wife of Carl Sagan), is an ancient idea, presented in scientific-sounding language that makes it politically correct for the new age. . . . The idea is rooted in ancient cultures and, until Lovelock, was generally known as 'paganism.'"

117. "Invasion of Green Religion," *ĕco•logic,* November/December 1995, page 27.

118. The video said the ceremony lasted 3 hours and involved nearly 1000 animals. William Bryant Logan, editor of the Cathedral's newsletter described the event: "I saw children lying in the laps of large dogs and a boy bringing his stuffed animals to be blessed. I saw the not-yet famous elephant and camel march up the aisle; a lawyer who scoops the poop and enjoys being clown-for-a-day; a priest who finds himself covered with wriggling ferrets; a man and a woman who meet when their leashes become enmeshed; a volunteer gardener marching to the altar with a bowl full of compost and worms; a sermon by Al Gore, in which he called on the congregants to recognize that 'God is not separate from the Earth.'" (This description was found in the article "The Rise of Global Governance," by Henry Lamb, in the book *Global Governance: Why? How? When?,* copyright © 1996 by National Review, Incorporated, reprinted by Murchison Chair of Free Enterprise, University of Texas at Austin, 1997, page 79.)

119. *Who's Who in America - 1996,* Reed Reference Publishing Company (now a Reed Elsevies Company), page 4022.

120. Berit Kjos, "Sex Ed and Global Values," *Media Bypass* magazine, August 1997, pages 24-26.

121. As reported in the Drudge Report (www.drudgereport.com), June 17, 1998.

122. Information reporting Dr. Spock's death (at age 94) found on the Internet at: www.yahoo.com/headlines/news/summary.html

123. *Who's Who in America - 1996,* Reed Reference Publishing Company (now a Reed Elsevies Company), page 3978.

124. ALSO: *Operation Vampire Killer 2000,* revised 1996, published by Police Against the New World Order, page 25.

125. *The Limbaugh Letter,* July 1996, page 7.

126. Murray Norris, *Weep for Your Children,* Valley Christian University, 1983.

127. "Sidelights," *The American Enterprise,* November/December 1997, page 8.

128. ALSO: *Operation Vampire Killer 2000,* revised 1996, published by Police Against the New World Order, page 12.

129. Shirley Correll, *Body Snatching and the New World "Odor,"* Florida Pro Family Forum, Incorporated, 1996, page 55.

130. *9*1*1,* June 1997, page 2.

131. *Ibid.*

132. *Ibid.*

133. Cliff Kincaid, *Global Taxes for World Government,* Huntington House Publishers, 1997, page 85.
134. Thomas W. Chittum, *Civil War Two,* American Eagle Publications, Incorporated, 1996, page 21.
135. David A. Russell, *Special Report - Who Is Leading the Attack on American Liberty?,* Citizens for Constitutional Property Rights, Incorporated, 1996, page 31.
136. *International Who's Who - 1990-91,* Europa Publications Limited, page 193.
137. ALSO: "Boutros Boutros-Ghali Dreams of UN Sovereignty," by Senator Jesse Helms, *Human Events,* March 15, 1996, page 14. ALSO: *The McAlvany Intelligence Advisor,* Don McAlvany, editor, September 1995, page 45.
138. As quoted in an undated solicitation letter by Jamey Wheeler, chairman, Fortress America, Washington, D.C.
139. "Insider Report," *The New American,* May 11, 1998, page 4.
140. *Who's Who in America - 1996,* Reed Reference Publishing Company (now a Reed Elsevies Company), page 1226.
141. ALSO: "Just Say No to the WTO," *Human Events,* March 7, 1997, page 1. ALSO: *Facts, Truth, Evidence that Will Affect All Americans,* support material for David Wegener's video *Barbed Wire on America,* page 2.
142. Senator James William Fulbright, *The Arrogance of Power,* Random House, Incorporated, 1967, 1970.
143. "Immigrant Rights," *The Washington Times,* National Weekly Edition, May 5, 1996, page 16.
144. Frank J. Murray, "Supreme Court Rejects Miami Beach Hispanic Voting-Rights Plea," *The Washington Times,* National Weekly Edition, June 22, 1997, page 10.
145. *Ibid.*
146. Thomas W. Chittum, *Civil War Two,* American Eagle Publications, Incorporated, 1996, page 175.
147. Joseph A. D'Agostino, "California Will Not Indict Illegal Foreign Voters," *Human Events,* March 13, 1998, page 4.
148. Reprinted with permission from *The Quotable Conservative,* compiled by Rod L. Evans and Irwin M. Berent, copyright © 1995, Rod L. Evans and Irwin M. Berent, published by Adams Media Corporation, page 37.
149. As quoted in the *The New American,* March 2, 1998, page 29.
150. Quoted by William Norman Grigg in the video *Tragedy by Design,* produced by the John Birch Society, 1997.
151. Quoted in the book *This Land Is Our Land,* by Richard Pombo and Joseph Farah, St. Martin's Press, 1996, pages 97, 98.
152. Daniel Oliver, "PETA Steps Up Pursuit of Radical Goals," *Human Events,* July 18, 1997, page 12.
153. Susan E. Paris, "Animal Rights Extremists Threaten Medical Research," *Human Events,* August 12, 1994, page 139.
154. David A. Russell, *Special Report - Who Is Leading the Attack on American Liberty?,* Citizens for Constitutional Property Rights, Incorporated, 1996, page 13. ALSO: Tom DeWeese, "Radical Greens Use Churches to Force Senate Support of UN's Global Warming Treaty," *Insider's Report,* October 1998, page 4.
155. As quoted in "Animal Rights Extremism at Princeton," by Wesely. J. Smith, *Heterodoxy,* September 1998, page 8. The article says, "Next year [1999], Singer will become a permanent member of the Princeton University faculty, where he will be the Ira W. DeCamp Professor of Bioethics, a prestigious, tenured academic chair, at the

university's Center for Human Values." Also in the same article: "Singer is now so mainstream that he even wrote the essay on ethics for the Encyclopedia Britannica." My reaction: If folks like Peter Singer are "in charge" of ethics in this country's leading institutes of learning, doesn't that sound like the inmates are running the insane asylums? Phyllis Schlafly describes Mr. Singer: "He is an advocate of abortion rights, animal rights, and euthanasia rights, and he teaches that the only reason we value life is the pleasure it produces. If cows lead pleasurable lives, don't butcher them. If handicapped [people lead] lives [that] are not pleasurable, kill them." (*The Phyllis Schlafly Report,* November 1998, page 3.)

156. Daniel T. Oliver, "PETA Steps Up Pursuit of Radical Goals, *Human Events,* July 18, 1997, page 13.
157. *Ibid.*
158. *Who's Who in America - 1996,* Reed Reference Publishing Company (now a Reed Elsevies Company), page 1710.
159. Holly Swanson, *Set Up and Sold Out,* CIN Publishing, Incorporated, 1995, page 17.
160. *Who's Who in America - 1996,* Reed Reference Publishing Company (now a Reed Elsevies Company), page 2813.
161. *Ibid,* page 2972.
162. "Meet Andy Kerr," *ĕco•logic,* July/August 1995, page 28.
163. William F. Jasper, "Conspiracy: Where's the Proof?" *The New American,* September 16, 1996, page 7.
164. Devvy Kidd, *Why a Bankrupt America,* Project Liberty, 1994, page 22. ALSO: "Is Socialism/Communism at Work in America? You Decide." *Freedom Alert,* Newsletter of the Defenders of Personal Property Rights, Citizens for Constitutional Property Rights, Incorporated, January 5, 1998, insert sheet. ALSO: Henry Lamb, "The Rise of Global Governance," in the book *Global Governance: Why? How? When?,* copyright © 1996 by National Review, Incorporated, reprinted by Murchison Chair of Free Enterprise, University of Texas at Austin, 1997, page 31.
165. Holly Swanson, *Set Up & Sold Out,* CIN Publishing, Incorporated, 1995, page 285.
166. Don McAlvany, *Toward a New World Order,* 2nd edition, Western Pacific Publishing Company, 1992, page 270.
167. Quoted from *The New American,* as contained in a pamphlet titled "Why Accountability NOW!" accompanied by a letter dated August 12, 1997, by Holly Swanson. ALSO: "Is Socialism/Communism at Work in America? You Decide." *Freedom Alert,* Newsletter of the Defenders of Personal Property Rights, Citizens for Constitutional Property Rights, Incorporated, January 5, 1998, insert sheet.
168. Fred Smith, "Reappraising Humanity's Challenges, Humanity's Opportunities," *The True State of the Planet,* edited by Ronald Bailey, The Free Press, division of Simon & Schuster, 1995, page 379.
169. *Ibid.*
170. Rifkin, friend of Bill Clinton, and recognized (by the *National Journal*) as one of the 150 most influential people in the nation, has close ties to the "Church of Euthanasia," the "Four Pillars" of which are "suicide, abortion, cannibalism, and sodomy." Some congregation! The church's reverend Chris Korda asserts: "We are for real. It's as simple as that." The church's new slogan: "Save the planet, kill yourself." "People have got to understand," says Reverend Korda, "That we really aren't too interested in whether or not the human species survives. That's the bottom line." All this is described in the *DeWeese Report,* Tom DeWeese, editor in chief, December 1997, pages 1, 2.

171. Information provided through the courtesy of *The American Sentinel,* in response to a request for information. The website address is: www.gci.ch/greencrossprograms/earthcharter/earth.html
172. *Ibid.* The website address is: www.gci.ch/greencrossprogram/earthcharter/earthcharterphilosophy.html
173. *Who's Who in America - 1996,* Reed Reference Publishing Company (now a Reed Elsevies Company), page 126.
174. ALSO: *America's Judgements, What Lies Ahead,* documentation supporting the Militia of Montana video, page 50.
175. Phyllis Schlafly, "UN Conferences Promote Feminist Agenda," *Phyllis Schlafly Report,* October 1997, page 2.
176. Cliff Kincaid, *Global Taxes for World Government,* Huntington House Publishers, 1997, page 103.
177. *The International Who's Who - 1990-91,* Europa Publications Limited, Reed Reference Publishing Company, page 1533.
178. ALSO: *Environmental Overkill,* by Dixy Lee Ray with Lou Guzzo, Regnery Publishing, Incorporated, 1993, page 11. ALSO: *The McAlvany Intelligence Advisor,* Donald McAlvany, editor, October 1997, pages 1, 21. ALSO: Tom DeWeese, "Radical Greens Use Churches to Force Senate Support of UN's Global Warming Treaty," *Insider's Report,* October 1998, page 1.
179. Definition of Sustainable Development, The World Commission on Environment and Development (The Brundtland Commission), *Our Common Future* (Oxford: Oxford University Press, 1987), page 43, as quoted in *Sustainable America - A New Consensus,* The President's Council on Sustainable Development, U.S. Government Printing Office, February 1996, page iv.
180. Floy Lilley, J.D. in *ēco•logic,* as quoted in *Media Bypass* magazine, June 1996, page 57.
181. David A. Russell, *Special Report - Who Is Leading the Attack on American Liberty?,* Citizens for Constitutional Property Rights, Incorporated, 1996, page 4.
182. Ronald Bailey, "Who Is Maurice Strong?" *National Review,* September 1, 1997, page 33.
183. Phyllis Schlafly, "Will America Be Caught in Clinton's 'Web'?" *The Phyllis Schlafly Report,* April 1998, page 1.
184. Michael S. Coffman, "Sold Down the River," *The New American,* January 5, 1998, page 14.
185. David A. Russell, president, Citizens for Constitutional Property Rights, "Sustainable Development: A Wolf in Sheep's Clothing," insert, *Freedom Alert,* November/December 1997, page 8
186. Peter LaBarbera, *Clinton's Crazies,* Eagle Publishing, Incorporated, 1994, page 16.
187. *Who's Who in America - 1996,* Reed Reference Publishing Company (now a Reed Elsevies Company), page 3495.
188. ALSO: "Bill Clinton's Goals 2000," *Media Bypass* magazine, February 1997, page 22. ALSO: *Set Up and Sold Out,* by Holly Swanson, CIN Publishing, Incorporated, 1995, page 131, which contains a somewhat modified version of Pierce's statement gleaned from *Educating for the New World Order.* ALSO: *Bill Clinton: Friend or Foe?* by Ann Wilson, J.W. Publishing Company, 1994, page 174.
189. Benton is quoted in the article "The Rise of Global Governance," by Henry Lamb, in the book *Global Governance: Why? How? When?,* copyright © 1996 by National Review, Incorporated, reprinted by Murchison Chair of Free Enterprise, University of Texas at Austin, 1997, page 9. He said: "As long as the child breathes the poisoned air of nationalism, education in world-mindedness can produce only precarious results. As we

have pointed out, it is frequently the family that infects the child with extreme nationalism. The school should therefore use the means described earlier to combat family attitudes that favor jingoism . . . . We shall presently recognize in nationalism the major obstacle to development of world-mindedness . . . ."

190. William Norman Grigg, "Service or Slavery?," *The New American,* July 21, 1997, page 46.

191. Maxine Shideler, "Mandatory National Service Is a Tool to Indoctrinate Youth into Socialism," *Colorado Christian News,* October 1994, page 15, as quoted in *Brave New Schools,* by Berit Kjos, Harvest House Publishers, 1995, page 149. Holly Swanson, in her book *Set Up and Sold Out* (CIN Publishing, Incorporated, 1995, page 132), identifies the source of Hitler's comment: *The Rise and Fall of the Third Reich.* ALSO: Henry Lamb, "The Rise of Global Governance," in the book *Global Governance: Why? How? When?,* copyright © 1996 by National Review, Incorporated, reprinted by Murchison Chair of Free Enterprise, University of Texas at Austin, 1997, pages 182-193.

192. *Dispatches,* News Publication of the Western Journalism Center, October 7, 1997, page 3.

193. Amy Fagan, "Group: Kinsey Report an Ill-Conceived Fraud," *The Washington Times,* National Weekly Edition, October 19, 1997, page 10. For additional information see the article by Col. Ronald D. Ray, USMC (Ret.), entitled "Kinsey's Legal Legacy," *The New American,* January 19, 1998, page 31.

194. *AIM Report,* Reed Irvine, editor, Accuracy In Media, Incorporated, December-A 1997, page 4.

195. *Ibid.*

196. *The New American,* June 9, 1997, page 24.

197. "Insider Report," *The New American,* November 24, 1997, page 10.

198. Judith Schumann Weizner, "Student Faces Graduation Ban," *Heterodoxy,* June 1997, page 20.

199. *Ibid.*

200. Berit Kjos, *Brave New Schools,* Harvest House Publishers, 1995, page 283.

201. Lori Aratani, "Out of the Classroom, into the Community," 1994, as quoted in *Brave New Schools,* by Berit Kjos, Harvest House Publishers, 1995, page 141.

202. Berit Kjos, *Brave New Schools,* Harvest House Publishers, 1995, page 50.

203. Phyllis Schlafly, *The Dangers of the School-to-Work Movement,* a presentation she gave at the 1997 Conservative Leadership Conference, Sheraton Hotel, Washington, D.C., November 22, 1997.

204. *Media Bypass* staff, "Ejukashun Nashun - Developments of Late on the Sorry State of America's Classrooms," *Media Bypass* magazine, September 1997, page 39. ALSO: Dr. Paul Clark, "Government Schools Endanger Children's Health," *Media Bypass* magazine, October 1998, page 12.

205. "Outcome-Based Education: The New Assault on Children," a pamphlet produced by The Foundation Endowment, Alexandria, Virginia, distributed in 1998.

206. "Turning Technology Against Children," *The DeWeese Report,* Tom DeWeese, editor, January 1998, page 2.

207. Don McAlvany, "Education Briefs," *The McAlvany Intelligence Advisor,* February 1998, page 22.

208. Rush Limbaugh, "What's Wrong with American Schools?" *The Limbaugh Letter,* March 1997, pages 3, 4.

209. Tom DeWeese, "Why Is Public Education Failing?" *The DeWeese Report,* February 1997, page 7.

210. As quoted in the article "The Rise of Global Governance," by Henry Lamb, in the book *Global Governance: Why? How? When?,* copyright © 1996 by National Review, Incorporated, reprinted by Murchison Chair of Free Enterprise, University of Texas at Austin, 1997, page 9.
211. Phyllis Schlafly, *The Phyllis Schlafly Report,* November 1997, page 4.
212. *Ibid.*
213. According to Jack Thompson in *The Truth about Janet Reno,* a video of his talk, sponsored by the American Forum, given April 14, 1997 at the Biltmore Hotel, Coral Gables, Florida. (Thompson ran for Dade County, Florida state attorney in 1988 but lost to Janet Reno.)
214. *Freedom Alert,* newsletter of Citizens for Constitutional Rights, Incorporated, David A. Russell, publisher, June 1998, page 2.
215. Holly Swanson, *Set Up and Sold Out,* CIN Publishing, Incorporated, 1995, page 39.
216. Although the source of this quotation attributes it to Thomas Jefferson, an expert on Jefferson's writings, Eyler Robert Coates, Sr., suspects it came from someone else. "While the idea expressed does sound 'Jeffersonian'," says Coates in an e-mail note, "the style is not Jefferson's, in my opinion. My experience with Jefferson's writings suggests that he was not given to making aphorisms with 'cute' contrasting sections as contained here. That was more Benjamin Franklin's 'Poor Richard' style."
217. *Federalist Papers.*
218. As quoted in *Toward a New World Order,* 2nd edition, by Don McAlvany, Western Pacific Publishing Company, 1992, page 43.
219. See endnote 213.
220. ALSO: *Media Bypass* magazine, March 1997, page 13.
221. *Who's Who in America - 1996,* Reed Reference Publishing Company (now a Reed Elsevies Company), page 2006.
222. "Gun Report," *The New American,* June 9, 1997, page 37.
223. "Gun Statistics: 1.9 Million Reasons to Bear Arms," by Morgan O. Reynolds and H. Sterling Burneff, *Midnight Messenger,* March/April 1998, page 3, quoting a study by John Lott and David Mustard of the University of Chicago, as published in the *Journal of Legal Studies.*
224. See endnote 221.
225. Don McAlvany, *Toward a New World Order,* 2nd edition, Western Pacific Publishing Company, 1992, page 59.
226. As quoted in *The American Sentinel,* March 1998, page 11. A comment indicates this quotation appeared in the January 1994 edition of *The National Educator,* on page 3, but an effort is under way to contact "a former editor of the now-defunct publication for stronger confirmation and more specific details surrounding the statement, purportedly made to former Senator Howard Metzenbaum of Ohio."
227. ALSO: *Global Taxes for World Government,* by Cliff Kincaid, Huntington House Publishers, 1997, page 72. ALSO: *The McAlvany Intelligence Advisor,* Don McAlvany, editor, October 1997, pages 5, 6.
228. ALSO: *Bill Clinton: Friend or Foe?* by Ann Wilson, J.W. Publishing Company, 1993, 1994, page 173. ALSO: *Operation Vampire Killer 2000,* revised 1996, published by Police Against the New World Order, page 19.
229. Who pulls the strings behind the scenes to "manage" the news? *The American Sentinel* (March 1998, page 6) answers the question: "Most of the big media organizations are part of a larger, interlocking corporation. In fact, just eight corporations control most of what you see or hear on the airwaves in the way of news in many urban areas. These

corporations control the three major television networks (CBS, NBC, ABC), own some 40 subsidiary television stations, control over 200 cable television stations and have more than 60 radio stations. Print sources are sometimes less controlled. But the trend is toward less freedom in the editorial room, not more. These same corporations have also covered this base. They control 59 magazines (including *Time* and *Newsweek*), have chains of newspapers (including *The New York Times, The Wall Street Journal, The Los Angeles Times,* and *The Washington Post*). They also control 41 book publishers and a few other major media enterprises thrown in for good measure . . . ."

230. Quotation from an ad sponsored by Accuracy in Media in the *The Washington Times,* National Weekly Edition, September 21, 1997, page 23.

231. "Bilderbergers Meet in Georgia," *The New American,* August 18, 1997, page 8.

232. ALSO: "The Rise of Global Governance," by Henry Lamb, in the book *Global Governance: Why? How? When?,* copyright © 1996 by National Review, Incorporated, reprinted by Murchison Chair of Free Enterprise, University of Texas at Austin, 1997, page 34.

233. From the *Wall Street Journal* editorial page, February 13, 1996, as quoted in the *AIM Report,* Reed Irvine, editor, Accuracy In Media, Incorporated, September 1997, page 11.

234. ALSO: Quoted in part in *ēco•logic,* November/December 1997, page 21, quoting *Forbes* Magazine, November 11, 1991, page 174.

235. "The Rise of Global Governance," by Henry Lamb, in the book *Global Governance: Why? How? When?,* copyright © 1996 by National Review, Incorporated, reprinted by Murchison Chair of Free Enterprise, University of Texas at Austin, 1997, page 34.

236. Ann Wilson, *Bill Clinton: Friend or Foe?* J.W. Publishing Company, 1994, page 173. ALSO: *Operation Vampire Killer 2000,* revised 1996, published by Police Against the New World Order, page 19.

237. *Ibid,* both sources.

238. *Ibid,* both sources.

239. *Who's Who in America - 1996,* Reed Reference Publishing Company (now a Reed Elsevies Company), page 459.

240. *Ibid,* page 4051.

241. ALSO: *Trashing the Planet,* by Dixy Lee Ray with Lou Guzzo, Regnery Gateway, 1990, page 76.

242. Reed Irvine, Joseph C. Goulden, and Cliff Kincaid, *The News Manipulators,* Book Distributors, Incorporated, 1993, page 300.

243. *Ibid,* page 303.

244. As quoted in the *ASAP Report,* The Newsletter of the American Sovereignty Action Project, Cliff Kincaid, editor, March 1998, page 4.

245. As quoted in *The Great Quotations,* compiled by George Seldes, The Citadel Press, 1983, page 367.

246. Dr. Gene Schroder, *Constitution: Fact or Fiction,* Buffalo Creek Press, 1995, page 2.

247. Donald McAlvany, *The McAlvany Intelligence Advisor,* April 1998, page 5. According to David Wegener's *Facts, Truth, Evidence that Will Affect All Americans* (support material for his video *Barbed Wire on America*), Executive Orders are poised to radically alter life in the good old USA. Executive Order #10995 lets the government seize all communications media in the country. EO #10997 lets the government seize all electric power, fuels, and minerals. EO #10998 lets the government seize all food supplies, all farms, and all farm equipment. EO #10999 lets the government seize the American population itself for a work force. EO #11000 allows the government to seize all health, education, and welfare facilities. EO #11003 lets the government seize all airports and

aircraft. EO #11004 lets the government seize all housing and finance authorities and force relocation. Can someone tell me why all these Executive Orders are necessary? How will they be used? Perhaps more importantly, when?

248. James "Bo" Gritz, *Called to Serve,* Lazarus Publishing Company, 1991, page 605.
249. CEOs of 100 American corporations were asked to "establish a regular practice at every annual shareholders meeting whereby you and the board of directors stand and, in the name of your domestically chartered corporation, 'pledge allegiance to the flag and to the Republic for which it stands.'" Kodak said no because the corporation "needs to maintain a global perspective to compete effectively in a global economy," and because it "would not be productive." Allstate said no because the pledge would be "inappropriate at a business meeting." Ford said no because "We do not believe that the concept of 'corporate allegiance' is possible.'" ("Super Patriot Ralph Nader," *The New American,* August 31, 1998, page 8.)
250. Holly Swanson, *Set Up and Sold Out,* CIN Publishing, Incorporated, 1995, pages 140, 141.
251. Berit Kjos, *Brave New Schools,* Harvest House Publishers, 1995, page 105.
252. Peter LaBarbera, *Clinton's Crazies,* Eagle Publishing, Incorporated, 1994, page 11.
253. "How the EPA Outflanks the GOP Congress," *The American Sentinel,* Lee Bellinger, editor, Issue #608, November 1997, page 3.
254. ALSO: *This Land Is Our Land,* by Richard Pombo and Joseph Farah, St. Martin's Press, 1996, page 78. ALSO: "Rewilding America," *ēco•logic,* November/December 1995, pages 22-23.
255. Dixy Lee Ray with Lou Guzzo, *Environmental Overkill,* Regnery Publishing, Incorporated, copyright © 1993 by Regnery Publishing, page 131. All rights reserved. Reprinted by special permission of Regnery Publishing, Incorporated.
256. Richard Pombo, Joseph Farah, *This Land Is Our Land,* St. Martin's Press, 1996, page 1.
257. *Ibid,* page vii.
258. *Who's Who in America - 1996,* Reed Reference Publishing Company (now a Reed Elsevies Company), page 1673.
259. *Ibid,* page 2037.
260. Wesley Pruden, "Anybody Looking for a Promise Breaker?" *The Washington Times,* National Weekly Edition, October 19, 1997, page 4.
261. *Cambridge Paperback Encyclopedia,* Cambridge University Press, 1995, page 536.
262. ALSO: "The Pagan Roots of Environmentalism," by Tom DeWeese, included in *Special Report, Who Is Leading the Attack on American Liberty?*, by David A. Russell, president, Citizens for Constitutional Property Rights, Incorporated, 1996, page 87. ALSO: Accountability Now flyer, undated.
263. Holly Swanson, *Set Up & Sold Out,* CIN Publishing, Incorporated, 1995, page 86. ALSO: "Is Socialism/Communism at Work in America? You Decide." *Freedom Alert,* Newsletter of the Defenders of Personal Property Rights, Citizens for Constitutional Property Rights, Incorporated, January 5, 1998, insert sheet.
264. F. A. Hayek, *The Road to Serfdom* (50th anniversary edition), The University of Chicago Press, 1994, page 115.
265. Brad Miner, *The Concise Conservative Encyclopedia,* Free Press Paperbooks, division of Simon & Schuster, Incorporated, 1996, page 196.
266. Nancie G. Marzulla, Esq., "The Magic of Property Rights," *NWI Resource,* Spring 1995, page 2.

267. Henry Lamb, in comments before the U.S. House of Representatives Committee on Resources, June 10, 1997, regarding the American Land Sovereignty Protection Act (HR901), as published in "Protecting American Land," *ĕco•logic,* May/June 1997, page 6.
268. *Ibid.*
269. Richard Pombo and Joseph Farah, *This Land Is Our Land,* St. Martin's Press, 1996, page 154.
270. *Ibid,* pages 5, 6.
271. *Ibid,* page 19.
272. Donald McAlvany, *The McAlvany Intelligence Advisor,* April 1998, page 10. See also Phyllis Schlafly's "Will America Be Caught in Clinton's 'Web'?," *The Phyllis Schlafly Report,* April 1998, page 4, in which she writes: "Clinton's Rivers Initiative would restrict the property rights of private property owners living along the banks of the [designated] rivers [and] would put hundreds of thousands of acres of land under the control of federal regulators with authority over the 'characteristics of the natural, economic, agricultural, scenic, historic, cultural, or recreational resources of a river.'" Says David Russell in his article "Sustainable Development: A Wolf in Sheep's Clothing" (*Freedom Alert,* Citizens for Constitutional Property Rights, Incorporated, November/December 1997, insert, page 8) "The American Heritage Rivers program is the final nail needed to seal the coffin on private property. Through this initiative, the government will be able to take control of all land use in America."
273. William Norman Grigg, "Celebrating the Hate," *The New American,* May 11, 1998, page 36.
274. ALSO: John F. McManus, "Remembering Barry Goldwater," *The New American,* July 6, 1998, page 52.
275. This statement was made by Ronald Reagan while campaigning for governor of California in 1965, as quoted in *The CSE Sentinel,* published by Citizens for a Sound Economy, January-February 1998, page 8.
276. *Media Bypass* staff, "Brock Turns Tables on TrooperGate Story," *Media Bypass* magazine, April 1998, page 60.
277. Albert Gore, *Earth in the Balance,* Houghton Mifflin, 1992.
278. ALSO: "Strangling Heterosexuality in the Schools," Insider Report, *The New American,* November 11, 1996, page 11. ALSO: "Sidelights," *The American Enterprise,* September/October 1996, page 8.
279. *The Homosexual Agenda: How the Gay Lobby Is Targeting America's Children,* compiled and written by the staff of Americans For Truth About Homosexuality, division of the Christian Defense Fund, Washington, D.C., 1997, page 57.
280. *Ibid,* page 43.
281. Don McAlvany, *Toward a New World Order,* 2nd edition, Western Pacific Publishing Company, 1992, page 16. It's not just the public schools that are celebrating and promoting the homosexual agenda. Phyllis Schlafly describes some courses presently offered in major U.S. universities: Dartmouth - "Queer Theory, Queer Texts." Yale - "Queer Histories." Cornell - "Gay Fiction." Brown - "Unnatural Acts: Introduction to Lesbian and Gay Literature." University of Michigan - "Crossing Erotic Boundaries." (*The Phyllis Schlafly Report,* November 1998, page 3.)
282. *Ibid,* pages 16, 17.
283. As described in a solicitation letter dated September 19, 1997 from Sharon Earls distributed by the Southeastern Legal Foundation, Merrifield, Virginia.

284. As described in an August 1997 solicitation letter from the Rutherford Institute, Charlottesville, Virginia.
285. Berit Kjos, "Sex Ed and Global Values," *Media Bypass* magazine, August 1997, page 24.
286. The Montpelier High School story was made available through the efforts of "Curt" Tomlin, Major, U.S. Army, who is also president of the Christian Alert Network.
287. Carol Innerst, "Some Kindergartners Are Taught about Homosexuality," *The Washington Times,* National Weekly Edition, December 7, 1997, page 23.
288. The NEA lobbying agenda for 1998, as described in *The Phyllis Schlafly Report* (August 1998, page 2), includes these items, among others: Support creation and maintenance of a national database on early childhood care and education programs. Support adding the Equal Rights Amendment to the Constitution. Support a tax-based, single-payer healthcare plan for all residents of the U.S., its territories, and Puerto Rico. Support bilingual education and affirmative action programs. Support funding for the National Endowment for the Arts. Support a national holiday honoring Cesar Chavez. Support U.S. participation in and financing of the United Nations and related bodies. Support ratification of the UN Convention on the Elimination of All forms of Discrimination Against Women. Support ratification of the UN Convention on the Rights of the Child. Support federal legislation emphasizing multicultural/multilingual education programs in public schools.
289. For a riveting, powerful presentation of the dangers of OBE, I recommend the video *OBE: Education or Social Engineering?,* copyright © 1996 by Ann Wilson, published by J.W. Publishing Company. I also strongly recommend another video, *Crisis in the Classroom - Hidden Agendas and Grassroots Opposition,* hosted by Phyllis Schlafly, copyright © 1996, produced by Eagle Forum. Both videos should be seen by every parent, teacher, and politician in America!
290. The library is located at 1350 East Sunrise Boulevard. The exhibit, shown in February 1998, presented "art" drawn by students from the Dillard School of Arts magnet program. In a letter to the editor, Carole Novielli wrote, "I was appalled by what I was forced to view hanging on the hallway walls going into the library . . . . If this is the education the City of Ft. Lauderdale and the library want to encourage for our students, it's no wonder we don't focus enough attention on reading, writing, and arithmetic."
291. Carol Innerst, "Some Kindergartners Are Taught about Homosexuality," *The Washington Times* National Weekly Edition, December 7, 1997, page 23.
292. *The Homosexual Agenda: How the Gay Lobby is Targeting America's Children,* compiled, written, and published by Americans for Truth about Homosexuality, a division of Christian Defense Fund, Washington, D.C., 1997, page 34.
293. Michael Swift, "Towards a Homoerotic Order," *Gay Community News,* November 7, 1987. This quotation was obtained through the courtesy and efforts of Concerned Women for America, Beverly LaHaye, chairperson, Washington, D.C.
294. Father James Thornton, "A Question of Morality," *The New American,* June 8, 1998, page 29.
295. *Who's Who in America - 1996,* Reed Reference Publishing Company (now a Reed Elsevies Company), page 4483.
296. Reed Irvine, *AIM Report,* Accuracy In Media, Incorporated, May-B 1997, page 3.
297. As quoted in *The home Book of American Quotations,* by Bruce Bohle, Dodd, Mead, and Company, 1967, page 182.
298. Don McAlvany, *Toward a New World Order,* 2nd edition, Western Pacific Publishing Company, 1992, page 214.

299. Gary Aldrich, *Unlimited Access,* Regnery Publishing, Incorporated, copyright © 1996 by Regnery Publishing, page 36. All rights reserved. Reprinted by special permission of Regnery Publishing, Incorporated.
300. *Ibid,* page 134.
301. Dick Morris, in a January 27, 1998 radio interview, quoting a Bill Clinton statement made in the 1980s, as reported by *Human Events,* "Quote of the Week," February 6, 1998, page 1.
302. ALSO: *Toward a New World Order,* 2nd edition, by Don McAlvany, Western Pacific Publishing Company, 1992, page 275. ALSO: *Set Up and Sold Out,* by Holly Swanson, CIN Publishing, Incorporated, 1995, page 258. ALSO: "Method Behind the Madness," by William F. Jasper, *The New American,* September 18, 1995, page 43. ALSO: *Tragedy by Design,* a video narrated by William Norman Grigg, John Birch Society, 1977. ALSO: *Bill Clinton: Friend or Foe?* by Ann Wilson, CIN Publishing, Incorporated, 1994, page vi. ALSO: "Is Socialism/Communism at Work in America? You Decide," *Freedom Alert,* Newsletter of the Defenders of Personal Property Rights, Citizens for Constitutional Property Rights, Incorporated, January 5, 1998, insert sheet.
303. Holly Swanson, *Set Up and Sold Out,* CIN Publishing, Incorporated, 1995, page 259.
304. The foundations are not alone in their aggressive support of liberal agendas. In the book *Patterns of Corporate Philanthropy* (published by Capital Research Center, 1996, pages 4-5), author Austin Fulk shows that in 1994 (the latest year analyzed), the top 250 U.S. corporations contributed $27 million to advocacy organizations. Agencies with leftist agendas received more than 75% of the money.
305. "Insider Report," *The New American,* May 25, 1998, page 8.
306. *Ibid,* page 5.
307. *Who's Who in America - 1996,* Reed Reference Publishing Company (now a Reed Elsevies Company), page 4266.
308. Devvy Kidd, *Why a Bankrupt America,* Project Liberty, 1994, page 20. ALSO: Ann Wilson, *Bill Clinton: Friend or Foe?* J.W. Publishing Company, 1994, page 170.
309. William F. Jasper, "His 'Simple Desire,'" *The New American,* February 16, 1998, page 31.
310. Quoted by William Norman Grigg from the October 30, 1993 *Washington Post* in the video *Tragedy by Design,* John Birch Society, 1997.
311. Devvy Kidd, *Why a Bankrupt America,* Project Liberty, 1994, page 20.
312. Quotation attributed to "unknown," in a posting found March 16, 1998 at the Right Now website on the Internet: www.rightnow.org.
313. Phyllis Schlafly, *The Phyllis Schlafly Report,* October 1997, page 4.
314. *Facts, Truth, Evidence that Will Affect All Americans,* support material for David Wegener's video *Barbed Wire on America*, page 31.
315. Dennis Cuddy (Raleigh, North Carolina), in a letter to the editor, *Human Events,* October 7, 1994, page 21.
316. *Facts, Truth, Evidence that Will Affect All Americans,* support material for David Wegener's video *Barbed Wire on America*, page 31, quoting from the book *Keys of This Blood,* by Malachi Martin, Simon and Schuster, 1990.
317. Shirley Correll, *Body Snatching and the New World "Odor,"* Florida Pro Family Forum, Incorporated, 1996, page 66.
318. From the *Congressional Record,* October 26, 1971, page S16764, quoted by Robert W. Lee, *The United Nations Conspiracy,* Western Islands, 1981, page 194, as quoted in *Global Tyranny . . . Step by Step,* by William F. Jasper, Western Islands, 1992, page 261.

319. For those who may think the UN acts in the interest of the U.S., take a look at the oath of office UN members pledge to uphold: "I solemnly swear to exercise in all loyalty, discretion, and conscience the functions entrusted to me as an international civil servant of the United Nations; to discharge these functions and regulate my conduct with the interest of the United Nations only in view and not to seek or accept instructions in any regard to the performance of my duties from any government or other authority external to the United Nations Organization." (As quoted by Dr. James Wardner in his April 1996 video "The Communist Infiltration of the Roman Catholic Church, 609-767-1593.) Check those words "with the interest of the United Nations *only* in view" and ask yourself, who there is looking out for the good, old U.S.A.? (The oath is also quoted in *Operation Vampire Killer 2000,* revised 1996, published by Police Against the New World Order, page 59.) For a sobering preview of life in the U.S. under expanded UN control, I recommend the video *The United Nations: A Look into the Future,* copyright © 1998 by the John Birch Society.
320. "Real Threat of United Nations Not Being Debated," *The DeWeese Report,* August 1997, page 7.
321. Written in a letter to Gideon Granger in 1800, as quoted in the "Favorite Jefferson Quotes" website (etext.lib.virginia.edu/jefferson/quotations/jeff4. htm), part 4.
322. *Who's Who in America - 1996,* Reed Reference Publishing Company (now a Reed Elsevies Company), page 2274.
323. Cliff Kincaid, *Global Bondage, The U.N. Plan to Rule the World,* Huntington House Publishers, 1995, page 7.
324. Devvy Kidd, *Why a Bankrupt America,* Project Liberty, 1994, page 20.
325. ALSO: *Global Tyranny . . . Step by Step,* by William F. Jasper, Western Islands, 1992, page 88. ALSO: *Bill Clinton: Friend or Foe?* by Ann Wilson, J.W. Publishing Company, 1994, page 171. ALSO: *Kill Zone,* by Craig Roberts, Typhoon Press, division of Christian Patriot Press, 1994, page 159. ALSO: *Facts, Truth, Evidence that Will Affect All Americans,* support material for David Wegener's video *Barbed Wire on America*, page 2.
326. Thomas W. Chittum, *Civil War Two,* American Eagle Publications, Incorporated, 1996, page 182.
327. Don McAlvany, "Meltdown in the Orient: the Asian Financial Crisis," *The McAlvany Intelligence Advisor,* December 1997, page 9.
328. Gus R. Stelzer, "It's Time to Tell the Truth about Free Trade," *Media Bypass* magazine, February 1998, page 49.
329. Devvy Kidd, *Why a Bankrupt America,* Project Liberty, 1994, page 21.
330. As quoted in *Set Up and Sold Out,* by Holly Swanson, CIN Publishing, Incorporated, 1995, page 106.
331. Cliff Kincaid, *Global Bondage, The UN Plan to Rule the World,* Huntington House Publishers, 1995, pages 23, 24.
332. Quoted by John F. McManus in "Remembering Barry Goldwater," *The New American,* July 6, 1998, page 52.
333. Dr. Stanley K. Monteith, M.D., "Population Control Agenda," *Midnight Messenger,* July-August 1997, page 8.
334. ALSO: *Environmental Overkill,* by Dixy Lee Ray with Lou Guzzo, Regnery Publishing, 1993, page 205. ALSO: *Global Tyranny . . . Step by Step,* by William F. Jasper, Western Islands, 1992, page 121. ALSO: "Scary Scenarios, Oversimplification Highlight Environmental Curricula," by Berit Kjos, *Media Bypass* magazine, June 1996, page 10.

335. Don McAlvany, *Toward a New World Order,* 2nd edition, Western Pacific Publishing Company, 1992, page 281.
336. *Dispatches,* June 3, 1997, page 8.
337. "Stupid Quotes," *The Limbaugh Letter,* June 1996, page 12.
338. Robert W. Lee, "Gun Report," *The New American,* September 15, 1997, page 42.
339. John Meredith, "The Alamo on the Bay," *The DeWeese Report,* August 1997, page 6.
340. As quoted by Gary Kah during his talk, titled "New World Order Current Events: Gorbachev/Education/Stock Market," presented at the Granada Forum (818-385-4003), September 18, 1997. For more information contact Hope for the World, PO Box 899, Noblesville, Indiana 46061-0899 (317-290-4673).
341. *Who's Who in America - 1996,* Reed Reference Publishing Company (now a Reed Elsevies Company), page 2764.
342. Ben Bolch and Harold Lyons, "Bad Chemistry," *National Review,* September 26, 1994, Page 58.
343. Paul Craig Roberts, "Commentary," *The Washington Times,* National Weekly Edition, September 5-11, 1994, page 35.
344. Pat Buchanan, "The Latest Fraud from the New Malthusians," *The Washington Times,* National Weekly Edition, October 19, 1997, page 31.
345. *Who's Who in America - 1996,* Reed Reference Publishing Company (now a Reed Elsevies Company), page 3221.
346. Tom DeWeese, "The Demented Genius of Earth First!" *Insiders Report,* June 1997, page 2.
347. *Human Events,* May 12, 1995, page 20.
348. Alan Caruba, "Spotlight on the left: Gore vs. the Automobile," *DeWeese Report,* August 1997, page 8.
349. David A. Russell, *Freedom Alert,* Citizens for Constitutional Property Rights, Incorporated, July/August 1997, page 6.
350. *Ibid.*
351. Holly Swanson, *Set Up and Sold Out,* CIN Publishing, Incorporated, 1995, page 35.
352. *Who's Who in America - 1996,* Reed Reference Publishing Company (now a Reed Elsevies Company), page 161.
353. This designation was bestowed by Jeremy Rifkin and Carol Grunewald Rifkin in their *Voting Green, Your Complete Environmental Guide to Making Political Choices in the 1990's,* as reported by Holly Swanson in her book, *Set Up and Sold Out,* CIN Publishing, Incorporated, 1995, pages 63, 64.
354. ALSO: "Explaining the Global Warming Myth so that Even Liberals Understand It," *The American Sentinel,* December 1997, page 8. ALSO: "Eco-Agenda Heating Up," by William Norman Grigg, *The New American,* December 8, 1997, page 13. ALSO: "The Rise of Global Governance," by Henry Lamb, in the book *Global Governance: Why? How? When?,* copyright © 1996 by National Review, Incorporated, reprinted by Murchison Chair of Free Enterprise, University of Texas at Austin, 1997, page 88.
355. Reed Irvine, Joseph C. Goulden, and Cliff Kincaid, *The News Manipulators,* Book Distributors, Incorporated, 1993, page 289-290.
356. Walter E. Williams, "Environmental Radicals Agenda Red, Not Green," *Human Events,* December 5, 1997, page 11.
357. As researched by Berit Kjos in her book *Brave New Schools,* Harvest House Publishers, 1995, page 120.

358. ALSO: From the website of the National Center for Policy Research: "Talking Points on the Environment," www.nationalcenter.org/tp2.html, accessed 5-23-98. ALSO: *AIM Report,* Reed Irvine, editor, Accuracy In Media, Incorporated, September-A 1996, page 1. ALSO: "Scary Scenarios, Oversimplification Highlight Environmental Curricula," by Berit Kjos, *Media Bypass* magazine, June 1996, page 10. ALSO: *Brave New Schools,* by Berit Kjos, Harvest House Publishers, 1995, page 120. ALSO: "Hot and Cold Running Arguments," by Gary Benoit, *The New American,* December 8, 1997, page 20. ALSO: "The Rise of Global Governance," by Henry Lamb, in the book *Global Governance: Why? How? When?,* copyright © 1996 by National Review, Incorporated, reprinted by Murchison Chair of Free Enterprise, University of Texas at Austin, 1997, page 88. ALSO: "Al Gore's Greatest Hoax," by Rush Limbaugh, *Limbaugh Letter,* December 1997, page 14.
359. William Norman Grigg, "Eco-Agenda Heating Up," *The New American,* December 8, 1997, page 13.
360. Dixy Lee Ray with Lou Guzzo, *Environmental Overkill,* Regnery Publishing, Incorporated, copyright © 1993 by Regnery Publishing, page 205. All rights reserved. Reprinted by special permission of Regnery Publishing, Incorporated.
361. *The ASAP Report,* The Newsletter of the American Sovereignty Action Project, Cliff Kincaid, editor, July 1997, page 1.
362. *Ibid,* page 8.
363. From an article in *Fortune,* July 7, 1987, as presented by Cliff Kincaid in a talk at the Lake Worth (Florida) Holiday Inn, October 23, 1997.
364. Cliff Kincaid, *Al Gore, the United Nations, and the Cult of Gaia,* a report published by the American Sovereignty Action Project, Fairfax, Virginia 1997, page 12.
365. ALSO: *Global Taxes for World Government,* by Cliff Kincaid, Huntington House Publishers, 1997, page 105. ALSO: *Toward a New World Order,* 2nd edition, by Don McAlvany, Western Pacific Publishing Company, 1992, page 326. ALSO: "One Man's Demented Vision Becomes a Nation's Nightmare," by Karen Anderson, *The DeWeese Report,* December 1997, page 3. ALSO: "The Green Genocide Agenda - Saving the Earth by killing humans," by Alan Caruba, *The DeWeese Report,* September 1998, page 2.
366. *Global Biodiversity Assessment,* Article 25(2)(a), quoted in *ēco•logic,* November/December 1996, page 21.
367. As quoted by Robert H. Goldsborough in his article, "Gore, Gorbachev, and GAIA," *Midnight Messenger,* March/April 1998, page 1.
368. ALSO: *Environmental Overkill,* by Dixy Lee Ray with Lou Guzzo, Regnery Publishing, Incorporated, 1993, page 204.
369. "The Earth Charter," *ēco•logic,* May/June 1997, page 11. ALSO: Henry Lamb, "Earth Charter: Analysis and Comment, *ēco•logic,* May/June 1997, pages 12-13.
370. *ēco•logic* staff, "Global Governance Marches Forward," *ēco•logic,* September/October 1997, pages 23-26.
371. *ēco•logic* staff, "Wildlands Project Update," *ēco•logic,* September/October 1997, pages 5-9.
372. *ēco•logic* staff, "The American Heritage Rivers Initiative," *ēco•logic,* May/June 1997, page 18. In an article titled "Clinton's 'River Initiative' Is Illegal," published in *Insider's Report* (May, 1998, page 1), Tom DeWeese states: "The American Heritage Rivers Initiative represents one of the greatest federal land grabs of all time. It is a bold move to literally impose federal zoning and federal control over local development and the use of private property."

373. *ēco•logic* staff, "The La Paz Agreement - Border Region XXI," *ēco•logic,* May/June 1997, pages 19-23. ALSO: Henry Lamb, "The Border XXI Program," *ēco•logic,* September/October 1997, pages 12-17.
374. *ēco•logic* staff, "PCSD Update" (President's Council on Sustainable Development), *ēco•logic,* September/October 1997, pages 19-22.
375. *Environmental Overkill,* by Dixy Lee Ray with Lou Guzzo, Regnery Publishing, Incorporated, 1993, page 204.
376. ALSO: "Globalized Grizzlies," by Michael S. Coffman, *The New American,* August 18, 1997, page 12. ALSO: *The McAlvany Intelligence Advisor,* Don McAlvany, editor, October 1997, page 12.
377. Richard Pombo and Joseph Farah, *This Land Is Our Land,* St. Martin's Press, 1996, page 99.
378. "Congressional Opposition to UN Land Grab Grows as Sovereignty Protection Act is Reintroduced," *Insiders Report,* March 1997, page 1.
379. ALSO: (quotation 2): Richard Pombo and Joseph Farah, *This Land Is Our Land,* St. Martin's Press, 1996, page 97.
380. Dixy Lee Ray with Lou Guzzo, *Trashing the Planet,* Regnery Gateway, copyright © 1990 by Regnery Publishing, page 168. All rights reserved. Reprinted by special permission of Regnery Publishing, Incorporated. ALSO: Holly Swanson, *Set Up and Sold Out,* CIN Publishing, Incorporated, 1995, page 171.
381. As quoted in an undated brochure titled "Accountability Now!", by Holly Swanson, Medford Oregon. ALSO: "Is Socialism/Communism at Work in America? You Decide." *Freedom Alert,* Newsletter of the Defenders of Personal Property Rights, Citizens for Constitutional Property Rights, Incorporated, January 5, 1998, insert sheet, page 1.
382. Dr. Walter E. Williams, professor of economics, George Mason University, as quoted on the book cover of *This Land is Our Land,* by Richard Pombo and Joseph Farah, St. Martin's Press, 1996.
383. ALSO: *The McAlvany Intelligence Advisor,* Don McAlvany, editor, October 1997, page 12. ALSO: *Special Report - Who Is Leading the Attack on American Liberty?*, by David A. Russell, president, Citizens for Constitutional Property Rights, Incorporated, 1996, page 5.
384. Cliff Kincaid, *Global Taxes for World Government,* Huntington House Publishers, 1997, page 103.
385. Dixy Lee Ray with Lou Guzzo, *Environmental Overkill,* Regnery Publishing, Incorporated, copyright © 1993 by Regnery Publishing, page 203. All rights reserved. Reprinted by special permission of Regnery Publishing, Incorporated.
386. As quoted in *Environmental Overkill,* by Dixy Lee Ray with Lou Guzzo, Regnery Publishing, Incorporated, 1993, page 203.
387. Dixy Lee Ray with Lou Guzzo, *Environmental Overkill,* Regnery Publishing, Incorporated, 1993, page 245.
388. *Who's Who in America - 1996,* Reed Reference Publishing Company (now a Reed Elsevies Company), page 3433.
389. *Ibid,* page 4210.
390. "Mountain Lion Kills Boy, 10," *Sun-Sentinel,* (South Florida) Broward Metro Edition, from the Associated Press, July 19, 1997, page 3A.
391. William Perry Pendley, "Colorado Cougar Kills 10-Year-Old Boy," *Human Events,* August 22, 1997, page 14.
392. Don McAlvany, *Toward a New World Order,* 2nd edition, Western Pacific Publishing Company, 1992, page 340.

393. Results of a Southern Focus Poll, Fall 1996, conducted by the University of North Carolina's Institute for Research in Social Science, co-sponsored by the *Atlanta Journal-Constitution* and the University's Center for the Study of the American South, as reported in "Opinion Pulse," edited by Karlyn Bowman, in the March/April 1998 issue of *The American Enterprise,* page 91.
394. *Cambridge Paperback Encyclopedia,* edited by David Crystal, Cambridge University Press, 1995, page 696.
395. David A. Russell, *Special Report - Who Is Leading the Attack on American Liberty?,* Citizens for Constitutional Property Rights, Incorporated, 1996, page 41.
396. ALSO: *Set Up and Sold Out,* by Holly Swanson, CIN Publishing, Incorporated, 1995, page 229. ALSO: *The McAlvany Intelligence Advisor,* Don McAlvany, editor, November 1997, page 7. ALSO: the October 1997 issue, pages 6, 19.
397. Holly Swanson, *Set Up and Sold Out,* CIN Publishing, Incorporated, 1995, page 171.
398. Dixy Lee Ray with Lou Guzzo, *Trashing the Planet,* Regnery Gateway, copyright © 1990 by Regnery Publishing, page 171. All rights reserved. Reprinted by special permission of Regnery Publishing, Incorporated.
399. *Who's Who in America - 1996,* Reed Reference Publishing Company (now a Reed Elsevies Company), page 485.
400. Cliff Kincaid, "Cronkite Endorses World Government," *ASAP Report,* September 1997, page 5.
401. ALSO: "The Fruits of Eco-Extremism," by Robert W. Lee, *The New American,* February 17, 1997, page 8. ALSO: "The Rise of Global Governance," by Henry Lamb, in the book *Global Governance: Why? How? When?,* copyright © 1996 by National Review, Incorporated, reprinted by Murchison Chair of Free Enterprise, University of Texas at Austin, 1997, page 95. ALSO:"The Green Agenda - Saving the Earth by killing Humans," by Alan Caruba, *The DeWeese Report,* September 1998, page 1.
402. See *Environmental Overkill,* by Dixy Lee Ray with Lou Guzzo, Regnery Publishing, Incorporated, 1993, pages 28-30, 32-38, 40, 45-49, 50-51, 189-191. See also the following articles referenced in the book: "The Ozone Scare," *Insight Magazine,* April 6, 1992, and "The Hole Story -- The Science Behind the Scare," *Reason,* June 1992.
403. "The President and the Media, Etc.," editorial, *The Washington Times,* National Weekly Edition, September 5-11, 1994, page 36.
404. Robert W. Lee, "The Fruits of Eco-Extremism," *The New American,* February 17, 1997, page 8.
405. Ronald Bailer, editor, *The True State of the Planet,* The Free Press, division of Simon & Schuster, 1995, page 95.
406. You may have heard President Clinton cite 1000 scientists who agree with his administration's stand that global warming is real. All 1000 are members of the Union of Concerned Scientists, an advocacy group organized to prevent use of nuclear energy. You may not have heard that 83% of more than 18,000 independent scientists who responded to a poll conducted by the Oregon Institute for Science and Medicine believe there's *no* convincing evidence of global warming. ("Let's Be Sure . . .," commentary, *ĕco•logic,* July/August 1998, age 20.) The article states: "Clinton proposed an additional $6 billion program to fight global warming while insisting that the science not be debated. Why not debate the science? The answer is easy: the more science learns, the clearer it becomes that human activity has little or nothing to do with climate change."
407. From a speech at the UN Earth Summit, reported by the AP, as quoted in *The Limbaugh Letter,* August 1997, page 13.

408. Walter E. Williams, "Environmental Radicals Agenda Red, Not Green," *Human Events,* December 5, 1997, page 11. ALSO: Sterling Burnett and Merrill Mathews, Jr., "Mr. Gore, Carbon Dioxide is Not a Pollutant," *Human Events,* March 6, 1998, page 22.
409. Sterling Burnett and Merrill Matthews, Jr, "Mr. Gore, Carbon Dioxide is Not a Pollutant," *Human Events,* March 6, 1998, page 22.
410. "Science or Superstition?" *Voices of the Florida Taxpayer,* George and Philip Blumel, editors, Winter 1998, page 8.
411. "The Rise of Global Governance," by Henry Lamb, in the book *Global Governance: Why? How? When?,* copyright © 1996 by National Review, Incorporated, reprinted by Murchison Chair of Free Enterprise, University of Texas at Austin, 1997, page 88.
412. Tom DeWeese, "Double Speak, Non-Speak and Lies . . . Government Scientists and the 'Non' News Conference," *Insider's Report,* February 1998, page 4.
413. Dr. Arthur B. Robinson, "Laying Out the Evidence," *The New American,* December 8, 1997, page 25.
414. Patrice Hill, "EPA Is Not Waiting for Senate to OK Global-Warming Treaty," *The Washington Times,* National Weekly Edition, March 22, 1998, page 1.
415. According to the National Center for Public Policy Research, "Four hundred and forty million years ago, atmospheric concentrations of CO_2 were up to ten times current levels. Yet, geologic evidence suggests that the planet was five to ten degrees Celsius cooler than today. Recent history also shows no solid connection between CO_2 levels and global warming. Since 1979, emissions from burning fossil fuels have increased by 19%, yet satellite data suggest the planet's temperature has cooled slightly over that period." This information was found on the Internet at www.nationalcenter.org/kyotofactsheet.html, and was accessed May 23, 1998.
416. Sterling Burnett and Merrill Matthews, Jr., "Mr. Gore, Carbon Dioxide Is Not a Pollutant," *Human Events,* March 6, 1998, page 22.
417. Phyllis Schlafly, *The Phyllis Schlafly Report,* January 1998, page 4.
418. Richard A. Kerr, *Science Magazine,* May 16, 1997, as reported in the *AIM Report,* Reed Irvine, editor, Accuracy In Media, Incorporated, November-A 1997, page 5.
419. Dixy Lee Ray with Lou Guzzo, *Trashing the Planet,* Regnery Gateway, copyright © 1990 by Regnery Publishing, page 189. All rights reserved. Reprinted by special permission of Regnery Publishing, Incorporated.
420. Dr. Stanley K. Monteith, M.D., "Population Control Agenda," *Midnight Messenger,* July-August 1997, page 8.
421. "Global Scare Over 'Climate Change,'" *The ASAP Report,* December 1997, page 6.
422. Dr. Stanley K. Monteith, M.D., "Population Control Agenda," *Midnight Messenger,* July-August 1997, page 8.
423. Holly Swanson, *Set Up and Sold Out,* CIN Publishing, Incorporated, 1995, page 156.
424. Dixy Lee Ray with Lou Guzzo, *Environmental Overkill,* Regnery Publishing, Incorporated, 1993, page 87.
425. Alan Caruba, "The Shame of Science Reporting in America," *Insider's Report,* February 1998, page 3.
426. As quoted in *This Land Is Our Land,* by Richard Pombo and Joseph Farah, St. Martin's Press, 1996, page 61.
427. *Ibid,* page 160.
428. Grover G. Norquest, "Defunding the Left," *The American Spectator,* September 1995, page 56.
429. *Who's Who in America - 1996,* Reed Reference Publishing Company (now a Reed Elsevies Company), page 4239.

430. Dixy Lee Ray with Lou Guzzo, *Environmental Overkill*, Regnery Publishing, Incorporated, 1993, page 80.
431. Don McAlvany, "Welcome to the New Civilization!" *Power & Money,* brochure published by the McAlvany Intelligence Advisor, Fall 1997, page 6. ALSO: Quoted in *The American Sentinel,* February 1998, page 7. ALSO: Same publication, April 1998, page 9. ALSO: "The Rise of Global Governance," by Henry Lamb, in the book *Global Governance: Why? How? When?,* copyright © 1996 by National Review, Incorporated, reprinted by Murchison Chair of Free Enterprise, University of Texas at Austin, 1997, page 49.
432. *The American Sentinel,* February 1998, page 6.
433. ALSO: "The Fruits of Eco-Extremism," *The New American,* February, 17, 1997, page 8.
434. Richard Pombo and Joseph Farah, *This Land Is Our Land,* St. Martin's Press, 1996, page 111.
435. William Norman Grigg, "Eco-Agenda Heating Up," *The New American,* December 8, 1997, page 17.
436. Henry Lamb, *Global Governance: Why? How? When?,* in a section titled "The Rise of Global Green Religion," copyright © 1996 by National Review, Incorporated, reprinted by Murchison Chair of Free Enterprise, University of Texas at Austin, 1997, pages 101-103.
437. *Ibid,* page 22.
438. Robert H. Goldborough, "Gore, Gorbachev, and GAIA," *Midnight Messenger,* March/April 1998, page 14. This quote by Father Marx was found in a June 6, 1997 issue of the Human Life International newsletter.
439. David A. Russell, president, Citizens for Constitutional Property Rights, Incorporated, "Sustainable Development: A Wolf in Sheep's Clothing," *Freedom Alert,* November/December 1997, insert, page 3.
440. Henry Lamb, *Global Governance: Why? How? When?,* in a section titled "The Rise of Global Green Religion," copyright © 1996 by National Review, Incorporated, reprinted by Murchison Chair of Free Enterprise, University of Texas at Austin, 1997, page 99.
441. *Ibid,* page 100.
442. *Operation Vampire Killer 2000,* revised 1996, published by Police Against the New World Order, page 21.
443. Henry Lamb, *Global Governance: Why? How? When?,* in a section titled "The Rise of Global Green Religion," copyright © 1996 by National Review, Incorporated, reprinted by Murchison Chair of Free Enterprise, University of Texas at Austin, 1997, page 105.
444. As quoted in *The Limbaugh Letter,* July 1996, page 7.
445. As quoted in *The Phyllis Schlafly Report,* November 1998, page 4.
446. As quoted by Robert W. Lee in "Kids, Guns, and Marilyn Manson," *The New American,* July 20, 1998, page 19.
447. As quoted in *Toward a New World Order,* 2nd edition, by Don McAlvany, Western Pacific Publishing Company, 1992, page 200.
448. George E. Lee, "Buchanan Brigades Storm Through Boston," *Human Events,* October 7, 1994, page 12.
449. As quoted by Walter E. Williams in his article "Environmental Radicals Agenda Red, Not Green," *Human Events,* December 5, 1997, page 11.
450. Father James Thornton, "Truth: Our Only Weapon," *The New American,* July 21, 1997, page 10.
451. Holly Swanson, *Set Up and Sold Out,* CIN Publishing, Incorporated, 1995, pages 99, 102.

452. As described in David A. Russell's *Freedom Alert,* Citizens for Constitutional Property Rights, Incorporated, March/April 1998, page 3.
453. As quoted in *Set Up and Sold Out,* by Holly Swanson, CIN Publishing, Incorporated, 1995, page 293.
454. James "Bo" Gritz, *Called to Serve,* Lazarus Publishing Company, 1991, page 623.
455. Joseph Farah, "The Growing Threat of Fascism," *Dispatches,* A news publication of the Western Journalism Center, July 22, 1997, page 6.
456. Richard M. Ebeling, "The Free Market and the Interventionist State," *Imprimis,* Hillsdale College, August 1997, page 5.
457. Reprinted with permission from *The Quotable Conservative,* compiled by Rod L. Evans and Irwin M. Berent, copyright © 1995, Rod L. Evans and Irwin M. Berent, published by Adams Media Corporation, page 24.
458. Richard M. Ebeling, "The Free Market and the Interventionist State," *Imprimis,* Hillsdale College, August 1997, page 5.
459. Joseph Farah, "The Growing Threat of Fascism," *Dispatches,* A News Publication of the Western Journalism Center, July 22, 1997, page 6.
460. Philip K. Howard, *The Death of Common Sense,* Random House, Incorporated, 1994, page 122.
461. James "Bo" Gritz, *Called to Serve,* Lazarus Publishing Company, 1991, pages 617-618.
462. As quoted in *The New American,* January 19, 1998, page 8.
463. As quoted in *Set Up and Sold Out,* by Holly Swanson, CIN Publishing, Incorporated, 1995, page 239.
464. *American Communications Association v. Douds* (339 U.S. 382, 442), 1950.
465. As quoted in the *Free American Newsmagazine,* September 1997, page 21.
466. James "Bo" Gritz, *Called to Serve,* Lazarus Publishing Company, 1991, page 423.
467. As quoted in *Blind Loyalty,* by Devvy Kidd, copyright 1996 by Devvy Kidd, page 43.
468. As quoted in *Media Bypass* magazine, February 1998, page 42.
469. Thanks to Henry Lamb's article "The Rise of Global Governance," in the book *Global Governance: Why? How? When?,* copyright © 1996 by National Review, Incorporated, reprinted by Murchison Chair of Free Enterprise, University of Texas at Austin, 1997, page 120.
470. Dixy Lee Ray with Lou Guzzo, *Environmental Overkill,* Regnery Publishing, Incorporated, copyright © 1993 by Regnery Publishing, page 208. All rights reserved. Reprinted by special permission of Regnery Publishing, Incorporated. ALSO: Don McAlvany, *Toward a New World Order,* 2nd edition, Western Pacific Publishing Company, 1992, page 7.
471. Don McAlvany, *Toward a New World Order,* 2nd edition, Western Pacific Publishing Company, 1992, page 109.
472. *Ibid,* page 352.
473. According to *Human Events,* January 13, 1995, page 1, the federal government consists of about 2000 departments, agencies, administrations, and other bureaucracies.
474. Paul Harvey, "A Time To Be Alive," *Imprimis,* October 1998, page 3.
475. As quoted in *Called to Serve,* by James "Bo" Gritz, Lazarus Publishing Company, 1991, page 385.
476. See endnote 216.
477. *Facts, Truth, Evidence that Will Affect All Americans* (support material for David Wegener's video *Barbed Wire on America*) presents a copy of this August 29, 1994 Army memo on page 21. The same memo is also referred to by Brenda Roberts in her article "Civilian Internment Camps Up for Review," *Free American Magazine,*

November 1997, pages 22, 23. The article was reprinted in the November 1998 issue, pages 46, 47.

478. *Ibid.*

479. David E. Rydel, "Government Admits Concentration Camp Plan," *Free American Magazine,* March 1998, page 24.

480. "Foreign Military," *Free American Magazine,* April 1998, page 52.

481. David Wegener, "Barbed Wire on America," in the video of his talk at the Prophecy Club®, 1997. ALSO: Jim Ammerman, "Imminent Military Takeover of the USA," a video tape of his presentation at the Prophecy Club®, 1996. In his video Jim Ammerman reports that in 1996 a total of three million foreign troops were stationed in the U.S., Mexico, and Canada.

482. *Ibid,* both sources.

483. *Ibid.* ALSO: The same statement appears in an article in the Midnight Messenger, July/August 1998, page 2.

484. Thomas Jefferson, *Letter to Lafayette on April 2, 1790,* as quoted in *Bartlett's Familiar Quotations,* 14th edition, by John Bartlett, Little, Brown, and Company, Incorporated, 1968, page 471.

485. Ralph Waldo Emerson, *May-Day and Other Pieces,* 1867, as quoted in *Bartlett's Familiar Quotations,* 14th edition, by John Bartlett, Little, Brown, and Company, Incorporated, 1968, page 604..

486. As quoted in *Midnight Messenger,* January/February 1998, page 2.

487. As quoted in *Bartlett's Familiar Quotations,* 14th edition, by John Bartlett, Little, Brown, and Company, Incorporated, 1968, page 901.

488. Tom DeWeese, "An Open Letter to the Republican Majority -- Why the Right Mistrusts You," *The DeWeese Report,* published by the American Policy Center, March 1998.

489. As quoted in *Set Up and Sold Out,* by Holly Swanson, CIN Publishing, Incorporated, 1995, page 93.

490. As quoted in *Called to Serve,* by James "Bo" Gritz, Lazarus Publishing Company, 1991, page 606.

491. As quoted in *Bartlett's Familiar Quotations,* 14th edition, by John Bartlett, Little, Brown, and Company, Incorporated, 1968, page 750.

492. Rush Limbaugh, "My Conservation with J.C. Watts," *The Limbaugh Letter,* November 1996, page 10.

493. Thomas W. Chittum, *Civil War II,* American Eagle Publications, Incorporated, 1996, page 144.

494. As quoted in *The New American,* March 2, 1998, page 29.

495. If indeed Oswald alone assassinated Kennedy by firing a shot to the back of the President's head, how is it JFK's brains were splattered all over the *rear* of the automobile in which he was riding? For those interested in learning more about the assassination, I recommend "The Men Who Killed Kennedy," a six-part series of television broadcasts that appears from time to time on The History Channel. A video of the broadcasts is available for purchase by calling: 800-708-1776. It is excellent. I also recommend the book *Kill Zone - A Sniper Looks at Dealey Plaza,* by Craig Roberts, Consolidated Press International, 1994.

496. If indeed Vince Foster killed himself in the park, how is it his car arrived at the park only *after* his dead body was found there? To those interested in learning more about the peculiar circumstances surrounding Mr. Foster's demise, I recommend the book *The Strange Death of Vincent Foster - An Investigation,* by Christopher Ruddy, The Free Press, a division of Simon & Schuster, Incorporated, 1997. I also recommend *The Secret*

Life of Bill Clinton - The Unreported Stories, by Ambrose Evans Pritchard, Regnery Publishing, Incorporated, an Eagle Publishing Company, 1997.

497. If indeed TWA 800 simply exploded on its own, how is it some 150 or so people saw what looked to them like "fireworks" streak up to the aircraft before it exploded and how is it all this evidence has been ignored by the federal investigators? To those interested in learning more about this tragedy I recommend the book *The Downing of TWA Flight 800,* by James D. Sanders, Zebra Books, Kensington Publishing Corporation, 1997. Note also the article, "Black Box Exposes TWA 800 Coverup," by Reed Irvine, in the January-A 1998 issue of the *AIM Report,* Accuracy In Media, Incorporated. Note also the July-B 1998 issue of the *AIM Report.* Note also Chapter 29 in the book *The Medusa File - Secret Crimes and Coverups of the U.S. Government,* by Craig Roberts, Consolidated Press International, 1997.

498. If indeed McVeigh, alone or with Nichols, brought down the building with a single "truck bomb," how is it that bomb experts agree the damage caused to the Murrah Building could not possibly have resulted from a single explosion? To those interested in more information on the subject, I recommend *The Secret Life of Bill Clinton - The Unreported Stories,* by Ambrose Evans Pritchard, Regnery Publishing, Incorporated, an Eagle Publishing Company, 1997. I also recommend *A Sniper's View of Dumitru's Warning,* a video of a talk by Craig Roberts at the Prophecy Club®. Roberts discusses the Murrah Building bombing (he assisted the FBI during the investigation) and he also sheds new light on the government's involvement in the New York City World Trade Center bombing, the TWA 800 explosion, the Amtrack derailment, and more.

499. If indeed the Branch Davidians were not fired upon, how is it surveillance evidence on video tape shows that countless shots were fired into the Branch Davidians' buildings? To those interested in more information on the subject, I recommend *Waco - The Rules of Engagement,* a video of a William Gazecki Film, Somford Production, 1997.

500. Joseph C. Goulden, "A Frightening Waco Documentary," *AIM Report,* Accuracy In Media, Incorporated, January-B 1998, page 4.

501. If indeed the UN is acting in our interests, how is it the UN is able to take action that directly violates the U.S. Constitution? To those interested in more information on the subject, I recommend *Global Governance - The Quiet War Against American Independence,* a video hosted by Phyllis Schlafly, Eagle Forum, 1997.

502. As reported by the *New York Times,* 1955. Quoted in *Set Up and Sold Out,* by Holly Swanson, CIN Publishing, Incorporated, 1995, page 150.

503. As reported by the *Washington Post,* 1957. Quoted in *Set Up and Sold Out,* by Holly Swanson, CIN Publishing, Incorporated, 1995 page 149.

504. Holly Swanson, *Set Up and Sold Out,* CIN Publishing, Incorporated, 1995, page 196.

505. As quoted in David Wegener's video, *Barbed Wire on America,* distributed by The Prophecy Club®, 1997.

506. As quoted in *Citizens Intelligence Digest,* newsletter of Citizens for Honest Government, every issue (in the masthead), page 1.

507. As quoted from *Of Men and Not of Law: How the Courts Are Usurping the Political Function,* by Lyman A. Garber, Devin-Adair, 1966, page 170, quoted in *Global Tyranny . . . Step by Step,* by William F. Jasper, Western Islands, 1992, page 268.

508. As quoted by Rush Limbaugh in "My Conversation with Dana Rohrabacher," *Limbaugh Letter,* June 1998, page 10.

SELECTED BIBLIOGRAPHY

The high office of the President has been used to foment a plot to destroy America's freedom and before I leave office, I must inform the citizens of their plight.

- President John F. Kennedy
At Columbia University, 1963, ten days prior to his assassination, as quoted in *Set Up and Sold Out,* by Holly Swanson, CIN Publishing, Incorporated, 1995, page 280

We are not going to achieve a new world order without paying for it in blood as well as in words and money.

- Arthur Schlesinger, Jr.
In the July/August 1995 issue of *Foreign Affairs,* as quoted in "Beasts in Blue Berets," by William Norman Grigg, *The New American,* September 29, 1997, page 16

Books

Al Gore, the United Nations, and the Cult of Gaia, by Cliff Kincaid, American Sovereignty Action Project, 11094-D Lee Highway, Suite 200, Fairfax, Virginia 22030. Copyright © 1997. PHONE: 703-352-4788. FAX: 301-855-3732. E-MAIL: antiun@earthlink.net WEBSITE: www.usasurvival.org

Are You a Conservative or a Liberal? by Bradley O'Leary (conservative) and Victor Kamber (liberal), Boru Publishing, Incorporated, 11212 Ladera Drive, Austin, Texas 78759. Copyright © 1996. PHONE: 202-944-4855. FAX: 202-944-4560.

Bill Clinton: Friend or Foe? by Ann Wilson, J.W. Publishing Company, PO Box 455, St. Clair, Missouri 63077. Copyright © 1993, 1994. PHONE: 314-629-1196. E-MAIL: jwpubl@fidnet.com

Blind Loyalty, by Devvy Kidd, 14253 West Baltic Avenue, Lakewood, Colorado 80228. Copyright © 1996 by Devvy Kidd.

Body Snatching and the New World "Odor" by Shirley Correll, Florida Pro Family Forum, Incorporated, PO Box 1059, Highland City, Florida 33846-1059. Copyright © 1996.

Brave New Schools, by Berit Kjos, Harvest House Publishers, Eugene, Oregon 97402. Copyright © 1995.

Called to Serve, by James "Bo" Gritz, Lazarus Publishing Company, Box 472 HCR-31, Sandy Valley, Nevada 89019. Copyright © 1991.

The Cambridge Paperback Encyclopedia, edited by David Crystal, The Press Syndicate of the University of Cambridge, 40 West 20th Street, New York, New York 10011-4211. Copyright © 1995. PHONE: 212-924-3900. FAX: 212-691-3239.

Civil War Two, by Thomas W. Chittum, American Eagle Publications, Incorporated, PO Box 1507, Show Low, Arizona 85902. Copyright © 1996. PHONE: 800-719-4957. FAX: 520-367-1621. WEBSITE: www.logoplex.com/resources/ameagle

Clinton's Crazies - The Loony Left is Alive and Well in the Clinton Administration, by Peter LaBarbera, Eagle Publishing, Incorporated, A Phillips Publishing International Company, 422 First Street, S.E., Suite 400, Washington, D.C. 20003. Copyright © 1994.

The Concise Conservative Encyclopedia, by Brad Miner, Free Press Paperbooks, a division of Simon & Schuster, Incorporated, 1230 Avenue of the Americas, New York, New York 10020. Copyright © 1996.

Constitution: Fact or Fiction, by Dr. Eugene Schroder with Micki Nellis, Buffalo Creek Press, 603 North Main Street, Cleburne, Texas 76031. Copyright © 1995. (For information on efforts to restore the Constitution, write: American Agriculture Movement, Box 130, Campo, Colorado 81029. Or call: 719-787-9958.) PHONE: 800-610-4908 or 817-641-4909. FAX: 817-641-0901. E-MAIL sales@buffalo-creek-press.com. WEBSITE: http://buffalo-creek-press.com.

The Death of Common Sense, by Philip K. Howard, Random House, Incorporated, 201 East 50th Street, New York, New York 10022. Copyright © 1994. PHONE: 212-751-2600.

The Disuniting of America - Reflections on a Multicultural Society, by Arthur M. Schlesinger, Jr., W.W. Norton & Company, Incorporated, 500 Fifth Avenue, New York, New York 10110. Copyright © 1991.

The Downing of TWA Flight 800, by James D. Sanders, Zebra Books, Kensington Publishing Corporation, 850 Third Avenue, New York, New York 10022. Copyright © 1997.

Environmental Overkill, by Dixy Lee Ray with Lou Guzzo, Regnery Publishing, Incorporated, An Eagle Publishing, Incorporated Company, One Massachusetts Avenue, NW, Washington, D.C. 20001. Copyright © 1993. PHONE: 202-216-0600. FAX: 202-216-0612.

Global Governance: Why? How? When? with sections written by Henry Lamb and Kenneth Minogue. Copyright © 1996 by National Review, Incorporated, reprinted by Murchison Chair of Free Enterprise, University of Texas at Austin, Petroleum/CPE 3.168, Austin, Texas 78712. Copyright © 1997. PHONE: 512-471-7501. FAX: 512-471-5120. E-MAIL: lilypad@mail.utexas.edu WEBSITE: www.engr.utexas.edu/cofe/

Global Bondage, The U.N. Plan to Rule the World, by Cliff Kincaid, Huntington House Publishers, PO Box 53788, Lafayette, Louisiana 70505. Copyright © 1995. PHONE: 318-237-7049. FAX: 318-237-7060. E-MAIL: ladawn@eatel.net

Global Taxes for World Government, by Cliff Kincaid, Huntington House Publishers, PO Box 53788, Lafayette, Louisiana 70505. Copyright © 1997. PHONE: 318-237-7049. FAX: 318-237-7060. E-MAIL: ladawn@eatel.net

Global Tyranny . . . Step by Step, by William F. Jasper, Western Islands, PO Box 8040, Appleton, Wisconsin 54913. Copyright © 1992. PHONE: 920-749-3780. FAX: 920-749-5062. E-MAIL: wjf@jbs.org WEBSITE: www.jbs.org

The Homosexual Agenda: How the Gay Lobby Is Targeting America's Children, (booklet) compiled and written by the staff of Americans for Truth about Homosexuality, Americans for Truth about Homosexuality, a division of the Christian Defense Fund, PO Box 97210, Washington, D.C. 20090-6779. Copyright © 1997. PHONE: 703-684-4871.

The International Who's Who, Fifty-Fourth Edition, Europa Publications, Limited, 18 Bedford Square, London WC1B 3JN, England. Copyright © 1990. PHONE: 44-171-580-8236. FAX: 44-171-636-1664. E-MAIL: sales@europapublications.co.uk WEBSITE: www.europapublications.co.uk

Kill Zone - A Sniper Looks at Dealey Plaza, by Craig Roberts, Consolidated Press International, 3171-A South 129th East Avenue, Suite 338, Tulsa, Oklahoma 74134. Copyright © 1994. PHONE: 918-664-0024. FAX: 918-664-0024. E-MAIL: centurion1@compuserve.com

The Medusa File - Secret Crimes and Coverups of the U.S. Government, by Craig Roberts, Consolidated Press International, 3171-A South 129th East Avenue, Suite 338, Tulsa, Oklahoma 74134. Copyright © 1994. PHONE: 918-664-0024. FAX: 918-664-0024. E-MAIL: centurion1@compuserve.com

The News Manipulators, by Reed Irvine, Joseph C. Goulden, and Cliff Kincaid, Book Distributors, Incorporated, PO Box 1413, Smithtown, New York 11787-0660. Copyright © 1993. PHONE: 202-364-4401. FAX: 202-364-4098. E-MAIL: ar@aim.org WEBSITE: www.aim.org

Partners in Power - The Clintons and Their America, by Roger Morris, Henry Holt and Company, Incorporated, 115 West 18th Street, New York, New York 10011. Copyright © 1996.

The Quotable Conservative, compiled by Rod L. Evans and Irwin M. Berent, Adams Media Corporation, 260 Center Street, Holbrook, Massachusetts 02343. Copyright © 1995. PHONE: 781-767-8100. FAX: 781-767-0994. E-MAIL: sacarfagna@aol.com WEBSITE: www.adamsonline.com

Right from the Beginning, by Patrick J. Buchanan, Regnery Publishing, Incorporated, an Eagle Publishing Company, One Massachusetts Avenue, NW, Washington, D.C. 20001. Copyright © 1990. PHONE: 202-216-0600. FAX: 202-216-0612.

Road to Serfdom (50th anniversary edition), by F. A. Hayek, The University of Chicago Press, Chicago, Illinois 60637. Copyright © 1944 (renewed 1972), 1994.

Secret Life of Bill Clinton - The Unreported Stories, by Ambrose Evans Pritchard, Regnery Publishing, Incorporated, an Eagle Publishing Company, 1 Massachusetts Avenue NW, Washington, D.C. 20001. Copyright © 1997.

Set Up & Sold Out, by Holly Swanson, CIN Publishing, Inc., PO Box 2645, White City, Oregon 97503. Copyright © 1995. (Updated second edition published 1998.) PHONE: 541-830-1447. FAX: 541-830-1448. E-MAIL: cwb@ednet.net WEBSITE: www.anow.home.ml.org

The Strange Death of Vincent Foster - An Investigation, by Christopher Ruddy, The Free Press, a division of Simon & Schuster, Incorporated, 1230 Avenue of the Americas, New York, New York 10020. Copyright © 1997.

Sustainable America - A New Consensus for Prosperity, Opportunity, and a Healthy Environment for the Future, by the President's Council on Sustainable Development, 730 Jackson Place, NW, Washington, D.C. 20503. Copyright © 1996.

This Land is Our Land - How to End the War on Private Property, by Richard Pombo and Joseph Farah, St. Martin's Press, 175 Fifth Avenue, New York, New York 10010. Copyright © 1996.

Toward a New World Order: The Countdown to Armageddon, 2nd edition, by Donald S. McAlvany, Western Pacific Publishing Company, PO Box 84900, Phoenix, Arizona 85071. Copyright © 1992. PHONE: 800-528-0559. FAX: 970-259-9396.

Trashing the Planet, by Dixy Lee Ray with Lou Guzzo, Regnery Publishing, Incorporated, an Eagle Publishing Company, One Massachusetts Avenue, NW, Washington, D.C. 20001. Copyright © 1990. PHONE: 202-216-0600. FAX: 202-216-0612.

The True State of the Planet, edited by Ronald Bailey, The Free Press, a Division of Simon & Schuster, Incorporated, 1230 Avenue of the Americas, New York, New York 10020. Copyright © 1995.

Unlimited Access, by Gary Aldrich, Regnery Publishing, Incorporated, An Eagle Publishing Company, One Massachusetts Avenue, NW, Washington, D.C. 20001. Copyright © 1996. PHONE: 202-216-0600. FAX: 202-216-0612.

Who's Who in America, Marquis Who's Who, a Reed Reference Publishing Company (now a Reed Elsevies Company), 121 Chanlon Road, New Providence, New Jersey 07974. Copyright © 1996.

Who's Who Among African Americans, edited by Shirelle Phelps, Gale Research, Incorporated, 835 Penobscot Building, Detroit, Michigan 48226-4094. Copyright © 1996. All rights reserved.

Who's Who of American Women 1997/1998, 20th Edition, Marquis Who's Who, a Reed Elsevies Company, 121 Chanlon Road, New Providence, New Jersey 07974. Copyright © 1996.

Why a Bankrupt America, by Devvy Kidd, Project Liberty, 4260 Dymic Way, Sacramento, California 95838. Revised: March 1, 1994. Copyright © 1994. (New revision published April 1997.)

The World Order - Our Secret Rulers, by Eustace Mullins, Second Edition, Ezra Pound Institute of Civilization, PO Box 1105, Staunton, Virginia 24401. Copyright © 1992.

A World Without Heros: The Modern Tragedy, by George Roche, The Hillsdale College Press, Hillsdale, Michigan 49242. Copyright © 1987. PHONE: 517-437-7341, extension 2319. FAX: 517-437-0654.

Other Sources

The 60-Minutes Deception, videotape produced by American Agenda, PO Box 702417, Tulsa, Oklahoma 74170, 1997. ADDRESS: Citizens for Honest Government, PO Box 220, Winchester, California 92596. PHONE: 757-465-4068. FAX: 909-652-5848. E-MAIL: jeremiah@pe.net WEBSITE: www.jeremiahfilm.com

*9*1*1,* newsletter published by the California Coalition for Immigration Reform, 5942 Edinger, Suite 113-117, Huntington Beach, California 92649. PHONE: 714-921-7142.

Accountability Now!, a campaign to create a citizen's lobby and watchdog group to ensure citizen interests are represented, founded by Holly Swanson, author of *Set Up & Sold Out, Find Out What Green Really Means,* South Grape #349, Medford, Oregon 97501. PHONE: 541-830-1446. FAX: 541-830-1448. E-MAIL: cwb@cdsnet.net WEBSITE: www.anow.home.ml.org

AIM Report, newsletter, Reed Irvine, editor, Accuracy In Media, Incorporated, 4455 Connecticut Avenue, N.W., Suite 330, Washington, D.C. 20008. PHONE: 202-364-4401. FAX: 202-364-4098. E-MAIL: ar@aim.org WEBSITE: www.aim.org

The American Enterprise, A National Magazine of Politics, Business, and Culture, Karl Zinsmeister, editor in chief, Christopher DeMuth, publisher, Enterprise Institute for Public Policy Research, 1150 17th Street N.W., Washington, D.C. 20036. *The American Enterprise,* 430 South Geneva Street, Ithaca, New York 14850. PHONE: 202-862-5886. FAX: 202-862-5867. E-MAIL: theamericanenterprise@compuserve.com WEBSITE: www.theamericanenterprise.org

American Leadership Magazine, Harold W. Bolinger, director, LEADERS (The Legislative Exchange Association, Drafting, Editing, and Research Service), PO Box 1851, Cumberland, Maryland 21502. E-MAIL: leaders@aol.com WEBSITE: http.logoplex.com/shops/leaders/

America's Judgments, What Lies Ahead? documentation in support of the video of the same name, Militia of Montana (M.O.M.), PO Box 1486, Noxon, Montana 59853. PHONE: 406-847-2735. FAX: 406-847-2246. WEBSITE: www.logoplex.com/resources/mom

The American Sentinel, newsletter, "Blowing the Lid Off the Liberal Left's Most Closely Guarded Secrets, (formerly *The Pink Sheet on the Left*)," Lee Bellinger, editor. Radio Center, Suite 2E, 3229 South Boulevard, Charlotte, North Carolina 28209. PHONE: 704-525-8807. FAX: 704-525-6779. E-MAIL: sentinel@caro.net

The American Spectator magazine, R. Emmett Tyrrell, Jr., editor-in-chief, 2020 North 14th Street, Suite 750, Arlington, Virginia 22201. PHONE: 703-243-3733. E-MAIL: amspec@ ix.netcom.com WEBSITE: www.spectator.org

ASAP Report, The Newsletter of the American Sovereignty Action Project, Cliff Kincaid, editor. ASAP is a campaign of Citizens United Foundation, 11094-D Lee Highway, Suite 200, Fairfax, Virginia 22030. PHONE: 703-352-4788. FAX: 301-855-3732. E-MAIL: antiun@earthlink.net WEBSITE: www.citizensunited.org/cu/asap

Barbed Wire on America, 1997 video of a presentation by David Wegener at a meeting of the Prophecy Club®, Box 750234, Topeka, Kansas 66675. PHONE: 785 478-1112. WEBSITE: www.prophecyclub.com

Border Watch, newsletter (ceased publication in 1996) of The American Immigration Control Foundation, PO Box 525, Monterey, Virginia 24465. PHONE: 540-468-2022. FAX: 540-468-2024. E-MAIL: aicf@cfw.com WEBSITE: www.cfw.com/naicf

Center for Action, newsletter published by Center for Action for the Center for Patriotic Activity, James "Bo" Gritz, editor, HC 11, Box 308, Kamiah, Idaho 83536. PHONE: 208-935-1325. FAX: 208-935-1328. E-MAIL: bogritz@camasnet.com WEBSITE: www.bogritz.com

Crisis in the Classroom - Hidden Agendas and Grassroots Opposition, video hosted by Phyllis Schlafly, produced by Eagle Forum, PO Box 618, Alton, Illinois 62002. Copyright © 1996. PHONE: 618-462-5415. FAX: 618-462-8909. E-MAIL: eagle@eagleforum.org WEBSITE: www.eagleforum.org

The DeWeese Report, newsletter, Thomas A. DeWeese, editor in chief, American Policy Center, 13873 Park Center Road, #316, Herndon, Virginia 20171. PHONE: 703-925-0881. FAX: 703-925-0991. E-MAIL: apc@americanpolicy.org WEBSITE: www.americanpolicy.org

Dispatches, newsletter, "A News Publication of the Western Journalism Center," Joseph Farah, editor/publisher, PO Box 2450, Fair Oaks, California 95628. PHONE: 916-852-9700. FAX: 916-852-6302. WEBSITE: www.worldnetdaily.com

ĕco•logic, Environmental Conservation Organization, Henry Lamb, publisher, PO Box 191, Hollow Rock, Tennessee 38342. PHONE: 901-986-0099. FAX: 901-986-2299.

Facts, Truth, Evidence that Will Affect All Americans, support material for David Wegener's video *Barbed Wire on America.* PHONE: 785-478-1113. FAX: 785-478-1115.

Fortress America, Jamey R. Wheeler, chairman, One America's Way, Washington, D.C. 20069. PHONE: 800-667-0056.

Foundation Endowment, Joseph M. Horn, president, 611 Cameron Street, Alexandria, Virginia 22314. PHONE: 703-683-1077. FAX: 703-683-1272. E-MAIL: tfe@laser.net

Free American Newsmagazine, Clayton R. Douglas, editor and publisher, US Highway 380, Box 2943, Bingham, New Mexico 87832. PHONE: 505-423-3250. FAX: 505-423-3258. E-MAIL: freeamerican@etsc.net WEBSITE: www.freeamerican.com

Freedom Alert, "Newsletter of the Defenders of Personal Property Rights," the Voice of Citizens for Constitutional Property Rights, Incorporated, David A. Russell, editor/publisher, PO Box 757, Crestview, Florida 32536. PHONE: 904-682-6156. FAX: 904-689-3637. E-MAIL: ccpr-prez @cyou.com WEBSITE: www.ccpr-fl.com

Global Governance - The Quiet War Against American Independence, video, hosted by Phyllis Schlafly of the Eagle Forum, PO Box 618, Alton, Illinois 62002, 1997. PHONE: 618-462-5415. FAX: 618-462-8909. E-MAIL: eagle@eagleforum.org WEBSITE: www.eagleforum.org

Heritage Foundation, Edwin J. Feulner, Jr., president, 214 Massachusetts Avenue, NE, Washington, D.C. 20002-4999. PHONE: 202-546-4400. WEBSITE: www.heritage.org

Heterodoxy, newspaper, "Articles and animadversions on political correctness and other follies," Peter Collier and David Horowitz, editors, published by the Center for the Study of Popular Culture, PO Box 67398, Los Angeles, California 90067. PHONE: 310-843-3699. FAX: 310-843-3692. E-MAIL: brdonaldson@cspc.org WEBSITE: www.frontpagemag.com ALSO: www.cspc.org

Human Events, The National Conservative Weekly, newspaper, Thomas S. Winter, editor in chief, 1 Massachusetts Avenue NW, 6th Floor, Washington, D.C. 20001. PHONE: 202-216-0600. FAX: 202-546-0611.

Imminent Military Takeover of the USA, video of a 1996 presentation by Jim Ammerman at the Prophecy Club®, PO Box 750234, Topeka, Kansas 66675. PHONE: 785-478-1112.

Imprimis, newsletter, Ronald L. Trowbridge, editor, Hillsdale College, 33 East College Street, Hillsdale, Michigan 49242. PHONE: 517-437-0388. FAX: 517-437-0654. WEBSITE: www.prophecyclub.com

Insider's Report, newsletter published by the American Policy Center, 13873 Park Center Road #316, Herndon, Virginia 20171. PHONE: 703-925-0881. FAX: 703-925-0991. E-MAIL: apc@americanpolicy.org WEBSITE: www.americanpolicy.org

The Limbaugh Letter, newsletter, Rush Limbaugh, editor-in-chief, EFM Publishing, Incorporated, 366 Madison Avenue, 7th Floor, New York, New York 10017. *The Limbaugh Letter,* 2 Penn Plaza, 17th Floor, New York, New York 10121. PHONE: 800-282-2882. FAX: 212-563-9166. E-MAIL: rush@eibnet.com

The McAlvany Intelligence Advisor, newsletter, Don McAlvany, editor, PO Box 84904, Phoenix, Arizona 85071. PHONE: 800-528-0559. FAX: 970-259-9396.

Media Bypass magazine, Gerald Carroll, editor, PO Box 5326, Evansville, Indiana 47716. PHONE: 812-477-8670. FAX: 812-477-8677. E-MAIL: ceo@4bypass.com WEBSITE: www.4bypass.com/

The Mena Cover-Up: Drugs, Deception, and the Making of a President, video produced by Citizens for Honest Government, John Wheeler, director, 1996, PO Box 220, Winchester, California 92596. PHONE: 757-465-4068. FAX: 909-652-5848. E-MAIL: jeremiah@pe.net WEBSITE: www.jeremiahfilm.com

The Men Who Killed Kennedy, six-part video presentation broadcast occasionally on the History Channel. For more information, call: 800-708-1776.

Midnight Messenger, newspaper, 9205 SE Clackamas Road, #1776, Clackamas, Oregon 97015. PHONE: 503-824-2050. FAX: 503-824-2050. E-MAIL: midnight@midnight-emissary.com WEBSITE: www.midnight-emissary.com

National Review, magazine, Richard Lowry, editor, 215 Lexington Avenue, New York, New York 10016. PHONE: 212-679-7330. FAX: 212-849-2835. WEBSITE: www.nationalreview.com

The New American, magazine, John F. McManus, publisher, 770 Westhill Boulevard, Appleton, Wisconsin 54914. PHONE: 920-749-3784. FAX: 920-749-3785. E-MAIL: tna@jbs.org WEBSITE: www.jbs.org/tna.htm

New World Order Current Events: Gorbachev/Education/Stock Market, video of Gary Kah at the Granada Forum, September 18, 1997. Hope for the World, PO Box 899, Noblesville, Indiana 46061-0899. PHONE: 818-385-1003 (Granada Hotline).

None Dare Call It Murder, video, produced by Mondo Libre Productions, available through Global Insights, 675 Fairview Drive, #246, Carson City, Nevada 89701. PHONE: 702-891-0703. FAX: 702-891-0704.

NWI Resource, National Wilderness Institute Magazine, Robert E. Gordon, executive director, National Wilderness Institute, PO Box 25766, Washington, D.C. 20007. PHONE: 703-836-7404. FAX: 703-836-7405. E-MAIL: nwi@nwi.org WEBSITE: www.nw.org

OBE: Education or Social Engineering?, video, published by J.W. Publishing Company, PO Box 455, St. Clair, Missouri 63077. Copyright © 1996 by Ann Wilson. PHONE: 314-629-1196. E-MAIL: jwpubl@fidnet.com

Operation Vampire Killer 2000, American Police/Military Action Plan for Stopping World Government Rule, revised 1996, published by Police Against the New World Order, PO Box 8712, Phoenix, Arizona. NEWSLETTER: Aid & Abet Police Newsletter, PO Box 8787, Phoenix, Arizona 85066. PHONE: 602-237-2533. FAX: 602-237-2444.

The Phyllis Schlafly Report, newsletter published by the Eagle Trust Fund, PO Box 618, Alton, Illinois 62002. PHONE: 618-462-5415. FAX: 618-462-8909. E-MAIL: eagle@eagleforum.org WEBSITE: www.eagleforum.org

The Rutherford Institute, John W. Whitehead, esquire, president, PO Box 7482, Charlottesville, Virginia 22906-7482. PHONE: 804-978-3888. FAX: 804-978-1789. E-MAIL: rutherford@fni.com WEBSITE: www.rutherford.org

A Sniper's View of Dumitru's Warning, video of a presentation by Craig Roberts at the Prophecy Club®, PO Box 750234, Topeka, Kansas 66675. PHONE: 785-478-1112. WEBSITE: www.prophecyclub.com

Special Report - Who Is Leading the Attack on American Liberty?, reference materials prepared by David A. Russell, president, Citizens for Constitutional Property Rights, Incorporated, 1996, PO Box 757, Crestview, Florida 32536-0757. PHONE: 904-682-6156. FAX: 904-689-3637. E-MAIL: ccpr-prez@cyou.com WEBSITE: www.ccpr-fl.com

Tragedy by Design, video narrated by William Norman Grigg, John Birch Society, 1997, PO Box 8040, Appleton, Wisconsin 54913. PHONE: 920-749-3783. FAX: 920-749-5062. E-MAIL: wng@jbs.org WEBSITE: www.jbs.org

The Truth about Janet Reno, video of a speech given by Jack Thompson April 14, 1997 at the Biltmore Hotel, Coral Gables, Florida, sponsored by the American Forum, 8128 SW 172 Terrace, Miami, Florida 33157.

The United Nations: A Look into the Future, video produced by the John Birch Society, 1998, 770 Westhill Boulevard, Appleton, Wisconsin 54914. PHONE: 920-749-3784. FAX: 920-749-3785. E-MAIL: tna@jbs.org WEBSITE: www.jbs.org/tna.htm

Waco - The Rules of Engagement, video, a William Gazecki Film, Somford Production/Fifth Estate Productions, 1997, 11940 Chaparal Street, Los Angeles, California 90049-2910. PHONE: 310-289-3900.

The Washington Times, newspaper, National Weekly Edition, Wesley Pruden, editor in chief, News World Communications, Inc., 3600 New York Avenue, N.E., Washington, D.C. 20002. FAX: 202-832-8285. E-MAIL: nated@wt.infi.net WEBSITE: www.washtimes-weekly.com

Who Runs the Global Economy? video of a presentation by Cliff Kincaid at the Granada Forum, December 4, 1997, America's Survival, PO Box 146, Owings, Maryland 20736. PHONE: 301-855-2679. FAX: 301-855-3732.

INDEX

The trouble with freedom is that most people don't know what to do with it.

- Jan Botwinich, as quoted in *Modern American Wit and Wisdom,* Random House, Incorporated, 1970

Either governments serve the ends of justice or they become vast criminal enterprises.

- Saint Augustine (354-430), as quoted in *Tragedy by Design,* video, with William Norman Grigg, John Birch Society, 1997

Governments will always do the right thing - after they have exhausted all other possibilities.

- John Fund, Editorial Board, *Wall Street Journal,* in remarks delivered at the Shavano Institute for National Leadership, October 1997

Underlined individuals authored the 76 major quotations.
Last names of individuals are shown in bold type.
Unless designated otherwise, references are to the Quotation Number.

Quotation Number or (Page Number)

B

C

F

G

H

L

M

N

O

S

T

U

V

W

X

Y

Z

PHOTO CREDITS

Photos are identified by quotation number and page number.

Quotation Number
(Page Number)

1. (p. 10) Laurence Agron, Archive Photos.
2. (p. 12) NBC Press Administration
5. (p. 18) John Duricka, AP Photo.
6. (p. 20) George Bennett, CNN, Turner Broadcasting System..
7. (p. 22) Jim Wells, Archive Photos.
8. (p. 24) Mark Wilson, Reuters, Archive Photos.
9. (p. 26) Fred Prouser, Reuters, Archive Photos.
10. (p. 30) Bob Scott, Archive Photos.
11. (p. 32) Lee Celano, Reuters, Archive Photos.
12. (p. 34) Archive Photos.
13. (p. 36) William Wilson Lewis, III, AP Photo.
14. (p. 40) Archive Photos.
15. (p. 44) Archive Photos.
16. (p. 46) Wide World Photos.
17. (p. 48) Wide World Photos.
18. (p. 50) Curry School of Education Foundation, Incorporated, University of Virginia
20. (p. 56) Popperfoto, Archive Photos.
23. (p. 62) Popperfoto, Archive Photos.
24. (p. 64) Don Kunkel, Harvard University Center for the Study of World Religions, Temple of Understanding.
25. (p. 66) Ken Howard, Archive Photos.
27. (p. 70) Wide World Photos.
29. (p. 74) Mike Segar, Reuters, Archive Photos.
30. (p. 76) Lee Celano, Reuters, Archive Photos.
31. (p. 78) Wide World Photos.
32. (p. 82) AP Newsfeatures Photo.
34. (p. 90) Reuters, Archive Photos.
35. (p. 92) Vanderlei Almeida, Reuters, Archive Photos.
38. (p. 102) Popperfoto, Archive Photos.
39. (p. 104) Chris Kleponis, Reuters, Archive Photos.
43. (p. 114) AP Wirephoto.
44. (p. 116) Wide World Photos.
45. (p. 118) Frank Capri, SAGA, Archive Photos.
46. (p. 120) Greg Gibson, Associated Press, AP.
48. (p. 124) AP Photo.
49. (p. 126) AP Photo.
50. (p. 130) Archive Photos.
51. (p. 132) AP Laserphoto.
53. (p. 140) Stelios Varias, Reuters, Archive Photos.
54. (p. 142) Stephen Jaffe, Reuters, Archive Photos.
55. (p. 144) AP Wirephoto.
56. (p. 146) Jules Geller, Pictorial Parade, Inc., Archive Photos.
57. (p. 150) Associated Press Photo.
59. (p. 156) Gene Puskar, Wide World Photos.
62. (p. 162) Patrick de Noirmont, Reuters, Archive Photos.
63. (p. 164) Vincent Laforet, Reuters, Archive Photos.
64. (p. 166) Linda Cicero, News and Publications Service, Stanford University News Service.
65. (p. 168) AP Photo.
68. (p. 174) Wide World Photos.
70. (p. 178) Dr. Beier's website (www.for.nau.edu/forestry/faculty/pb.html). Thanks, too, to the staff at Northern Arizona State University.
72. (p. 182) John Redman, Associated Press, London.
73. (p. 184) Arch de France, Archive Photos.
74. (p. 190) Evy Mages, Reuters, Archive Photos.

Our Constitution was made only for a moral and religious people. It is wholly inadequate for the government of any other.

- John Adams
1789, as quoted in "Local Police under Siege," by William F. Jasper, *The New American,* May 4, 1998, page 25

Indeed I tremble for my country when I reflect that God is just.

- Thomas Jefferson
Notes on the State of Virginia, 1781-1785, as quoted in *Bartlett's Familiar Quotations,* 14th edition, by John Bartlett, Little, Brown, and Company, Incorporated, 1968, page 471

All that is necessary for evil to triumph is for good men to do nothing.

- Oliver Wendell Holmes, as quoted in *Freedom Alert*, November/December 1997, page 8

You Don't Say Comment Sheet

(Please make a copy to submit your comments.)

How satisfied are you with this book?

☐--------☐--------☐--------☐--------☐

Very Satisfied	Somewhat Satisfied	Neither Satisfied nor Unsatisfied	Somewhat Unsatisfied	Very Unsatisfied

Comments: ______________________________

____

____

____

____

____

____

____

Did you find any errors? (Please indicate page number and paragraph.)

____

____

____

Would you be willing to allow your comments to be used in the promotion of this book? ☐-Yes ☐-No

Would you be willing to allow your name to be used in the promotion of this book? ☐-Yes ☐-No

Name: ______________________________

(Name and address are optional.)

Address: ______________________________

City, State, ZIP: ______________________________

Send to: Fred Gielow, Care of Freedom Books
17234 Boca Club Boulevard #102
Boca Raton, Florida 33487-1268

You Don't Say Order Form

(Please make a copy to submit your order.)

You don't Say is available for purchase through the courtesy of Accuracy In Media (AIM). When you order a copy of this book, why not join AIM. You'll receive the *AIM Report* and perhaps for the first time find fairness, balance, and accuracy in news reporting.

		Amount
You Don't Say $16.00 per copy plus $4.00 P&H ($2.00 P&H per book for quantity orders)	Number of books:______	$_______
AIM Membership $35.00 per year		$_______
Tax-deductible contribution to **AIM**		$_______
Total amount enclosed:		$_______

Enclosed: ☐-Check ☐-Money Order ☐-Credit card order

Credit Card: ☐-AMEX ☐-Discover ☐-MasterCard ☐-VISA

Credit card account number: ☐☐☐☐☐☐☐☐☐☐☐☐☐☐☐☐ Expiration date: ____/____

Signature: ______________________________

(Required for credit card orders only.)

Name: ____________________ Phone:______________

Address: ______________________________

City, State, ZIP: ________________________

If books are to be shipped to another address, indicate ship-to address:

Name: ______________________________

Address: ______________________________

City, State, ZIP: ________________________

Send to: Accuracy In Media (Phone: 800-787-4567. Fax: 202-364-4098)
4455 Connecticut Avenue, Suite #330
Washington, DC 20008-2302

Worse is better.

- Vladimir Lenin, as quoted in *The McAlvany Intelligence Advisor*, Donald S. McAlvany, editor, October 1998, page 32

Life is just one damned thing after another.

- Attributed to Frank Ward O'Malley (1875-1932)
- Also attributed to Elbert Hubbard (1856-1915)
- *Bartlett's Familiar Quotations* suggests the phrase precedes both

---

Victory at all costs, victory in spite of all terror, victory however long and hard the road may be; for without victory there is no survival.

- Sir Winston Spencer Churchill

First Statement as Prime Minister, House of Commons, May 13, 1940, as quoted in *Bartlett's Familiar Quotations,* 14th edition, by John Bartlett, Little, Brown, and Company, Incorporated, 1968, page 920

About the Author

Long ago in the early days of television, when screens were tiny and the colors were only black and white, one of the networks was Du Mont and one of its programs was the New York Times Youth Forum. This once-a-week panel show featured six students from around the country discussing national issues. On Sunday, February 1, 1953 the question was "Can We Maintain Ethics in Government?" and one of the panelists was teenager Fred Gielow.

He recalls: "I can't remember much about our discussion, but I vividly recall taking issue with the basic premise of the program. I questioned how ethics could be *maintained,* if as I suspected, ethics were largely *absent* to begin with. Such an attitude wasn't much appreciated by moderator Dorothy Gordon or special guest Ellis Arnall, former governor of Georgia."

That television debut and debate may have planted a political seed in Fred's subconsciousness, but if so, it certainly remained dormant for a long time. Long enough for him to finish school, get a job, marry, raise a family, even retire, before germinating. But now that seed has blossomed into a full-time interest as his recent appearances on local radio programs, his co-hosted public-access television interview program (InfoQuest), his appearances on the Rush Limbaugh television show, and now this book attest.

"There are many sources of truth to refute what liberals and the mainstream media tell us," says Fred, "but you have to dig around a little to find them. If you really expect both sides of an issue to be fully and fairly presented in the major newspapers and magazines and on television, I'd say you've bought into the mainstream media scam. You're a victim of the Propaganda Machine. But, sadly, it appears you're in the majority. The media seem to be winning their clever con game."

Fred continues: "I wrote this book to present a perspective that seems to go largely unnoticed in the U.S. today. It's a real tragedy when lies are regularly masqueraded as the truth. What's even more tragic is when a majority of the public buys into the big deception, or worse yet, when the public doesn't even care.

"By using quotations direct from the mouths of liberals, quotations generally unreported by the mighty Propaganda Machine, I think it's possible to demonstrate the kind of world our liberal friends wish to impose upon the rest of us. It takes but a few remarks, during rare, unguarded moments, for liberals to vividly and unambiguously show their true colors."

Fred Gielow also authored the book *Laughter, Love, and a Barbershop Song,* published 1980.